Praise for *Connection*

"This is one of the best books on personal growth I've ever read. With warm encouragement and easy, practical steps, Dr. Klussman brings us home to a natural connection, confidence, and ease. You can trust what she says since her path is grounded in science and she's walked it herself. Clear, brilliant, and so hopeful, this book is a gem."

RICK HANSON, PHD
author of *Resilient*

"In refreshingly skillfully ways, Kristine invites us into deep connection and well-being underneath all our busy, separate lives. This is a wise vision and a transformative way to awaken."

JACK KORNFIELD, PHD
author of *A Path with Heart* and cofounder of Spirit Rock Meditation Center

"I think it is a very important addition to our understanding of how and why people metabolize challenges differently. It offers an important perspective for doctors, nurses, therapists, teachers . . . everyone in helping professions."

SYLVIA BOORSTEIN, PHD
author of *Happiness Is an Inside Job*

"This book helps us answer the fundamental WHY question—*Why do I get up in the morning?*—and then guides us to authentically stay awake on purpose."

RICHARD LEIDER
author of *The Power of Purpose* and coauthor of *Repacking Your Bags*

"This is a remarkable handbook for transformation. Kristine offers life-changing insights on what true satisfaction looks and feels like. This message will light the way to the world we all want: a more just, sustainable, and meaningful future for all."

LYNNE TWIST
author of *The Soul of Money*

"The greatest pandemic in modern history is loneliness. We are so digitally 'connected' and yet many feel so disconnected within ourselves. This book is not just timely, it is essential. Kristine's unique approach of blending science, practice, and her own personal journey makes for a compelling read."

PHILIP MCKERNAN
author of *One Last Talk*

"Ready for a clear roadmap to a meaningful life? Striving for a deeper connection to yourself and the world around you? Dr. Kristine Klussman has laid the path to get you there in her new book *Connection*. Using her expansive experience and personal dedication to evolution, Klussman provides the keys to understanding yourself and how you fit, happily, into every day of your life."

ELIZABETH HAMILTON-GUARINO

author of *Percolate*

"This is THE go-to guide for awakening the mind and body while cultivating emotional mastery, deep meaning, and a profound sense of purpose fulfillment in every area of life. Kristine's support and in-depth protocols offered throughout the *Connection* program are not only tried-and-true strategies proven effective in countless clinical sessions and community practice—they're clearly designed to be accessible and likewise activating for anyone and everyone ready to awaken into greater connection with themselves and with all of life."

SYDNEY CAMPOS

spiritual healer and author of *The Empath Experience*

"Self-awareness, acceptance, and alignment set the foundation for peace and joy. In this book, Dr. Kristine Klussman presents a beautiful roadmap to get you there."

SHANNON KAISER

author of *The Self-Love Experiment* and *Joy Seeker*

"Kristine Klussman has written a very important book. No, actually, it's a critical guide to help us navigate these unprecedented times of disconnection. Her book, all about connection, points out how the lack of it is negatively impacting every single area of life that matters to us on every level—physical, emotional, psychological, and spiritual—and shows us how to shift things in the right direction. I'll be recommending this book to everyone."

KAREN JONES

relationship coach and author of *Men Are Great*

connection

connection

HOW TO FIND
THE LIFE YOU'RE
LOOKING FOR
IN THE LIFE
YOU HAVE

KRISTINE KLUSSMAN, PHD

sounds true
BOULDER, COLORADO

Sounds True
Boulder, CO 80306

Published 2021

Book design by Linsey Dodaro
Illustrations © Purpose Project, Inc. Used with permssion.

The wood used to produce this book is from Forest Stewardship Council (FSC)
certified forests, recycled materials, or controlled wood.

Printed in the United States of America

Library of Congress Cataloging-in-Publication Data

Names: Klussman, Kristine, author.
Title: Connection : how to find the life you're looking for in the life you
    have / Kristine Klussman.
Description: Boulder : Sounds True, 2021. | Includes bibliographical
    references.
Identifiers: LCCN 2020029975 (print) | LCCN 2020029976 (ebook) | ISBN
    9781683647157 (hardcover) | ISBN 9781683647164 (ebook)
Subjects: LCSH: Self-actualization (Psychology) | Mindfulness (Psychology)
    | Self. | Happiness.
Classification: LCC BF637.S4 K558 2021 (print) | LCC BF637.S4 (ebook) |
    DDC 158.1--dc23
LC record available at https://lccn.loc.gov/2020029975
LC ebook record available at https://lccn.loc.gov/2020029976

10 9 8 7 6 5 4 3 2 1

Contents

For Max and Dakota.
Live long and prosper, dudes.

The Roots of Self-Connection

MEANING
PURPOSE
PHYSICAL SELF CARE
VALUES
EMOTIONAL SELF CARE
TIME MANAGEMENT

Introduction

I saw her leaning against the wall of the hospital's radiation oncology center. Young, dressed in athletic gear, bee-bopping to music through a set of headphones, she was a pleasant-looking woman, much too sunny in disposition to be a cancer patient. I assumed she was a bike messenger making a delivery as I began my rounds that Monday morning. I was there to see how patients and their families were adjusting to life with cancer, a disease that brought with it a whole range of emotions, most of them heart-wrenching. But when I called the first name on my list, the young woman raised her hand and met me with a smile. "Sunny" was my first appointment of the day—a recently diagnosed cancer patient on the verge of radiation therapy.

As we began to chat, I learned how grim her circumstances truly were. Having just moved to the Bay Area, she had no living family to help her with getting to and from appointments and no emotional or financial support for her treatments. She'd caught a bus before dawn that day to make the earliest appointment time because she needed to get back to work. I expected her to talk about how awful her circumstances were and how emotionally wrung out she was. I was wrong.

Sunny told me how grateful she was for the kind staff at the hospital and for her employer's flexibility, which allowed her time off for her treatments. Convinced the woman was in denial, I probed further and questioned the incongruence between her jovial mood and her circumstances.

"Why do you seem so lighthearted when you're dealing with so much?" I asked.

"What do I have to be sad about?" was her response.

She acknowledged that her situation was harrowing and that she wished none of it were happening, but she pointed out that being sad about it wouldn't change her circumstances.

"I've wasted my whole life being sad and feeling sorry for myself for things that didn't really matter. Now I finally see how much I have, and I refuse to spend precious time on being resentful."

Sunny told me that her cancer diagnosis had really woken her up. She could clearly see what mattered in her life, and she was able to be clear and honest with herself and those around her in a new and unique way. Handling cancer treatment was just like a job to this woman—something she needed to do every day. But it would in no way detract from her ultimate goal of being fully alive in every way she knew how.

"I will not waste my entire life being asleep at the wheel," was how she put it.

For perhaps the first time in my career, I was speechless. And embarrassed. I had argued with my partner that morning, then spent my drive to work obsessing about the absurdity of so many areas of my own life. What right did I have to complain? It had definitely been a cup-half-empty sort of morning, until now. I struggled to regain my professional composure as I listened to Sunny exude gratitude for so much less. Perhaps I was the one who needed a wake-up call.

As I got to know this woman better, she displayed the range of emotions I'd expect for her situation—including, at times, overwhelm, sadness, and grief. But what remained constant was how grounded she was, how completely she lived in her truth. She seemed utterly and authentically connected to herself and everything in her life, with an unshakable sense of her own true north.

It was that first conversation that touched a nerve in me . . . sparking a thirst to understand the truths that enabled such enviable grace and contentment. I met other patients like her who found they were living more fully after discovering that they might not have very long to live. At first I thought these patients with their uplifting attitudes were rare, but I came across them frequently. With so much to teach and share, these patients became the catalyst for a new psychological approach to well-being that I call *connection theory*.

LEARNING FROM THE BRIGHT SPOTS

Psychiatry and psychology have long been mired in controversy, primarily due to their slavish obsession with assigning a disorder to most human experience. Critics of psychiatry consider the *DSM-5*, the deeply flawed and controversial diagnostic handbook of mental disorders, as a collection of fad diagnoses that often does more harm than good. These "disorders" have in most cases been dreamed up by a committee of "experts" who have their own conflicted agendas. Although many mental disorders within it have not been empirically validated, many have become household names and contributed to an over-medicated society.

One of the many outspoken critics of psychiatry is Dr. Allen Frances, who served as chairman of the task force who actually wrote the *DSM-IV*. In his bestselling book, *Saving Normal: An Insider's Revolt Against Out-of-Control Psychiatric Diagnosis, DSM-5, Big Pharma, and the Medicalization of Ordinary Life*, he describes how much harm has come from psychiatry's tendency to medicalize normal behavior—over-pathologizing, overtreatment, over-medicating of the "worried well," as well as severe neglect of those with extreme mental illness, who are the ones who need treatment the most—and all while the pharmaceutical companies profit shamelessly.[1] He believes that rampant diagnostic inflation and unreliable diagnostic labels were responsible for launching false epidemics of mental disorders in children, creating what we in the field refer to as garbage-can diagnoses—an overly broad, catch-all diagnosis where you throw anything that's in doubt. Attention deficit disorders are a great example.

Only recently has the scientific community begun to realize the importance of studying what was right with people, instead of what was wrong with them. The positive psychology movement, which began in 1998 with the work of Drs. Martin Seligman, Barbara Fredrickson, Mihaly Csikszentmihalyi, Christopher Peterson, and others, finally shifted our focus from the shadows to the bright spots, studying what enables individuals and communities to truly thrive. This field has opened the door to some of the greatest achievements in and contributions to our understanding of mental well-being and health.

But as much as I have embraced and devoured the findings of my positive psychology peers, it has been frustrating that the scientific community encourages psychologists to work in their own little corners of the world, left to substantiate their own ideas, often with blinders on and to the exclusion of others. I remember being advised as a graduate student that, in order to stand out and be successful in the field, I needed to find a niche—the sooner and the narrower the better—and stick with it, lest I become the dreaded generalist.

Then and now, there has been little emphasis on synthesizing one's ideas with the brilliant ideas of others in order to gain an understanding of how they work together. As a result, the fields of psychology and psychiatry are still full of competing theories, turf battles, and overly niched areas of specialization that remain in isolation. Commonly, mental health clinicians and researchers become blinded by one approach to wellness (or lack thereof) and neither share nor partake in the viewpoints of others.

While mini-theories can help with understanding certain aspects of human behavior and emotion, they are often arcane or difficult to remember and don't shed light on how to achieve a more global sense of fulfillment—the goal I've been chasing for much of my career.

Grander, more comprehensive theories of human behavior do exist in psychology—Erik Erikson's theory of psychosocial development, Dr. Jean Piaget's theory of cognitive development, Maslow's hierarchy of needs, and Pavlov's and Skinner's contributions to learning theory, to name a few—and, while some of these theories remain useful (like classical conditioning) and have held up over time, others have proven incomplete, have not stood up to modern research, or have not been relatable to people's everyday lived experiences (such as Freud's psychoanalytic theories). Even in their heyday, however, these theories did little to shed light on well-being and the art of living well, since that was not the focus of the people articulating them.

Still missing from the practice and science of mental health are overarching theories or organizational approaches to living well in the modern world that incorporate the best, most well-established principles across all niches and specializations. I have yet to see someone articulate a truly informed, holistic approach to happiness and well-being.

Instead, it has been left to the lay person to sift through and analyze the vast collection of tips, tricks, ideas, research, and belief systems available, creating an individual but bulging self-help "tool kit." With the modern-day deluge of wellness tips and advice available, it is a daunting task to know which tools to apply to your life, and when. I was frustrated both professionally and personally. If we focus only on the most pressing needs, how do we ever make the great quantum leaps that can truly upgrade our lives, our relationships, and our existence to a higher level? This frustration pushed me to come up with a new, holistic approach.

I am not so arrogant or ignorant as to say that my focus on connection is more correct than or superior to other theories. What I can confidently say is this: a piecemeal, diagnosis-driven approach to optimal well-being has never gotten me or my clients very far. Conversely, a comprehensive approach to well-being that incorporates the best available research and is anchored in an intuitive, cornerstone concept has transformed my life. I believe it offers a simple approach to transform yours.

This guiding principle is the cultivation of authentic connection, which I define as the self-actualization born of profound self-knowledge, whole-hearted relationships, and meaningful engagement that I first observed in my cancer patients.

We all know intuitively what it feels like to be in the presence of someone who is deeply connected. It's a quality that makes people irresistibly magnetic, hard to take your eyes or ears off of. They look you in the eye, listen actively, and speak their truth. These are people who know what matters most to them and who align their lives with those profound, personal priorities. They are "authentic," which literally means "true to one's own personality, spirit, or character"—someone who acts according to their most sincerely held, cherished ideals.[2]

When you regularly pay attention to how you really feel and align your daily actions with what matters most to you, you exude a peaceful countenance, well-being, and a confidence about your life path that escapes most people. In the process, you avail yourself of important tools such as mindful awareness, compassion for self and others, gratitude, forgiveness, self-care, and meditation.

The beauty of this approach is that you really only have to remember one thing in order to increase your ability to effect meaningful change across multiple dimensions of your life: make achieving authentic connection your goal. The many individual practices and techniques that we know promote greater well-being fit logically within that framework. Connection provides a single, reliable compass that guides you through the many aspects of life and helps you make decisions day-to-day. It points out your own true north in virtually all contexts, challenges, and crossroads of life.

Learning to read this compass of authentic connection enables you to gain the closer, more satisfying relationship to yourself, to others, and to the world around you that humans crave. I hope you will find it as transformative as I have.

MY STORY

Most of my life, this question of whether or not I felt "connected" never would have occurred to me. Like most people, I lived my life on the run, with little thoughtfulness, self-reflection, or deep intention. I had my ups and downs, good years and bad years, but on the whole, I figured my life was fine and that whatever I was experiencing was to be expected.

What I realize now is that I never really knew myself that well. I knew that I preferred chicken over beef, but I never knew what my deepest longings were, what things meant the most to me, what moved me to my core, what my most deeply held beliefs were, what I stood for, what I valued above all else, what things nourished my soul, what I needed to feel healthy and whole, what made me feel alive, what made my heart leap. . . In reality, I had lived most of my life remarkably disconnected from myself.

My story is not unique. Our modern culture encourages us to be disconnected from our inner truth at every turn and instead encourages us to be enchanted by shallow pursuits. We strive to keep up with goals that have been set for us by others, struggling on a treadmill to nowhere. Most of us have never felt empowered to discover our own unique path, needs, and gifts. It's the rare few, graced with enough inherent wisdom, an enlightened upbringing, or debilitating illness, who are in touch with their deepest truth and living their lives in alignment with that truth.

It wasn't until my thirties that I started to question the "why" behind everything I thought mattered in life. For me, it was a series of major losses and life events that had rocked my world—the loss of a late-term pregnancy, the crushing realization that my marriage was a poor fit and doomed to fail, the fallout of certain friends and family after the eventual divorce—which left me feeling unsure of who I was or what I believed in anymore.

These lost years were marked by much confusion and pain. I felt compelled to examine my life more deeply, and slowly I began to realize that so much of what used to matter no longer did. What I didn't realize at the time was that this destruction of my belief systems and the process of scrutinizing the "why" behind all my choices would eventually lead to my own awakening. I was destined to realize the deep contentment and satisfaction of authentic self-connection.

THE INSPIRATION FOR CONNECTION THEORY

Concurrent with my own personal losses, my professional work shifted to working with medically ill and dying patients at a hospital in San Francisco. When I told people what I was doing for a living, they typically assumed that my job was depressing and difficult. It was actually the opposite.

These medically ill and dying patients were some of the most inspiring, *awake* individuals I had ever met. They had achieved self-awareness and found contentment amidst some of the most challenging circumstances imaginable. Working with these terminally ill men and women, I truly began the most important phase of my training. I was honored and inspired to be among the awake, and I learned much from their example. This experience was my first glimpse of what I would later understand as true, authentic connection.

In a surprisingly large subset of the people I worked with, patients were crystal clear about their viewpoints, their priorities, and the things that truly mattered to them. They cared about spending time with family and close friends and being emotionally available and open. They felt strongly about healing rifts, speaking truth, and being present. They prioritized slowing down, simplifying their activities, and showing gratitude to others.

More than anything, they cared about meaning. They reflected upon meaningful people and events in their lives and what unfinished business they still had. I seldom witnessed these patients reciting details of their work identity, their accomplishments, their belongings or acquisitions. They typically didn't want to expend energy on disagreements, disappointments, or resentments. They were adamant about connecting with loved ones, expressing their feelings or opinions, and living their remaining days in alignment with what mattered the most.

While the hospital patients differed in many ways, including how they ordered their priorities, their overarching attitudes were largely the same regardless of their prognosis. Some of the patients had aggressive life-ending illnesses, and medical treatment was only buying them a little more time—a few months or years. Others had to deal with the maddening uncertainty of ambiguous illnesses, where prognosis and outcome were tenuous. Would remission mean months, days, or years? There was no real answer. Some patients, such as those in cardiac rehabilitation, had just narrowly escaped death and exhibited an overwhelming joy, gratitude, and motivation to make healthy behavioral changes—to restructure their second lease on life in alignment with their newly recognized priorities. Yet regardless of their situation and how much time remained to them, these patients had all shifted their outlooks and were living according to their truths.

My hospital team and I frequently discussed the paradox. This subset of gravely ill patients seemed more content and authentic than people (like me) who did not consider themselves close to death. Despite their enormous health challenges, these patients were usually not suffering much emotionally—they were in a heightened state of awareness, in touch with the deepest parts of themselves, and living those truths every day. When facing death, they were connected to their truths and living each day in harmony with their values. This brought them a deep, lasting peace that sat comfortably side by side with grief and loss.

There were, of course, exceptions. And to be clear, there is no right or wrong way to react to a life-threatening illness. A multitude of individual circumstances and factors causes everyone to react in their own, equally valid way. I became particularly interested and surprised by the individuals who reacted by discovering their true selves and making stronger connections to others, which led them to embrace their inner truths and live in an enviable state of grace and authenticity.

I wanted to learn from those patients and to incorporate their elevated states of mind into my own fractured life, but I failed to master their secrets to deep fulfillment during my time with them. I was not yet awake enough myself to truly understand and appreciate their unique perspectives. Yet my experiences with these patients galvanized me to seek out my own clarity of purpose and learn whether it is possible to live that way every day—rather than waiting for a health crisis to prompt a change. As I worked through my personal challenges and began rebuilding my life, I also set to work exploring these themes of connection and meaning, combining the best of what Western science has taught us about well-being with the wisdom and practices of Eastern traditions.

Eventually, I developed a theory of well-being inspired by the grace, authenticity, and peace I'd first observed in those end-of-life patients who, in contemplating the end of life, better understood how to live it. I came to call my approach *connection theory*.

THE PURPOSE OF A THEORY

Theories answer the question *why*. They try to explain what causes what and what is associated with what. A solid theory needs to meet two important criteria: (1) to be credible in its field and to peers in that area of expertise and (2) to be useful—it needs to help us understand something important and illuminate ways that we can influence the process at hand. Theories are usually developed to help explain phenomena that are not well understood in a way that can be verified through scientific inquiry. They are also useful for providing tentative explanations for phenomena and trends that we are seeing in the world yet don't fully understand.

Theories are what enable science and society to move forward, beyond the knowledge we already have. Without the solid factual footing of a tested theory, ideas are just ideas, like the litany of pop-psychology tips, tricks, techniques, and anecdotal conjecture that we see in so many online forums and self-help books. While these ideas may be momentarily helpful in the short term, they typically lack a coherent framework for widespread application or the reliable, valid information grounding necessary for making significant and lasting behavioral shifts.

Connection theory is a response to the alarming accelerations of human unhappiness and suffering worldwide along with the continual increases in rates of depression, anxiety, suicide, gun violence, loneliness, and isolation in the United States. It attempts to identify and understand the fundamental issues that lead to the breakdown of individuals and society as a whole—and to offer a comprehensive road map for individual thriving and well-being that is logical, intuitive, accessible, and built upon the best information we have about how to achieve life satisfaction and ease suffering.

Connection theory highlights the irony of the digital age—that as we become more constantly and intimately connected by technology, we are nonetheless living more isolated, virtual lives with shallow relationships, with a lack of conscious presence in our physical selves, and with atrophying skills for understanding ourselves and others. Digital connection has created a society starved for true, authentic connection—that elusive sense of contentment, engagement, and unity we all crave as human beings.

THE PURPOSE PROJECT AND CONNECTION LAB

I founded the Purpose Project, a nonprofit think tank and research lab in San Francisco, with the goal of improving individual and societal well-being through research, education, and community programming. This work is my own personal purpose (hence the name): we work to help people understand the role that connection plays in well-being and how to foster it in their everyday lives.

The Connection Lab arm of the Purpose Project develops, supports, and conducts original research on well-being and the impact of authentic connection. We examine factors that promote feelings of connectedness and ways we can help people connect to themselves and each other. Our work utilizes both qualitative and quantitative methods of research, as appropriate for the nature of our inquiry.

When we gather experiences of connection—a qualitative approach to research—we analyze the stories and experiences people share with us to better understand the role that connection plays in our lives, especially as it relates to well-being. We also rely on quantitative research methods—more traditional scientific studies where the impact of different variables is measured against a control—for rigorous testing of hypotheses, such as whether a specific intervention or practice is effective.

We publish our research in peer-reviewed academic journals, present our findings at professional conferences, and incorporate what we learn into our theory of connection to help refine our understanding and approach. Our work at the Connection Lab profoundly informs the programs and educational offerings of the Purpose Project as well as the ideas and suggestions in this book.

INTRODUCTION TO CONNECTION THEORY

Over the last twenty years or so, we've seen an explosion of books about how to become happier. While some of these books are based on solid scientific research about subjective well-being, the pursuit of "happiness" is really the wrong angle.

Happiness is an emotion—and like all emotions, it comes and it goes. We feel happy when we get what we want—a raise, a special dinner out, the latest tech gadget—but in most cases the feeling doesn't linger long after Christmas morning. We get used to the new normal as our baseline, and it stops giving us pleasure. So to find happiness again, we have to start looking for something better than what we have. This never-ending, escalating cycle of selfish craving and taking continues in what's known as the *hedonic treadmill*—and like most treadmills, the pursuit of happiness doesn't get you far.[3]

What we truly yearn for is lasting fulfillment and a sense of living life with meaning and purpose grounded in something bigger than ourselves. But chasing down more happiness doesn't necessarily get us there. Research shows that what promotes happiness—getting what we want—has relatively little to do with a meaningful life.[4] These findings are consistent with the conventional wisdom that money can't solve everything. No matter how often we're able to cheer ourselves up with toys or indulgences, our lives will still feel empty unless we've identified and connected with some larger purpose for ourselves.

Tapping into what is meaningful for you and making life decisions that align with those priorities is the essence of connection. By orienting life around our souls' deepest truths, we gain the tranquility, comfort, and gratitude that enable us to experience enduring satisfaction and joy.

What I call connection is a holistic approach to well-being that focuses on the notion of *connectedness* . . . to oneself, to others, and to the world around us. This approach defines "connection" as the level of familiarity, closeness, intimacy, and understanding a person enjoys in relation to the various aspects of their life.

For example: How in touch are you with your priorities, deepest yearnings, or the truth of your relationships? How much are you living your life in alignment with your highest values and doing the things that bring you the most meaning and sense of purpose?

Grounded in the established psychological research and theoretical constructs of the last hundred years, my theory of connection brings together the most powerful tools and techniques known to promote satisfaction and well-being: engagement, purpose, meaning, self-knowledge, self-compassion, forgiveness, gratitude, self-expression, and mindfulness, to name a few.

Our understanding of connection acknowledges the need to tend to certain primal human cravings—for social relationships, nature, physical activity, sensory experiences, and other key features of hunter-gatherer societies—in order to optimize our well-being. It blends the best of what Western psychology and medicine already know about good living with the wisdom of Eastern philosophies to help us thrive in a modern world we are not physically or psychologically evolved to inhabit. Connection keeps us oriented as we tend to our bodies' physical and mental needs in the context of our complex, isolating, and technology-driven world.

These many, varied contributors to well-being are all brought together through this intuitive concept of *connection*—tapping into a present place of peace and power to transcend the challenges of being human in the modern world.

Connection is the doorway to our higher selves, where we find the life purpose, meaning, contentment, and lasting peace that all human beings seek. Learning how to achieve this state of connectedness is the key to achieving self-actualization and ending personal conflict. Relative to other behavioral change, connection requires very little effort since it lights a fire within, instead of a fire beneath. Feeling more connected is intrinsically rewarding and provides the missing *why* that undermines so many lofty pursuits in life.

I've observed in both my personal and clinical experience that some people—the lucky few—are natural aces at living deeply connected lives, but that most of us struggle with it in one form or another. Research and personal experience have also proven to me that connection is a skill that *can* be (re)taught and (re)learned. Just a little effort and practice can dramatically boost our abilities, illuminate our truths, and transform our lives.

Connection is the lens or compass through which we can see our path to well-being. It unites in a single word the contentment of authenticity, the profound peace of purposeful living, and the rapture of giving and receiving love. By learning to connect, reconnect, and cultivate connection across all different aspects of life, I believe people can dramatically change their lives for the better . . . and in doing so, hopefully improve society, as well.

WHO IS THIS FOR?

I sincerely believe that connection theory is an approach to well-being that can benefit everyone to one degree or another. It is not a miracle cure or panacea, but even people with depression and other serious mental illness can improve their health and satisfaction through connection-promoting practices—though of course I encourage such people to work closely with their own mental health-care professionals in deciding which practices to emphasize or omit.

A health or personal crisis (like the ones my patients and I experienced) sometimes helps catalyze transformative life changes, but it's not strictly necessary. Everyone inherently has this possibility for growth. At some point, each of us is confronted with the question of whether the life we lead is the life we wanted.

Whenever you are ready to face those scary questions and begin to find the answers, I believe that connection will help show you the way.

I recognize that not all of the real-life examples and suggestions in this book will be feasible for everyone to try for various reasons, and I hope my point is clear that there is no one way to cultivate connection. The range of human experience is vast and breathtaking in its diversity. Connection is about learning to find your own best self and living as that person as best you can in your day-to-day reality. Since it was impossible to include suggestions for every life scenario, I have attempted to include a range of ideas taken from my experiences working and talking with people from a variety of backgrounds and circumstances.

I encourage you to share the practices that resonate with you, as well as those that don't, so that we can all continue learning together. You can contact me through my website, kristineklussman.com.

WHAT'S AHEAD

This book discusses the importance of connection to oneself in several key areas: connection to one's own personal values, meaning, and purpose (or work); connection to the physical self and body; and connection to the world of emotions. Each chapter builds on what has come before, starting with the connection to your own personal values that will guide you through all other areas of life. In each section, I offer real-life stories, advice, and guidance taken from real-world experiences and established scientific research to help you recognize and address the habits that block connection in your own life, build new habits that nurture connection in everyday activities, and achieve deep, enduring life satisfaction that transcends ordinary happiness. The final chapter offers practical advice on making time and space for connection so you can implement lasting change that makes a real difference in your health and well-being. The appendix provides some simple worksheets for exercises mentioned in the main text to help get you started on your connection journey *today*.

Connection theory provides a simple but comprehensive framework for finding answers to your life's biggest questions. My hope is that it will help all of us live the best life we can, in the time we have remaining.

Chapter 1

BEGIN WITH SELF-CONNECTION

How true are you to yourself?
That is the degree of your contentment.

VERNON HOWARD[1]

L ife is about relationships . . . the relationships we have with ourselves, with others, with our communities, the earth, and life itself. Our experience of life is defined by the quality of these relationships. The path to being a better worker, partner, or parent begins by discovering and following our own truth first and foremost. When you're right with yourself, you're right with the world. This is why connection theory starts with connection to the self.

When we are connected to ourselves, it is usually experienced as a time of growth, expansion, and clarity—something we as human beings covet. When you are connected to yourself, connection to others and the world you live in flows naturally and effortlessly from there. Being in tune with and in touch with your own deepest truths is what enables you to move forward in the world from a place of confidence and purposefulness.

Most importantly, being connected to yourself is a loving act that enables your heart to open first to yourself and then to all that you encounter. This intimate knowledge and acceptance of yourself is the foundation that supports your ability to connect deeply with others. So it is wise to first examine your relationship to yourself before considering other relationships.

Self-Connection, as defined by Connection Lab research participants

We sometimes discover deeper connection to the self as a byproduct of experiencing profound connection to something else first, such as a moment of awe in nature or a transcendent relationship with another human being. When falling in love, for example, we typically experience a surge of vitality, compassion, openness to new experiences, and a desire to take better care of ourselves—this is being more connected. Such wondrous and treasured moments in life can and often do open up different sides of us and enable deeper understanding of ourselves. This haphazard and almost "accidental" learning is how the vast majority of people become more connected to themselves. Those moments of enlightened connection seem beyond our control and are not easily "conjured up."

Throughout my career as a health psychologist specializing in serious medical illness and end-of-life care, I witnessed so many of my clients find the clarity and the connection to themselves and others that had eluded them for a lifetime. I've also learned that we don't have to wait for a crisis or external event in our lives to come into this more enlightened state. We can cultivate this awareness at will.

DEFINING SELF-CONNECTION

Our academic research at the Connection Lab has defined *self-connection* as consisting of three components: (1) an *awareness* of oneself, (2) an *acceptance* of oneself based on this awareness, and (3) an *alignment* of one's behavior with this awareness.[2]

Simply put, being connected to yourself means that you are in touch with your deepest feelings, wants, and needs and are taking action aligned with those needs. When you are self-connected, you are in tune with yourself and can slow down enough to hear and listen to your gut in order to know what the next right action is. You are able to feel and discern things that easily hurt your feelings, what kind of movement your body is aching for, when you need alone time, and what you need to nourish yourself. In our research, people frequently describe it as feeling alive, present, calm, awake . . . "like I'm walking in my bones."[3]

When you are connected to yourself, you are thoughtful about time and use it wisely. You gravitate toward the meaningful and avoid the meaningless. You check in with yourself each day to acknowledge and fulfill any unmet needs. You take care of yourself in fundamental ways and are thoughtful about good nutrition, exercise, and sleep. You are not tempted to chase fool's gold and instead scrutinize the real value of things.

You consult regularly with your internal guidance system and have a strong inner compass that alerts you to when you are off track. You are able to do quick inventories or scans of your possibilities and make better choices. You are able to pause and easily access what your highest priorities are in any given situation.

You are honest with yourself and with others. You recognize and express your emotions. You are able to take stock and be grateful. You are curious about where you source true joy, and you follow your bliss. More often than not, your actions are aligned with your deepest truths. You feel fulfilled in the moment and in the big picture, knowing that you are tending to your deepest needs. You are proud of yourself and feel good about your choices. Above all, you know and honor yourself each day in a multitude of ways, small and large.

Self-connection manifests in different ways, depending on the context. It can mean experiencing a state of flow as you make art, feeling fully present and unblocked in your relationships, feeling at ease and at peace as you fold laundry, or being fully engaged and excited as you prepare a challenging recipe. You may feel acutely aware of your experience, your oneness with other living things. You may also feel emotionally vulnerable as you *let yourself be* with important or difficult emotions.

You feel at one with the world, relaxed and grateful. Questions are answered. You want for nothing. You feel full and exquisitely alive, aware of your surroundings, and there's no place you'd rather be. You are where you should be, doing what you should be doing, without a doubt.

Our research at the Connection Lab shows that higher levels of self-connection are also strongly linked to greater well-being.[4] In several of our studies, we asked people to report on their level of self-connection and then examined how it predicted their levels of eudaimonic well-being (flourishing) and hedonic well-being (life satisfaction). Even after accounting for the effects of important demographic factors, including age, area of residence, education, gender, and race, we found that self-connection was strongly associated with both kinds of well-being.

Interestingly, our results also showed that the more mindful people were, the more self-connected they were—and that the more self-connected they were, the greater their well-being. These findings suggest that self-connection is an important result of developing an effective mindfulness practice and helps explain how mindfulness fosters overall well-being.

More recently, Connection Lab research found that greater self-connection also seems to inoculate people against stress-related burnout.[5] Our study of business school students found that more self-connected students had lower rates of personal and school-related burnout than students with lower levels of self-connection, regardless of how much they thought stress was a debilitating force in their life. Generally speaking, self-connection seems to help us cope more effectively with life and enjoy a richer, more rewarding existence.

DISCONNECTION: WHAT IT LOOKS LIKE AND HOW IT HAPPENS

Modern societies have become disconnected and cut off from so many of the things that bring us our greatest sense of joy and fulfillment. We are bombarded with advertisements, obligations, distractions, and temptations virtually 24/7. We live and work in an attention economy, where businesses buy and sell us for the value of our attention. We're constantly being told what we "should" be doing, wearing, eating, and thinking by businesses selling whatever that is. We spend hours staring at what other people are doing, wearing, eating, and thinking through the magic of the internet and social media. It's a small wonder people often feel they are churning their wheels with everyday demands and minutiae rather than progressing through life to achieve something important. We don't have a clear idea of where we want to go, what we want to do, or who we really are. In the constant clamor for our attention, life gets shrunk down to the "practical considerations" and stream of to-dos we face each day. Gone are the days of reflection about who we are, where we come from, and our purpose on Earth.

One of the biggest challenges we face is learning how to connect with ourselves and others in this wildly disconnecting daily existence . . . what we call, ironically, the "connected" age. Digital connection has not made us more authentically connected—and I would argue it has caused more disconnection than it has resolved. Social media and email facilitate the act of communication, but not necessarily connection in the sense that we're talking about here.

In fact, few of us have ever been taught how to connect authentically with ourselves, others, or the world. We don't learn it in school—even in psychology classes—and we don't learn at home. Our teachers and families don't teach us, because they themselves have never learned how. Disconnection is a distinctly modern malady, and we need to teach ourselves how to recognize, treat, and overcome it.

In the United States, disconnection is rampant. So many of us are filled with distrust of political institutions, media, technology, industry leaders, religious leaders, and "friends" and neighbors. Many people live in a state of permanent unease and defensive aggression, trying to protect what we have so no one else can take it—not because we actually want it. Many of us feel rudderless, disempowered, lonely, and disappointed. In this state, we are easily swayed by appeals to tribalism and in-group/out-group divisions. Feeling part of a group is primally rewarding on one level—but it's not enough. We need also to understand and embrace who we are as individuals and the purpose we have in our daily actions.

The symptoms of disconnection are many and quite familiar. Friend A seems to have their mind on something else as they talk to you, and there is no emotional resonance between you. Friend B is always busy or in a hurry, forever chasing something, never truly satisfied with the present moment. A relative asks, "How are you?" but doesn't seem interested in your answer.

One of our study participants described disconnection as "the person who walks past me on the sidewalk and I call it 'looking for a quarter'—they won't bring up their head, they won't look up, certainly aren't gonna say hi. . . . It's adrift, sad, searching, resentful, cold, dark, alone, selfish, self-centered."[6]

Disconnected people may feel like they're doing what they think they're supposed to be doing, following the social script—but their hearts aren't in it. They may come across as distracted or insincere. Engagement and interest tend to be driven by secondary gain, rather than an internal satisfaction. It may feel unrewarding to spend time with disconnected people because they are emotionally blocked and preoccupied with themselves. They may seem deathly afraid of making big decisions, choosing wrong, and settling for less. They may lack compassion or empathy for others. They may keep everyone emotionally at arm's length, living in a thick layer of defensive armor.

One of our Connection Lab study participants described feeling disconnected as a kind of disembodied experience: "Like my mind could make my body do everything it needed to in order to be 'productive,' but I was still not me. Almost like my soul and head were separated and in different hemispheres."[7]

Disconnection often comes on slowly, imperceptibly. But, like the fable about the frog being slowly boiled alive, before we know it, the "heat" of disconnection has crept up on us gradually, and we've learned to live with it. It has become part of our culture without us even realizing it. This chronic, insidious disconnection often manifests as a nagging sense of dissatisfaction, even though there may be lots of great things happening in our lives. It can feel like unease, uncertainty, indecision; we don't really know what we need or want, what the next right action to take is. Disconnected people don't feel completely comfortable in their own skin. You're robbed of self-worth, and you seek constant external validation. When you're disconnected, you feel inauthentic, even to yourself.

You may often feel like you're on autopilot, just going through the motions, rudderless, and without a strong sense of purpose. Your life may feel too busy and complex, but you can't fathom how to change it. When you do have downtime, it may be difficult to determine what you truly need or want, so you fall into old routines instead. Life might feel like it's happening *to* you, instead of being authored *by* you. Anytime you start to consciously notice signs of disconnection, you feel anxious and shy away from confronting them.

Disconnected individuals experience a sense of narrowed options. They may not be able to see the big picture or have faith in the unfolding nature of life, yet they envy those who seem at peace with themselves. The disconnected are often operating from a place of fear and rarely from a place of courage. As a result, they are full of easy judgment, talking too much and listening too little. Even when these people are highly functional and accomplished, they are typically not truly satisfied or thriving.

In the presence of others, you may appear slightly unsettled, distracted, and frenetic. You might find it difficult to make consistent eye contact and uncomfortable to go beneath surface conversations. You may give the people around you the impression that you don't quite have time for them and are going to bounce soon, not because you truly need to leave, but because your attention is divided.

Dealing with a disconnected individual can be problematic, but imagine what it's like to be that person! The sense of disconnection may lead to depression, which—if viewed positively—is the body's wake-up call, and a potentially life-changing one.

These symptoms of disconnection can manifest in countless different ways and combinations for different people, and may be slight or extreme. Disconnection itself might be continuous, lasting days, weeks, and years . . . or on and off within a single day. You might experience interludes of being connected but slip back into disconnection frequently.

Connection Lab's research shows that many internal and external factors typically contribute to disconnection, and looking closely at these can help us better understand how to reconnect.[8]

HOW DO WE BECOME DISCONNECTED FROM OURSELVES?

Do you remember the timeless classic "Logical Song," by the '80s progressive rock band, Supertramp? As a teenager, I couldn't get enough of this song, and when my parents weren't home I would walk around the house with my Sony Walkman on, belting the lyrics at the top of my lungs.

Then and now, this song perfectly captures the natural, eyes-wide-open joy of connection we experience as kids and the way that easy self-awareness is eaten away by parental and societal expectations as we grow into adulthood and are taught to be rational, responsible grown-ups.[9] Our blissful, openhearted sense of wonder and self-knowledge are chipped away as we're taught the values of conformity, practicality, and so-called maturity in our decision-making. At the end of this education, we're left wondering, as the singer does, who we really are.

Disconnection comes on slowly and in subtle ways—it's death by a thousand self-betrayals. And then we wake up with a start, realizing that we have lost touch with ourselves and the things we hold dear. We are sleepwalking in a narrow band of emotion, lost and drifting without a clear path home.

The sad irony is that the more disconnected somebody is, the more unlikely they are to even realize it. Our hardwired human psychological defenses kick in and try to protect us from the pain of our unhappiness, particularly if it is chronic and ongoing—which disconnection usually is.

I wrote my dissertation in graduate school on psychological defenses, focusing primarily on the classic Freudian defenses (repression, denial, projection, etc.). But what ended up becoming far more fascinating and relevant to me in my own life was learning about the subtler and seemingly harmless defensive strategies we use to stay blissfully ignorant of our own unmet needs.

In her seminal book about the power of vulnerability, Dr. Brené Brown describes these strategies in a more modern way as "numbing" techniques, and they include all the variety of ways that we comfort and soothe ourselves, helping us avoid dealing with our real feelings and deeper needs. These numbing strategies can include anything from eating unhealthy "comfort" foods, staying busy, watching mindless TV, procrastinating, off-loading onto other people, and other ways we carve out a temporary reprieve from our underlying feelings. Reprieves can be positive, but they allow us to avoid confronting the underlying problem. And, as Brown points out, when we numb ourselves from the bad feelings, we also numb our ability to feel joy and gratitude, as well as our ability to connect.[10]

According to neuroscientist and psychologist Dr. Rick Hanson, there is another more "evolutionary reason why our brain interferes with our ability to feel oneness and sublime connection." Hanson explains:

> To keep our ancestors alive, the brain evolved strong tendencies toward fear, including an ongoing internal trickle of unease. This little whisper of worry keeps you scanning your inner and outer worlds for signs of trouble.
> This background of unsettledness and watchfulness is so automatic that you can forget it's there. . . .
> The brain's default setting of apprehensiveness is a great way to keep a monkey looking over its shoulder for something about to pounce. But it's a crummy way to live. It wears down well-being, feeds anxiety and depression, and makes people play small in life.
> Even worse, it's based on a lie.[11]

Another evolutionary obstacle making it difficult for us to incline our minds toward well-being is the negativity bias. Hanson's book *Hardwiring Happiness* discusses how for survival and self-protection, the human brain is far more adapted to remembering negative events in our lives than positive events in order to ward off future threats. Hanson describes the brain as "Velcro for bad experiences but Teflon for good ones."[12]

Emotions related to well-being do not naturally sink in with humans, so we must do our part to cultivate habits and incline our minds toward the states that truly serve us best. Fortunately, as Hanson's book goes on to explain, it is possible to reshape, rewire, and modify our brain tendencies and structure.

This relatively new theory of neuroplasticity is an incredibly exciting area of research that offers both hope and actionable strategies for improving our lives.

In short: though it can be difficult to overcome our natural hardwiring and achieve true, blissful connection, it can be done. And it's so worth it.

RECONNECTING TO SELF REQUIRES INTENTION, ATTENTION, AND ONE SIMPLE QUESTION

As much as the deck seems psychologically stacked against us being able to maintain positive connections, it really is possible—and even natural. Sometimes, we can experience spontaneous moments of natural connection without consciously trying. More often, though, we clear the path to connection by inclining our minds toward it—deliberately setting out to connect or reconnect. This is the most effective way to retrain our brains and supercharge connection. The more we incline our minds to connection, the better our brains become at doing it. Just as muscles become stronger when we use them regularly, our brains create and bolster the neural connections that make connection easier every time we do it.

But you may be asking, how and where do we begin? Reconnecting to self is fundamentally about getting to know yourself better—becoming familiar with your needs and desires, and then attending to those priorities in your day-to-day actions. Once you have clear-eyed self-knowledge, you can set an intention to become more connected and give that goal your fully engaged attention. These two ingredients—intention and attention—can solve virtually all of life's problems.

The third key tool in the reconnection toolbox is asking yourself the simple question: *Am I feeling connected to myself right now?*

We'll tackle each of these in turn.

Start with Setting an Intention

Setting, declaring, writing down, and discussing an intention are all very powerful ways of setting change in motion. The act of physically writing things out forces us to articulate what we want—and to behold what that is, every time we see it. It primes our attention to the goal, making it easier for us to spot and move toward it in our daily lives. We literally rewire our brain to see and pursue the end result we want. By writing down the goal or sharing it with others, we also create some external accountability for ourselves—something many people need in order to follow through on projects done solely for their own benefit.

Why do you want to make a change? Why are you unwilling to carry on the way you have been? Why did you buy this book?

The first and most important step is getting clear about why living a connected life matters to you. The "why" behind anything we do is what determines our success. A good friend, author Karen Jones, has a great saying that I frequently conjure up when I am wobbling in my commitment: "The greater the why, the easier the how."

For me, my "why" stemmed from a very slow realization that time, and consequently my life, was speeding past, the years flying by at warp speed. Yet no matter how hard I tried or how much I chased good experiences, I was never fully able to savor my life and feel satisfied by the overall picture. I often had the subtle feeling that time was being wasted and that priorities were not completely in sync with my real needs and truth. I also saw my kids growing up before my eyes and had the aching feeling that for as long as I was not truly clear on who I was and what I wanted, I would be limited in my ability to be fully present and connected to them.

Once I became clear on my "why," it was easy for me to set a very strong intention to become more in tune with and connected to myself.

Why do you want to make a change? Asking the question and answering it honestly gets you closer to achieving the life that you crave. The reasons "why" will bolster you in your moments of weakness and galvanize you to keep working toward your goal. Keep them somewhere you will see them often.

Add a Dose of Mindful Awareness

Mindfulness, in simple terms, is about paying attention without judgment. Using mindfulness in the service of becoming more connected to our lives brings a gentle awareness and intentional observation of life, with the goal of discovering what leads you to feeling more or less connected each day. Multiple studies at Connection Lab have confirmed that mindfulness bolsters self-connection (which in turn boosts well-being) and aids us in feeling that our lives have meaning.[13]

It's important to remember a couple of things about mindfulness. First, try to stay neutral when you observe yourself—otherwise probing your feelings can become too provocative and lead you into unhelpful reactivity, which might discourage further inquiry. Dr. Jon Kabat-Zinn, the father of the Western world's modern-day understanding of mindfulness, describes its essence as a loving awareness: "Mindfulness is a particular way of paying attention that is on purpose, in the present moment, and nonjudgmentally."[14]

When Kabat-Zinn speaks of awareness that comes from paying attention to the present moment without judgment, he is speaking of connected, loving, and intimate attention. The purpose of mindfulness is to reach clarity and understanding so we are better able to live wisely. We begin to see how we get consumed in our thoughts, reactive patterns, and sources of suffering. It is about creating spaciousness. Without awareness, there's no space; with no space, there's no room to choose our response.[15]

Kabat-Zinn also refers to the importance of having a "beginner's mind" and describes how this stance of openness, curiosity, and lack of preconceived ideas leads to true clarity and wisdom. So, if you feel confused about where this inquiry is headed, it's okay. Just keep going with a curious, open mind toward what you discover. The "aha" moments will eventually start pouring in, and you will be rewarded.

Awareness is your key to freedom. The more practiced you become, the more attainable connection will be. Mindful attention is an essential skill for cultivating connection in every aspect of life.

The Simple Question to Ask

When you are trying to learn a new skill or make a major change in your life, it helps to focus on a guiding light—or in this case, a single guiding question. It's concise, easy to remember, and, therefore, effective.

When I began my journey to understand connection, I had no clear understanding of what it looked like or felt like to be more "connected" to myself. So I started simply asking myself, Am I feeling connected to myself right now? I asked the question as often as I could remember, eager to see what I might discover.

At first, I felt no real connection to myself or my activities. Honestly, I wasn't even sure what I was looking for, but I thought I'd know it when I felt it.

Am I feeling connected to myself right now? Often, it seemed like I was going through the motions on autopilot, sometimes more or less satisfied—but never really connected. I was mildly content as I volunteered at the kids' school, drove to work, attended a meeting, made dinner. But I wasn't excited about any of it, and I didn't feel stimulated by my usual activities.

I learned that I wasn't feeling particularly connected to the food I was eating, to my colleagues as we were having our team meetings, to the conversations I was having with other mothers at school pickup, or to my boys as I was ushering them from one after-school activity to another. This initial act of checking in with myself often and asking this simple question led to an avalanche of information that helped me realize that indeed there were times when I felt more connected in my life and times when I felt completely disconnected.

Am I feeling connected to myself right now? A quick body scan and a deep breath alongside this contemplative question helped highlight if I was holding tension anywhere in my body. Often the body can answer the question better than the thinking mind. I also started jotting my observations down in a journal, making it easier to track and notice patterns.

This simple technique soon became a cornerstone for helping others learn how to become more connected. Participants in one of my parenting groups reported that tracking their own level of self-connection this way—a quick body scan, a deep breath, and asking themselves how connected they were feeling at that moment—seemed to heighten the quality of the interaction with their children. One of my clients noticed a sense of unease when she was blow-drying her hair in the morning and found her mind whirling around with negative thoughts every evening just before her husband came home and while they were catching up about the day.

At first, it's not important to figure out why you are feeling unease or disconnection, and it may bog you down to over-focus on that part. Try to let go of any judgmental reactions or interpretations as your mind seeks out the meaning behind the disconnection. This part is really important, because if you beat up yourself (or other people) about what you are noticing, you may never gain true insight. And you're likely to stop your inquiry altogether.

The goal of this exercise is simply to become more aware of the causes and conditions that influence your level of connection. Try to observe your moments of ease and contentment (and moments of unease) throughout the day. Continue to question yourself and listen for the answer, and you will notice change. In a way, you are priming your brain to search for connection.

Be a curious, neutral, passive observer of yourself. When you discover a moment of connection or disconnection, note it mentally or in your journal, and say to yourself, *That's interesting*. Within a day or two, you should have many observations and begin to see patterns emerging.

Trust that simply asking this one question throughout the day and noticing how your activities impact the answer will unearth useful information. You may discover (as I did) that much of your time is spent thoughtlessly, just responding to the demands of life and getting caught up with whatever is right in front of you.

Asking this one simple question—Am I feeling connected to myself?—is a beautiful and easy starting place to begin a journey of self-discovery. As the poet

Rainer Maria Rilke wrote, "try to love the questions themselves. . . . [S]omeday far in the future, you will gradually, without even noticing it, live your way into the answer."[16]

Chapter 2

CONNECTING WITH YOUR TRUE SELF

Knowing yourself is the beginning of all wisdom.

UNKNOWN

We all seek to know ourselves, to discover what we stand for, and to learn more about that which has meaning in our lives.

While some people take an "ignorance is bliss" approach to life, most of us would jump at the opportunity to know our true, inner selves. This desire explains the timeless appeal of fortune-tellers, mystics, and astrologers, all of whom promise to reveal hidden truths. It's a somewhat romantic and age-old concept that profound, secret truths are lurking beneath the surface inside of each of us. Yet many of the greatest thinkers and philosophers of all time also considered the quest for the true self to be a noble life pursuit.

In spite of the shroud of magic and mystery around the notion of the "true self," becoming more acquainted with and connected to your true self is a straightforward process of investigating your most deeply held truths. This path involves understanding where you already source meaning, learning new ways you can make and identify meaning, finding your small and large life purposes, and discovering the values and priorities you stand for. Most authors and experts discuss these concepts as distinct efforts and processes, while neglecting the bigger picture. But understanding how these powerful concepts work together is the key to finding your way. That 360-degree view empowers you to create a unique road map and mission statement for life and to tap into the bliss of knowing you are on the right track.

If you are like most people, you probably feel like you know yourself decently well, and yet, at the same time you recognize you have deeper yearnings, undiscovered passions, and unmet needs. You crave a better or more complete understanding of your true self.

But what is the true self, and why is it important? Until recently, the notion was defined primarily by philosophers, theologians, and great thinkers of the past. The psychological and scientific community dedicated little attention or research into the concept of a true self or how it might relate to well-being. Our research lab is one of only a few places dedicated to defining this construct and measuring its relevance to life satisfaction.

As part of that process, we're rejecting the description of an "inner truth" as something hidden or lurking just beneath our awareness, since it implies that it is beyond our grasp or requires major excavating to uncover . . . neither of which is true. In our experience, our deepest truths are everywhere, all around us every day. We are just not in the habit of paying attention to them. Our lives tend to get so habituated to narrow routines, we rarely have the time, the space, or the inclination to ponder our greater selves, our choices, our honest feelings and reactions, and our dreams. Chances to take stock of our lives or to ask whether we are at odds with our vision—or if we even have a vision—are few and far between.

Most people use some level of avoidance as a coping technique to prevent becoming too aware of areas of their lives that are out of alignment with their deepest truths. This is human nature and the way the brain protects itself from feeling too much pain. For some, it's far too threatening to open up to bigger truths and realities that may no longer serve them well, particularly since digging around in the psyche may lead to conclusions they are not ready to face.

We typically avoid misaligned areas in our life that would require change, such as ending a relationship, changing jobs, moving, switching majors at school, confronting someone, or breaking a destructive habit. Only when the pain gets so bad that we can no longer maintain the denial do we make the change. Our lives may feel like they are falling apart, but we often emerge from the turmoil as better versions of ourselves.

Marriage was once an area of massive misalignment in my own life, but I refused to address it. The arrival of our children brought to light a disturbing realization that my husband and I had nearly opposite values and priorities when it came to family and parenting. Neither of us felt that our true needs were being honored or met. We went through the usual period of trying everything we could think of to repair things, not quite sure if the relationship had truly reached its end. That line can be a gray area, and it's hard to know when you've crossed it. Our fear of ending our relationship, facing the unknown, and dealing with enormous change compelled us to stay together well after we'd passed that line—two years too long. During that time, I repeatedly ignored the signs, symptoms, and voices in my head. I *knew* the truth of the matter yet remained in denial that our marriage was doomed.

Interestingly, it was during those two years that we did the most damage to each other, ourselves, our bodies, and our children by living so out of alignment with our truth. Those two years are the biggest regret from my divorce. They have also been the hardest to recover from and forgive myself for in spite of the fact that all of our lives were improved dramatically when we finally split up.

This torturous pattern arises when we refuse to see or listen to our inner truth—what some people refer to as our soul's guidance. Putting aside the question of what a soul is, or if it even exists, this guidance comes from our intuitive understanding of our most fundamental needs and values. We frequently reject or ignore this guidance when it conflicts with other values we feel we "should" prioritize, as Dr. Lissa Rankin describes so vividly here:

- *The wedding invites are already sent, so you should go through with the wedding.*
- *You've already spent so many years training for the job your soul wants you to leave. The money is good. It's a secure job in an insecure economy. You should stay.*
- *Your soul is telling you that you don't have to take care of the elderly relative who treats you like dirt, but another part of you thinks you should.*
- *You're working yourself to death to pay for the fancy house and the private school, and your soul is telling you to simplify, downsize, and send the kids to public school. But you don't think you should sacrifice their quality of life for yours.*
- *Your soul doesn't want to go to church anymore, but you should.*
- *Your soul doesn't want to hang out with the friend you've known for twenty years anymore, but you should. . . .*
- *Your soul wants to dance under the moonlight, but you should go to the gym.*[1]

Often our inner guidance is telling us to make radical changes in our lives—changes that buck what we think we *should* do, changes that require radical acts of courage. It's terrifying to take a leap into the unknown. So we enslave ourselves with endless shoulds based on fear of uncertainty, guilt, or the desire to please others. Brick by brick, we imprison ourselves in incredibly complex lives, surrounded by unchallenged structures and obligations that have been handed to us by our parents, our culture, or our partners.

Reconnecting and communing with these inner truths, however, is essential to reclaiming our lives from the *shoulds* that so often control them.

CLARIFYING YOUR VALUES

What do you stand for? What do you believe in?

I'm not talking about dogmatic beliefs that are narrow and rigid. I mean concepts like believing in a just world, ending violence against children, and treating others with respect. Connected living is having a set of deeply held values and beliefs that guide you. It's knowing who we are and what we stand for and living in integrity with those values. While uncovering and cultivating meaning in your life will give you incredible information about the types of things that truly matter to you, these are only clues to uncovering your deepest truths—your values.

As you come to recognize what you actually stand for across a variety of topics and domains, it will become easier to identify the types of activities and people that will be meaningful for you. Some people know themselves better than others in this regard. But it's likely you have big blind spots in important areas of your life—like work, romantic partnership, parenting, civic responsibilities, community—where your belief system may never have truly coalesced, or perhaps has lost its sharp focus with time.

As a society, we constantly talk about our values and refer to them in an abstract way, but do we really know what we're talking about? If someone were to give you a pop quiz on naming your top ten values, how would you score? Most people, when confronted about their value systems, feel unsure of themselves.

Those values we state off the cuff might also be quite dated compared with who we are today and probably include components we've inherited from our parents, spouses, teachers, and bosses, as well as things that we think we *should* stand for but that don't reflect our real truths. Rarely do people take the time as adults to inventory their values and try and work to discern which ones *truly* matter to them versus which ones are outdated or have been handed down from another generation.

At a week-long workshop on values, one young man had a tearful revelation that his top values of achievement, self-sacrifice, and responsibility weren't at all *his* true values, but were instead ideals that he'd absorbed from his father's preaching. It became clear as he described his life and relationship with his wife that adherence to these values had enslaved him to a life he never felt was truly his own and led to an underlying resentment. At the time of our workshop, he was working in finance, a job he hated, playing out traditional gender roles with his wife. He was the overly responsible breadwinner, and she was the stay-at-home mom. He was frightened and almost ashamed at first to admit that his real, most treasured values were play, humor, and fun. He shared his long-time fantasy of working as a stand-up comedian.

It was easy for everyone in the workshop to affirm the authenticity of these values, given what a fun-loving, lighthearted, hilarious goofball this guy was underneath his façade of seriousness. Though he was scared to death of destabilizing his family and letting others down, and he had no clear idea how to start living more in alignment with his values, he admitted feeling relieved to have voiced his inner truth and agreed to have a conversation with his wife as a starting point. A few days later, he exuberantly reported to us that—to his amazement—his wife's reaction had been positive and that she admitted feeling trapped herself and unfulfilled by being at home with the kids. His commitment to action was to enroll in an acting class.

Years later, the couple is still blossoming as they embrace their own true values and needs. He has become the stay-at-home dad who delights in working on his comedy with his kids and friends, and she has launched a business and is now fulfilling her own dreams.

In order to succeed in any area of your life, or in order to have a prayer of being "true to yourself," you have to know where you stand and what you truly value. If you don't, then it's time for you to allow yourself some space to contemplate the various areas of your life and to develop your own core set of beliefs. Attempting to collect, examine, and reflect on all of your values in a holistic fashion is a turbocharged way to quickly get to "know thyself!" as the ancient Greeks prescribed. It's also an incredibly empowering and rewarding experience.

TOOLS FOR IDENTIFYING YOUR VALUES

The simplest and most direct way to get started is to look at a thorough list of values (there are several wonderful ones on the internet) and see which resonate with you. Note the ones that speak to you—as many as you want. If you hold particular values that aren't on these lists, just add them to your own.

Now, the hard part: prioritizing. Think about which twenty are truly the most important to you, and then look for common themes among them (kindness, caring, and compassion might all fit under "love," for example) to help you condense the list down to the top ten. From those, you will draw your top three most important values. (More on this prioritizing process shortly.)

Some examples of common values are:

- Creativity
- Courage
- Authenticity
- Excellence
- Belonging
- Caring
- Commitment
- Health
- Lifelong learning
- Parenting
- Honesty
- Independence

- Initiative
- Integrity
- Reliability
- Resourcefulness
- Safety
- Self-discipline
- Self-expression
- Self-respect
- Order
- Usefulness
- Leadership

FROM MACRO TO MICRO

I also recommend using a journaling exercise to go deeper into understanding values in particular arenas of life. I typically ask people to dedicate a full page to each major area of importance. Each person may have their own way of identifying different areas of life, but all may include some version of health, well-being, work, finance, romantic partnership, self-care, parenting, friendships, learning, personal growth, play, creativity, community involvement, and service. There's a worksheet with these categories in the appendix for your convenience.

Set aside an hour to take a stab at jotting down some initial things that you stand for in each category. Don't expect to conquer the whole thing all at once. This will become a living, breathing record that you populate over time, and especially over the course of this book.

There are so many values, multiplied across so many areas of our lives, that it's nearly impossible to keep them straight in our head, making it even more impossible to live by them. But it's extraordinarily powerful to look back at your page on work, as I did recently to check in, and see that you have four key things that matter most to you. In my case, it was autonomy, flexibility, the ability to be creative, and the ability to elevate and touch people's lives. Seeing that list of values makes it very clear to me what kind of work would and wouldn't be satisfying. Clarity is what we're going for here, and it's a welcome relief compared to the usual fog and ambiguity that we live in. This process puts down in writing a measured, well-thought-out, balanced belief system that reflects your true nature.

As you consider what your values are, don't worry about semantics—whether what you are considering qualifies as a virtue, a value, an important goal, or something you stand for. Your list is likely to be a combination of things, and they are all relevant to figuring out what matters to you most. I suggest you keep a running list of your values with you that you can add to spontaneously as they occur to you. (Smartphone notes apps are great for this.) Start a values collection. When you collect things like blue glass or vinyl LPs, you start to notice them everywhere you go. It's the same with values.

I often do this exercise alongside my group participants and am amazed at what new gems I discover whenever I take time to check in with myself. One of my biggest revelations emerged around the topic of parenting. I had always considered myself an ace in this regard—a good mom who was devoted and dutiful—and always assumed that my actions were aligned with my values. After a mini-brainstorm with a group of fellow participants, I noticed that most of the values I wrote down about parenting emphasized fostering a true closeness with my kids, a kind of closeness far beyond what I had with my own parents. Most of the words I used to convey my values centered on having a deeply trusting relationship that was characterized by honesty, transparency, emotional vulnerability, play, laughter, and meaningful experiences together.

When I later compared this list to my typical actions, I was horrified to discover that, in fact, that was not at all how I was parenting. In reality, I was on autopilot, a facilitator who shuffled the kids through their day, made sure their needs were taken care of, and consistently emphasized compliance over connection. I rarely interacted with them in a way that strengthened bonds. I was more inclined to ask them if their homework was finished than about what they were learning or how they felt about school. My emphasis was more on maintaining an orderly house and being on time to unimportant events, which tended to suck the fun out of things and squash natural moments of joy and laughter. Realizing these tendencies in my parenting was a major kick in the pants for me, and, thankfully, it led to one of the most profound shifts in my behavior.

Now, I can honestly say that I know exactly what my parenting values are and am living them. I must add that I'm by no means living them perfectly, but at least now I know where home plate is, so I'm alert to when I am swinging wide and need to adjust. I can tell you from firsthand experience that there is nothing more rewarding and deeply satisfying at a core level than knowing what you stand for and then living that truth.

Discovering your inner truth is not about being struck by lightning with all-encompassing clarity and insight. It's a process of peeling back the layers of an onion to finally discover your real self. Nothing feels better than operating from a place of knowing and honoring your real self. That kind of authenticity cultivates incredible confidence, certainty, and life satisfaction.

THE SECRET POWER OF DECLARING PRIORITIES

Values are like spokes on a wheel that guide you to the center of understanding your life purpose(s). But without a clear sense of their relative importance in our lives, the competing values in our lives immobilize us, preventing us from breaking through to higher levels. That is why prioritizing values is so critical and leads to greater self-awareness and connection. Many motivational speakers and time-management gurus tout the importance of knowing your priorities, but I invite you to consider them from a more personal point of view—how *you* can live a more authentically connected life.

Forcing yourself to narrow your world of values down to your top twenty, then ten, then top three—what you stand for above all else—is a very telling exercise. For example, it's empowering and liberating to know that when push comes to shove, honesty ranks in your top three. That clarity will help you enormously as you contemplate other areas of your life, like your ideal version of work or friends. But what happens when your top values conflict? Generally, a lot of personal turmoil.

Often people claim to know their top priorities but can't list them in order of importance when put on the spot. For instance, they declare that family, health, and work success are important, but they stumble when asked to rank them order of importance. It's a very different answer to list your priorities as (1) work, (2) family, (3) health than in reverse order. Priorities and their specific order dictate how we approach life and resolve difficult choices.

It can be uncomfortable for some people to create a hierarchical list, particularly when societal values differ from their own. Society may tell you that parenting or work success should be top priorities, when they're not actually your own. When we release self-judgment about what we think our priorities should or shouldn't be, there is tremendous empowerment, freedom, and relief that can come from stating—out loud and on paper—what our priorities actually are.

There are quite a few myths about priorities. Let's tackle a few of the common ones.

1. *Priorities are fixed.* While some priorities might remain relatively stable throughout a lifetime, many others are dynamic and can fluctuate in their relative importance over time. Because of this, it's important to check in about them frequently and honestly. One of our study participants noted during a journaling exercise that she no longer seemed to care as much about her physical appearance, which had been an important priority for her in the past. Instead, she now was prioritizing thoughtfulness and altruism: "I think I am both of those people at the same time. And I love both of those sides to myself. While writing this I realize I have always been these two people. I think there are times when one or the other version of me takes center stage. Right now, it's the frumpy, kind, pushover, loving, thoughtful version of me that dresses like a forty-five-year-old mom. I am okay with that."[2]

2. *A stated priority is true in all circumstances.* Don't get caught up in untenable, black-or-white thinking. Priorities change as circumstances do. Your health might not be your number-one priority now, but that could change in an instant if you were diagnosed with a serious illness. Check in often to see if what was true a month ago still holds true. So often we lose touch with ourselves by not updating our priorities. During the year I lived in Bali—a time of explosive personal growth and extraordinary experiences—I made it a habit to check my priorities once a month. Sure enough, I found they were constantly changing. Checking in with myself frequently helped me keep my finger on the pulse of what was emerging for me, enabling me to quickly pivot to honor my reshuffled priorities. If I felt a yearning to pursue more spiritual sides of the culture, I allowed myself to prioritize that over my earlier priorities of seeing as much of the new continent as I possibly could.

3. *There can be several top priorities.* Many people resist declaring a hierarchy of priorities, wanting or wishing to rank them equally. Resisting this reality keeps us in the dark when it comes to making difficult decisions. We find ourselves blindsided when we make the wrong decision between two competing priorities. Knowing which priority trumps the others enables you to confidently feel your way to the right choice when faced with conflicts that seem to be unresolvable. Doing your homework ahead of time illuminates the deciding factors for you and allows you to make these kinds of decisions more easily. For example, when trying to decide between attending a back-to-school night with your kids or an important client dinner, it helps to know where your priorities are landing. It may be that you are in a phase where work needs your attention and you are intentionally putting that first for a period of time—or vice versa. You may feel that your connection to your kids is not as strong as you'd like it to be and that showing up for their small stuff supports your current top priority of growing that relationship.

4. *Priorities below the top one are inferior or subject to neglect.* This is simply not true. You can enjoy a close, healthy relationship with priorities that occupy lower levels of importance for you. A couple who puts their children first may shift gears when the marriage needs more attention even if it doesn't always play out in a perfectly convenient, friction-free way. This is another example of how priorities can be fluid and situation specific.

There are a few key things to remember as you begin homing in on your true priorities:

No judgment allowed. As with all connection-cultivating activities, the platform upon which you begin your inquiry should be free from self-judgment and anticipated judgment from others. If you drop the internalized expectations from others and give yourself permission to declare what your true priorities actually are, you will gain much more from the experience. Let go of any guilt or shame that might be associated with admitting that the career you've worked your whole life to develop (or that others have paid enormous sums of money to prepare you for) may not be your number-one priority. Eliminating self-judgment allows you to tap in to your more honest feelings and true self.

Rigorous honesty. This is easier said than done since most of us have internalized priorities that others handed down to us, unquestioned. Many of us are subconsciously living our lives dedicated to priorities that are not really our own.

Andre Agassi, a world-famous tennis player with eight Grand Slam championships under his belt, admitted after he retired in 2009: "I play tennis for a living, even though I hate tennis, hate it with a dark and secret passion, and always have."[3] While Agassi's declaration may be viewed as tragic, imagine the incredible relief he must have felt after finally declaring his real truth and the inherent possibilities that lay ahead for him as he began to live his true priorities. Giving yourself permission to say the unsayable and think the unthinkable is where the possibilities emerge.

Be unattached to consequences. One reason we often resist being brutally honest about our true priorities is that we are afraid of the implications—they may shine a light on drastic or painful changes we are not ready to make. But so often, we exaggerate these implications. When a top priority turns out *not* to be a top priority, more often the opposite is true—we can embrace it even more and with greater peace of mind since the internal conflict is resolved.

In the case of Andre Agassi, admitting he hated tennis didn't necessarily mean he needed to quit the sport. Rather, he reframed his reason to be involved in the sport and simply said, "I play tennis for a living." The sport served a purpose that he did value and prioritize, and I imagine that understanding that role helped him find greater peace in his involvement.

Deprioritizing something doesn't mean it's not important or that you need to delete it from your life. My partner and I used to fight incessantly about being each other's number-one priority. We would both take umbrage whenever one of us hinted at a decision that conflicted with that expectation. We finally had a liberating conversation where we admitted to each other that in reality, during our phase of having young children, parenting our respective children from prior marriages was most often our first priority. Admitting this to each other released much of the pressure from the equation and enabled us to both support and deprioritize each other without taking it personally.

Make multiple lists. When we don't take the time to consider and rank all our priorities relative to one another, we make decisions according to knee-jerk, spur-of-the-moment priorities. We live without a template to guide us. I have found multiple lists are the best way to track and organize priorities.

The lists I'm talking about are dynamic, ones that you frequently review, add to, delete, and reorder. There is no wrong or right method to them, but I recommend you make one for each of the important domains of your life. For example, in the domain of self-care, my top priorities are mindful nutrition, gratitude journaling, and morning meditation. Getting specific with details within the major arenas of your life (which might include romantic partnership, work, parenting, self-care, spirituality, etc.) can help shed light on what it is you care most about in that context. While you may have many goals and aspirations within your various life domains, it's important to zero in on your top priorities.

Another list that is often helpful is one that ranks the relative importance of these major domains of your life. If you had to choose, is spirituality or personal health most important—or is it your work or your family? Knowing where you stand on the big topics is extremely illuminating, both for understanding how you tick and for guidance when it comes to making tough choices.

Instead of setting resolutions or goals, my New Year's ritual is to make a list of my anticipated priorities for the year according to the important areas of my life. I then refer back to it often throughout the year to see if I'm on track with those priorities and also to assess whether the priorities have changed. This is the simplest way I have found to stay in tune with myself.

Making lists of priorities has been so extraordinarily effective for helping me stay connected to my true desires that I use the technique all the time, in a variety of contexts. I even jot down some priorities and intentions for a vacation as I'm sitting on the plane, which reminds me to scale back ambitious sightseeing plans if my priority is to relax.

Pressure test your lists. Ask yourself the tough questions in order to better figure out which priorities win out over others. If you had to choose between two, which would you pick? If money and other obstructive practicalities were no object, what would really mean the most to you? As you do this, it's helpful to take big, obvious categories, like work or family, off the table for a moment and see what else emerges on your priority list. Sometimes you need to get the mountains out of your field of vision in order to see your less obvious priorities, such as creativity, play, or service to others. These subtler priorities often hold enormous possibilities for enhancing our life satisfaction and growth.

Periodically, check in on your lists and ask yourself whether the hierarchy you created is still a true reflection of what matters to you most or whether your feelings have changed. If you're not sure about a priority's position on the list, put a question mark next to it to remind yourself that this area needs further observation. As you review, consider how your life is changing and how your priorities are allowed to change as well. If you are becoming an empty nester, it might be time for other priorities to emerge or become more prominent. Try not to let too much time go by between heart-to-hearts with yourself on this topic.

There's no particular magic to figuring out or ranking your priorities. It's simply a process of taking the time to consider them and checking in periodically for any changes. Keeping your priorities list on your smartphone is a great way to be able to keep these ideas close to you, available at the spur of the moment when inspiration hits and can be easily updated. In my workshops, we spend an entire day working on priorities, values, and meaning. It's amazing to see how much the lists change from the morning to the end of the day. In my experience, it's the rare person who is perfectly clear about their priorities, but most people feel inspired with new direction and a sense of purpose after clarifying this important part of life.

ALIGNING BEHAVIOR WITH YOUR PRIORITIES, VALUES, AND BELIEFS

Alignment is the ultimate goal of true connection. It is the physical manifestation of what it feels and looks like to be connected with yourself, living in harmony with your deepest truths. It is also the source of great satisfaction and peace of mind.

When you are in alignment, your thoughts and behaviors match your priorities, values, and beliefs, and there is no longer a need to chase after anything in life. Scarcity disappears, and abundance enters. You no longer experience your life on a treadmill, since each act of your day is tied to a clear intention that holds meaning for you. Time slows down and is plentiful because your time is spent wisely and purposefully. Ambivalence and ambiguity disappear; you have clarity on where you stand and what you need. Fear of mortality or a wasted existence dissolves because you are living thoughtfully and intentionally. You become someone of character, with the daily courage to live by your deepest values.

The Indian philosopher Jiddu Krishnamurti described alignment in terms of living an integrated life: "To integrate is to bring together, to make complete. If you are integrated, your thoughts, feelings, and actions are entirely one, moving in one direction; they are not in contradiction with each other. You are a whole human being, without conflict. That is what is implied by integration."[4]

Alignment honors you and your deepest truths, sending a powerful message that you are worthy and that you matter. There is no greater, faster, more potent way to build unshakable self-esteem and self-confidence than to live in alignment.

Unfortunately, though, alignment is not a magical place that you hike to once and live in blissfully forever-after. It's something you fight for each and every day by vigilantly saying no to activities that do not fit you and yes to activities that align with your soul. It's something you put brief thought into each morning when you wake up and every night before you go to bed. You ask yourself, *How did I do acting in alignment today, and is there anything I need to change to improve?* It's a level of integrity that you hold yourself to and strive never to lose sight of. Yet when you do lose sight of it, as you inevitably will, you compassionately course-correct and recommit to your vision.

Once you mentally engage with who you are, where you are, and how connected you feel in your life, you climb into the driver's seat, where you are empowered to make insightful observations about yourself, consider new options, and become curious about your situation. You go from being a passive follower to an active leader of your life, enabling expanded thinking, more creative problem-solving, and inspired action in accordance with your beliefs.

Once you know who you are and what you stand for, and once you align your daily life with those values on both macro- and micro-levels, you achieve a solid and sustainable sense of well-being that transcends ordinary happiness.

Chapter 3

CONNECTING
WITH MEANING

While happiness is an emotion felt in the here and now, it ultimately fades away, just as all emotions do. . . . Meaning, on the other hand, is enduring. It connects the past to the present to the future.

EMILY ESFAHANI SMITH[1]

Human beings are hardwired to seek meaning in their lives. It's something we all crave and yearn for, and research shows that having high levels of meaning in our lives is correlated with high levels of well-being.[2] Happiness. Satisfaction. Physical health. Mental health. Self-esteem. Better immune response. It's the Holy Grail for a good life. A lack of meaning often is at the root of depressive disorders and is, in fact, the subject of one of the primary diagnostic questions trained health practitioners ask to determine if someone is suffering from depression.

Meaning is the significance a person ascribes to their experience of reality. At a macro-level, meaning relates to understanding one's life in a greater context and feeling that it makes sense and has significance.[3] At the micro-level, it is the significance and importance with which we imbue certain activities, people, memories, objects, and life events based in part on the pleasure, value, and satisfaction we derive from them. A meaningful act can be as small as exchanging a smile with someone who has just held the elevator door for you or as huge as the exchange of wedding vows. Meaning is highly subjective, determined by an individual's values and interpretation.

Meaningful activities feel important, worthwhile, fulfilling. Some people experience a warm, cleansing sensation washing over them during meaningful moments, which temporarily mutes other physical distractions. When we're aware that we're doing something meaningful, we are fully in the moment. These are experiences or activities we want to remember—things we don't want to forget.

Meaning is often contextual and dynamic, and it can evolve or change over time as our life experiences unfold and our perspectives change. Our perception of meaning is even impacted by mood.

In an edition of the *American Psychologist*, Drs. Samantha J. Heintzelman and Laura A. King noted another strange paradox of how we most often describe this elusive meaning: "It is portrayed simultaneously as a necessity of life *and* as something that is next to impossible to attain."[4] This essential part of daily living is treated like a rare phenomenon most of us cannot begin to understand until we have studied it for a lifetime.

While our research lab certainly encourages lifelong consideration of these concepts, we don't believe it takes a lifetime to find meaning and purpose in life. Connection Lab's research shows that self-connection is the tool we need to recognize and cultivate truly meaningful existence.[5] We argue that both meaning and purpose are achievable in short order, just by applying intention and attention (the wings of awareness) to the matter.

HOW MEANINGFUL IS YOUR LIFE?

Because of the relationship of meaning to well-being, and the relationship between the lack of meaning and depression, it is critically important to take stock of your life in this arena. Even if you think your life is already full of meaning, specifically identifying your areas of strength and weakness can help you to sharpen your appreciation for the meaning that is there as well as to cultivate meaning in areas you hadn't considered rewarding.

Interestingly, current research shows that *most people* rate their lives as very full of meaning. As rates of depression, anxiety, and social isolation are at an all-time high in our culture, something doesn't quite add up about this. In our research lab, we are questioning whether most people's lives are truly filled with an abundance of meaning or whether we might just be saying that our lives are full of meaning due to social conditioning or wishful thinking. We suspect that social bias is more often responsible for people reporting or believing that their lives are full of meaning—when, in fact, people may find their jobs, friendships, romantic relationships, and other major life categories sorely lacking in meaning. We are currently examining whether we can get more accurate responses by having people track meaning in their day-to-day lives more granularly, looking at hour-by-hour changes in levels of meaning experienced, as well as examining meaning separately in each sector of life (i.e., work, family, spiritual).

One of the biggest challenges of studying meaning and the way we tend to think about it in our own lives is that we typically pose the question in a very broad, simplistic way: *Is your life meaningful?* So the answer is a brutal yes or no. We don't believe that this binary breakdown is a very useful barometer, however, because it's too global, requires a snap judgment, and invites us to answer in the more socially acceptable affirmative: *Yes, of course my life has meaning!* To admit otherwise might force the interviewee to confront a very different and possibly depressing reality than they would like to believe exists. A yes/no answer also misses the nuances of everyday life, in which we source meaning from many different areas of life. In any given hour, on any given day, we can experience meaning at different levels, depending on our activities.

We think that in assessing meaning, it is better to use a ten-point scale, where one is utterly meaningless and ten is one of the most meaningful things you've ever experienced. And, we also believe it's more helpful to consider each of the major areas of your life separately, rather than trying to do a global assessment. The list of primary areas might vary from person to person, but most commonly includes romantic partnership, family, work, social, and spiritual.

Using the ten-point scale (again, one is totally meaningless, ten is a life-defining moment), try rating each of your major areas of life on how meaningful they feel to you. (There's a worksheet in the appendix to guide you.) Be honest with yourself. Does your work feel meaningful? Do your interactions with your kids feel meaningful? Are you more often than not just going through the motions in a particular area?

Keep in mind, no one can honestly score all areas of life at maximal meaning. It's usually the case that some areas of our lives enjoy the benefits of more attention and nurturing, and the others feel less meaningful. But taking stock of where you are now will give you enormous insight into where your dissatisfaction lies.

THE TWENTY-FOUR-HOUR INVENTORY

A great next step for assessing meaning is to conduct a twenty-four-hour experiment where, for one day, you focus hour to hour (or as often as you change activity) on the level of meaning you are experiencing, noting down each time what you're doing and how meaningful it feels.

Make sure you document your impressions. Keeping a list of all the things that struck you as meaningful, or particularly meaningless, is the best way to remember, gain true awareness, and begin to discover patterns.

You will likely be surprised at some of the things that you note. Our brains are primed to remember threats, disappointments, frustration, and negative stimuli of any kind far better than the meaningful moments. So, creating a list of the meaningful activities always seems to surprise and delight, even for the skeptics. (Our research at Connection Lab shows that logging meaning in daily activities also tends to lead to higher levels of job- and life-satisfaction as well as greater mindfulness longer term.[6])

I was certainly surprised by the many things I listed as meaningful, such as tucking in my boys at night, watching the birds visit the bird feeder, hearing "Clair de Lune" on the radio, feeding a stray dog and her puppy a can of dog food, sitting down to read a new fiction book, and learning a recipe from my sister over the phone. I discovered that I found meaning mostly in the tiny, simple moments of the day, moments that I would never normally have noticed or predicted. I also noticed the irony that I frequently rushed through the moments that actually felt the most meaningful to me.

To my surprise, quite a few of my daily activities felt low in meaning. I discovered that driving is totally meaningless to me—and that I spent a ton of time doing it. I also realized that chatting with acquaintances before and after school pickup felt empty to me rather than worthwhile. I went to lunch with a friend and recorded that this interaction depleted me. After some reflection, I realized my reaction to this person was not atypical. Back home with my family, I noticed we were all doing our own thing around the house with nothing meaningful happening.

My results from this experiment inspired me to take action—deleting meaningless and avoidable activities from my routine. For the activities that were unavoidable, I challenged myself to cultivate meaning there. We'll get into this more in the sections that follow.

Scanning your activities, behaviors, and environment for areas of meaningfulness or meaninglessness is not about berating or discounting your life, yourself, or the people in it. It's about becoming more curious about what *you* value as meaningful and more familiar with the kinds of things that move your needle or make your heart leap, as well as the kinds of things that leave you flat. These discoveries offer tremendous opportunities to optimize our lives and connect more deeply to the things we truly care about. For only when we realize something can we do something about it.

MEANING-MAKING: TECHNIQUES FOR CULTIVATING MEANING IN YOUR REALITY

Meaning is an intensely subjective area of life over which we have far more influence and control than most people realize—we ourselves choose the meaning we assign to activities. Even though there are some nearly universally meaningful moments in life—such as connecting with people we care about—meaning is completely unique to the individual, and how we define and experience it is totally different for each of us. For example, meaning for me can come in the form of making and serving my first lasagna, versus just heating up a perfectly good frozen one from the store. I'm beaming with pride and satisfaction when I pull mine out—not so much with the frozen one.

Meaning and connection are intertwined concepts that tend to fuel each other. Nothing is more disconnecting and energy draining than spending time and effort on things that are not meaningful to you. Conversely, the more meaningful an activity is to us, the more enjoyment and satisfaction we get out of it and the more connected we will be in that moment. Think about the difference between buying a thoughtless, obligatory, last-minute birthday gift for someone, versus framing and wrapping a cherished picture of the two of you, or the difference between a quick email note and a hand-written, deeply sentimental letter.

But meaning is not always linked with happiness or states of immediate joy. Often, deeply meaningful experiences come from encounters that might feel quite unpleasant in the moment, like having a much-needed but difficult conversation, facing fears, sitting with someone in their final moments of life, working as an activist for emotionally fraught causes (such as battling child sex trafficking), and other activities that require courage and resilience to accomplish.

A teenage boy I worked with declared adamantly that his life was devoid of any meaning and confided in me that he intensely disliked his peers, his classes, and most especially, his parents—he either avoided spending time with them altogether or escaped into gaming whenever they were around. While his parents and the school were exploring diagnostic labels and associated medications to address his withdrawal, he and I pursued the topic of meaning. We worked together to create a list of actions that might cultivate more meaningful encounters.

The first assignment required a lot of courage: he agreed to tell his parents how he felt about them. They were distraught to hear him describe the extent of his contempt, and for a while things felt even more hopeless for all involved. But in the end, sharing such potent feelings proved to be a deeply meaningful and unforgettable encounter for all of them, a real turning point in their relationships. After that experience, he agreed to try the same approach with his teachers and was surprised to learn how much they valued him and how interested they were in satisfying his needs. While not everyone may respond so constructively to it, radical honesty proved to be a painful, but productive, pathway for this teenager to find his way back to meaningful relationships and encounters.

In instances such as these, meaning arises from the satisfaction of being true to oneself, deepening relationships through sharing honest feelings, and standing up for values. When we look outside of the confines of our own immediate pleasure and self-interests, we can often find an abundance of opportunities for meaning-making.

And we truly are the meaning-makers: we can become more aware of areas of existing meaning in our lives, we can optimize and enhance the existing meaning, and we can learn to cultivate meaning where it previously did not exist. We will discuss these techniques in detail in the sections that follow.

USE VALUES TO CULTIVATE MEANING

One of the single most powerful tools to find meaning in our lives is reflective journaling—thinking back on and writing about what has happened to us.[7] Multiple research studies show that journaling about our experiences through the lens of our most important values can actually transform daily stress into an empowering force for better mental and physical health.

Stanford University did an amazing study in the 1990s that launched dozens of similar studies with the same results. The researchers asked undergraduate students on spring break to journal about their most important personal values and also about their daily activities; others were asked to write only about the good things that had happened to them in their day. When break was over three weeks later, the students who had written about their values were happier, healthier, and more confident about their ability to handle stress than the ones who had only focused on the good stuff.

How could this be? The researchers analyzed the journals to see what the kids had been thinking. By reflecting on how their daily activities supported their values, students had gained a new perspective on those activities and choices.

Little stresses and hassles, like having to fill out job applications or give younger siblings a lift, were now demonstrations of their values in action—bold and important steps toward their future careers or loving gestures of their commitment to family. Suddenly, their lives were full of meaningful activities. And all they had to do was reflect and write about it—positively reframing their experiences with their personal values.

Numerous research studies now confirm that journaling about how our daily activities relate to our most important values can reduce daily stress levels, boost mood and confidence, and actually reduce incidences of illness.[8] In the

Sometimes all you need is a new frame

short term, journaling empowers people, making us feel strong, in control, and proud of our lives. We feel more empathetic and loving toward others, and we ruminate less. We have greater self-control and better pain tolerance. In the long term, writing about our values has even been shown to improve GPAs, mental and physical health, weight loss, and outcomes for quitting smoking and reducing problem drinking.[9] Amazingly, the impact of positively reframing experiences is actually greater the more stressed out that we are.

Clearly, journaling is something we should all be doing on a regular basis for better mental and physical health. Learning to cultivate meaning this way is also a beautiful process on truly enjoyable terrain.

GETTING STARTED WITH JOURNALING

There are many processes at play when we journal that contribute to deepening awareness, learning, memory, and clarity. If you already like to journal, then this is an easy tool for cultivating meaning. If you aren't accustomed to journaling, the power of this approach may make you a convert.

In my workshops, we find it more successful to look for meaning on a micro-level, working our way up to the macro-level over time. It's the small raindrops that lead to a stream, that eventually take us to a river, and finally an ocean. Start by creating a list of all the things in your life that bring you meaning. Try to be as specific and diverse in your categories as possible. In my list, for example, I wrote about my photographs, my paintings, laughing with friends, helping my kids with homework, and other common activities. Dedicate a couple of pages in your journal to this list because even though you may not come up with much at first, it's likely that more and more things will occur to you later on. I keep my list on my phone so I can capture those "butterflies" as they occur to me.

This exercise allows you to end up with a long list of the things you care about the most. You will get to know yourself better, and even without making a conscious effort you'll be reminded to steer your ship in a more meaningful direction. You'll develop a clearer sense of what you value.

Then, at the end of each day, take five or ten minutes to reflect and write about what was most meaningful to you that day. Think about the obviously meaningful and pleasant events—you tend to relive the experience as you remember it, complete with the chemical reactions in your body. The release of oxytocin from experiencing something positive, for example, increases the likelihood that your brain will start to rewire and be more inclined toward noticing and experiencing meaning.

But don't forget to also write about how that day's stressful activities might have been related to the issues that matter to you. Write about the ways your actions advanced a cause or issue you believe in. Perhaps you were prioritizing your children's education by shuttling them across town to music lessons or some other enriching activity. Maybe your stressful confrontation at the office with a coworker demonstrated your commitment to integrity and open communication, or maybe it just was proof of how much you're willing to endure to support your company's mission. Reframe stressful events as demonstrations of your values in action, as the Stanford college kids did, and savor the satisfaction and well-being that flow forth.

After just a few days of journaling about meaning, you will be amazed at how your brain becomes more attuned to notice, pause, and more deeply appreciate and relive meaningful encounters in your life—both in the moment and when you reflect upon those moments later in the day. You're more than doubling your emotional and physiological reward.

This journaling exercise is similar in feel and content to a gratitude journal, which is another powerfully beneficial habit discussed in later chapters. My meaning journal ultimately morphed into a gratitude journal, and I found it to be such a positive and rewarding way to end my day that I have kept it going for three years straight, recording the most meaningful daily encounters. Today, my journal is a gorgeous, leather-bound piece of art that includes famous quotes from my kids, memorable interactions with people, beautiful moments I noticed, and things I am proud of myself for. It has turned into a golden bible, filled with precious and priceless moments of my life—my most prized possession. I hope that I'll be fortunate enough to live a long life because I love to imagine how gratifying it would be to relive these cherished, beautiful moments that would otherwise fade away.

My friends and I used to joke to each other, "If I die, find my journal and burn it." Like many people, we used journals to vent our negativity. Now I tell them, "If I die, find my journal, and let everyone I love read it."

PHOTOGRAPHING MEANING

Another profound meaning-cultivating exercise I recommend started as a photo experiment. I was craving a way to capture and collect meaning clues throughout the day—a way that was easier and more immediate than journaling. I was tired of the normal criteria I use to take pictures (e.g., it needs to be worthy of a photograph) and excited for permission to photograph nonsensical and mundane things that would only make sense to me. I decided to use my son's Polaroid camera for immediate gratification because there's something so satisfying about the way it spits out little pictures on demand.

The activity felt like an Easter egg hunt. At first, I walked around my house looking for things I loved, with just one question in mind: *Does this person, place, or thing feel meaningful to me?* At first, I took photos of the usual suspects—my family, the animals in our house. But then something interesting started to happen, and my photos expanded into richer and more subtle territory.

I took a photo of the hammock I love to lie in, a favorite meal I made for the kids, and a thank-you card from the kids I worked with on a TEDxYouth conference. I took a picture of a picture of me holding my sister as a baby, something that stirs deep feelings of love. I photographed the flowers growing in the garden, the kids' clubhouse in the backyard, the kale I love to grow and eat, the plant in my office that I lovingly tend, my kids sitting on the kitchen floor watching the pizza dough rise in the oven, the chapter book we are obsessively reading together, my favorite coffee cup, the friendly receptionist at my coworking space who makes me smile every day.

The rapid acceleration of my awareness of meaning was incredible. At the start, I felt awkward in this experiment. I worried about wasting expensive Polaroid film, taking stupid pictures of things that would seem meaningless to others. I had all kinds of small resistances and was convinced I wouldn't be able to think of anything meaningful or that I'd quickly run out of subjects. But a half day into the project, suddenly I was on fire. I noticed things that held deep meaning for me everywhere. My favorite tree in the front yard. The remnants of a family board game from the prior night. The stuffed animals on my son's bed. A sweet reminder note my partner left on my computer. The empty bottle of wine we enjoyed while comparing notes about our day. When I later looked at the collection of photos I had amassed, I was amazed and surprised to feel such strong emotion for this collection of photos. What had seemed like unworthy objects of photography had coalesced into a beautiful collage of my life—a small treasure chest of cherished moments and beloved encounters that would normally be forgotten but were now memorialized to be savored over and over again.

I pasted these photos into a notebook. Every time I look at them, I'm amazed how profoundly they capture the essence of who I am, what matters to me, and where I derive my greatest sources of meaning. This quirky photo essay was created in just one day of looking under rocks for meaning. And it grew from being something I was not sure I would bother to keep when I was done to one of the few objects in my house I would absolutely grab in a fire.

CULTIVATE EVEN GREATER MEANING THROUGH CONNECTION TO OTHERS

Humans find the greatest opportunity for meaning through relationships and connections to other humans. We are fundamentally social animals, and a growing body of research shows that our social connections have an astoundingly powerful influence on our lives, from our general satisfaction to our cognitive skills, longevity, and even things like how resistant we are to infections and chronic diseases.[10] Not surprisingly, then, learning ways to boost meaning in your social relationships can supercharge your life with new levels of satisfaction.

Most people have a cadre of close relationships over the course of a lifetime, drawn from friends, family, children, and coworkers. But how much do you nurture, value, and maintain those relationships? A commonly expressed regret among those who are facing the end of life is that they wished they'd stayed in better touch with friends. Relationships with the people "who knew us when," or who've shared an important part of life experience with us, can offer a deep trove of meaning and satisfaction if we pay them the respect they deserve. Yet all too often, we let these people drift out of our lives because of geographical distance or petty grievances, and we cut ourselves off from experiencing that rich reward.

It's interesting to consider which relationships you prioritize and nurture. Do you tend to spend most of your time around people with whom you can share vulnerabilities, laugh your face off, or feel loved unconditionally? Or are you more often interacting with virtual (i.e., online) connections or acquaintances, friends of convenience, colleagues, or "contacts" for the purposes of networking or social climbing? You might be surprised at the answer.

Take the time to ask yourself which relationships and relationship encounters provide you with the most meaning. You may decide to stop investing time and energy in the relationships that feel hollow, or you may realize you need to invest more meaning-making attention to the important relationships that aren't currently fulfilling.

When I considered this question for myself, for example, I realized, sadly, that my encounters with my dad often didn't feel very meaningful. Thinking about it further, I realized my dad's TV tends to be blaring in the background whenever I stop by to visit, and he is prone to distraction. I decided to experiment by eliminating that variable and invited him over to my house to teach me an old family recipe. And it worked like a charm: the next time we got together, he taught me how to make a dynamite potato-leek soup. Now cooking together is one of the most endearing and meaningful ways I have found to spend time with my dad. By making the effort to cultivate greater meaning in our time together, we have created unforgettable memories, and we feel closer and more fulfilled afterward.

Consciously tending our relationships can make the difference between ordinary and extraordinary levels of meaning.

Authentic Expression

Having a heart-to-heart of any kind tends to be a deeply meaningful experience for all involved. Vulnerable and authentic self-expression of this kind is unparalleled when it comes to filling your cup (or an encounter) with meaning. It's the opposite of the shallow, superficial banter that dominates so many of our social interactions. When you share your heart—your true feelings—with people, others are captivated because what is coming out of your mouth is so meaningful.

Think about how moved you are when you watch an actor—a complete stranger—show vulnerability on stage. You feel as if you have shared a special experience and had a glimpse into the actor's soul. In the same vein, delivering difficult, unexpressed communications or uncensored joy can make your relationships deeper and more meaningful. Abandon the pent-up grudges or unspoken grievances that can suck the closeness (and by extension, meaning) out of any good relationship.

On the flip side, taking the time to declare your feelings of love, admiration, or appreciation for another generates enormous amounts of mutual meaning. After one of my workshops, a participant I'll call Mary chose to write a love letter each week to someone who had touched her life. Mary described the exercise as having a profound effect on her—it brought tremendous meaning to her life, whether or not the letter recipients replied. She wrote to a random assortment of old teachers, lovers, mentors, current friends, or friends she had lost touch with in order to let each of them know how her life had been touched by their presence. Mary said in her letter that she had been unable to properly thank these people, but that she had never forgotten their impact. Mary's cup of gratitude was overflowing as she penned these letters even before she sent them into the world and whether or not she got a reply.

All too often we fail to express to others how we really feel, good or bad. Making the time and having the courage to share your heart with people throws open the doors, windows, and roof—allowing meaning to appear all around us.

Helping Other People

One of the most scientifically established pathways to a happier and more meaningful life is through helping others. Acts of service enable us to transcend self-absorbed thinking and to experience both the joy of being needed and the satisfaction of adding value. When we give our time, advice, expertise, or support, we are transported out of our own heads and focused on the purpose of improving someone else's condition. By volunteering to help others in need, we make meaningful contributions to individuals, families, or whole communities of people. It feels incredibly, soulfully good to help lift others up. And research shows that helping others actually minimizes depression and chronic pain.

Your act of service doesn't have to be a years-long commitment—even small acts of kindness and support can be powerful sources of meaning. Hold the door for someone who has their hands full. Let that driver trapped by traffic merge in front of you. Smile at a stranger on the street. Pick up lunch for your harried coworker. Run an errand for a friend or family member. Whenever we find a way to help our fellow humans, we find a powerful source of meaning in our own lives.

MAKE IT A HABIT

Cultivating meaning can and should become a lifelong habit. While you may be fired up when you begin, it's easy to lose that fiery motivation over time. This is where external accountability can help. We go farther, try harder, and sustain our changes for longer periods of time when we share a goal and receive support from like-minded others

So, to help cultivate meaning in your life, invite a friend to join you in the challenge. Every day for thirty days, each of you should send a quick, bullet-pointed email to the other, listing the most meaningful parts of your day. Maybe you'll mutually decide to list the top three moments that most profoundly touched your hearts—it's up to you! The point is that you're strengthening the meaning in your lives through attention and intention, and you're doing so with a buddy for best success. In addition to the commitment that holds you each accountable, you will also find yourself with new material, inspiration, and ideas about what moves someone else's needle.

The side benefit of this exercise is how it bonds people together. As we've just discussed, any act that promotes connection tends to be extraordinarily meaningful, above and beyond other activities. There's something endearing about learning what makes someone else's heart leap. You get to know a human in a whole new way. This poignant experience can be shared with someone you are close to or someone you barely know. I intentionally chose to work with somebody I didn't know very well in the hope that the exercise would bring us closer—and it did. Today, that friendship is still a source of great meaning for me.

Accountability buddies can be a tremendous resource as you progress along your path to greater connection. If you're struggling to keep up the habit of reflecting on meaning, give this technique a try.

CULTIVATING MEANING WHERE THERE SEEMS TO BE NONE

As we've discussed, our brains are primed to notice and remember negativity—things we don't like or abhor doing—while barely registering the positive. Because of this negativity bias, we have to make a special effort to get our brains to notice, register, and savor the good. It's the same with meaning. All too often, we assume activities and tasks (like cleaning, cooking, commuting, responding to emails) are meaningless. It's not that these are inherently negative activities, but because most people view them as necessary evils, the acts themselves seem devoid of value.

But, as with so many things in life, perspective is everything. Sylvia Boorstein, a witty and engaging mindfulness practitioner, gave a beautiful talk about how to turn the ordinary into the extraordinary. The chore of washing dishes can make us cranky. But try interrupting your negative emotion by pushing yourself in the opposite emotion, Boorstein suggests. Feel grateful, proud, and fulfilled. Force yourself to think of reasons that this simple chore is a privilege and a pleasure: You *have* dishes to wash, unlike many people in the world. You also have enough food to serve your family, thus the dirty dishes. You are personally contributing to your family's well-being by cleaning up the home you are lucky enough to live in. You have indoor plumbing and a functioning sink and don't have to carry dishes to the river to wash outside.

Come up with as many reasons as you can. Don't worry if it feels, at first, that you're faking it. Expand your mind as much as possible, looking for every reason to make a mundane task worthy. You might surprise yourself how easy it turns out to be, once you get going.

This classic cognitive behavioral technique (called "opposite emotion/action" by cognitive behavioral therapists) is very effective at reframing your most banal, least enjoyed activities. Instead of staying mired in your boredom, joylessness, or resentment, you're challenged to feel grateful and to explore the added value to the activity.

This technique is not designed to suppress emotions; it's designed to widen the lens you are looking through, break habitual reactions, and develop the skill of considering different perspectives. It's also a powerful tool for consciously injecting meaning into the inescapable tasks you have to do throughout your day, causing you, by extension, to feel more deeply connected. The key is to do the thought exercise—thinking of all the reasons why you might feel grateful or proud for this opportunity—every time you do it to strengthen the positive association in your brain's neural connections.

If you have mandatory activities in your life that are devoid of meaning, try this technique and see if you can't find some kernel of significance in performing them—how do they relate to something that matters to you? I think you'll be surprised. With time, these activities may come to be some of your most reliable sources of meaning in your everyday life.

FINDING MEANING IN YOUR LIFE STORY

Many people are plagued by what they feel is a less than idyllic childhood or life story and carry that around as a burden or something to turn away from, forget, or feel ashamed about. Regardless of what happened to us, when we view our lives that way, we are disconnecting from our past by believing that our history was devoid of meaning. This is often a huge area of disconnection for people who turn away from events of the past that appeared to serve no purpose other than causing pain and suffering.

Your life story is a golden opportunity for meaning-making. If yours includes pain and turmoil, you can rewrite it in a way that feels personally meaningful—a version you can be proud of. Narrative therapy is a form of psychotherapy that is based in part on just such a goal: the therapist helps the client coauthor a new story of their life that is constructive and meaningful, and that emphasizes strengths and resilience. This type of therapy has been shown to be enormously successful, particularly with veterans, troubled teens, and those in the social justice realm.

I had the opportunity to experience firsthand the life-changing impact of rewriting my life story at a women's retreat—forever changing my relationship to my past for the better. The instructions were simple: Write your life story in a form you can share with the group in under ten minutes. Be as honest as possible, and feel free to cast yourself as the hero of the story, using some creative analogy. This was a novel concept to me, and I was totally unprepared. Though my history had many tales of goodness, it had always felt overshadowed by sorrow and a series of unfortunate events related to a dramatic parental divorce, family members' substance abuse, and my sisters and I being raised apart. For so long, I had dismissed my life story as not worth telling because of the seeming pointlessness of those unfortunate aspects. But this invitation to cast myself as the heroine somehow changed everything and helped me rewrite my understanding of my history.

After struggling and feeling blocked for some time, I finally picked Katniss Everdeen from *The Hunger Games* as my heroine analogy since I resonated with her primary motivation of taking care of her younger sister. As I prepared my narrative to share with the group, I rewrote the unfortunate and traumatic events of my life as necessary challenges that were preparing me for who I was meant to become, and I recast myself as the fiercely protective older sister who slayed dragons with my bow and arrow in the name of justice. Suddenly my life story felt like a story of triumph and courage, rather than of shame and wasted opportunity. That simple exercise, which took only a couple of hours, enabled me to understand the meaning and significance of my life history in a whole new way, providing life-changing perspective. For the first time, I felt connected to, and even thankful for, my past. Even more surprising, rather than seeming farcical or like wishful thinking, my revised life story feels like a truer version than the old one.

I now frequently use this exercise in my workshops to invite people to reconstruct and reframe their pasts. If you're doing this at home, I recommend following Joseph Campbell's *hero's journey* as a starting point. This iconic narrative follows a hero who is unexpectedly called to adventure or challenge and who faces internal and external obstacles, setbacks, and triumphs along the way. (The YouTube cartoon of the hero's journey beautifully articulates this allegory for those who prefer videos to reading.) Campbell's narrative trajectory is the basis of nearly every dramatic plot or movie we have ever seen—and for good reason, since it is each of our stories as well.

Other, nonwriting methods of reflection can also be helpful for connecting our past with our present. One of our Connection Lab study participants shared the experience of listening to old music albums on a long car ride and how self-connected it made her feel:

> When I first started listening, I thought, Wow, I can't believe I used to be so into this. However, as I listened more closely to the lyrics, I

realized how perfectly they fit those times of my life. It is not who I am anymore, but it is a complete reminder of all the good and bad times I have had, the different friends and relationships I have made it through, and all the times that have led me to where I am today. Those times are another thing I am grateful for. Without having lived all of my—as I like to call them—"past lives," I wouldn't know myself as well as I do today, and I am proud of who I am.[11]

The broader lesson from this exercise is to consider the adversity in your life as a gift. Instead of things that happened *to you*, think of them as things that happened *for you* in order for you to learn the lessons you needed to become the person you are. It can feel like a stretch, but try it on. Look for the lesson and the ensuing personal growth or for the strength that occurred through each phase of difficulty, and recast your villains as your perfect teachers who were there to teach you something you needed to learn in order to move forward on your journey.

Chapter 4

CONNECTING WITH YOUR
LIFE PURPOSE(S)

After fifteen years of social-work education, I was sure of one thing: Connection is why we're here; it is what gives purpose and meaning to our lives.

BRENÉ BROWN[1]

There are many different names for what is classically referred to as your "purpose"—the most common in mythology and literature being "a calling." It's important to distinguish between of the idea of *the* purpose of life and having purpose *in* one's life. The purpose of life is a heady, heavy topic that has fascinated and perplexed humankind through the ages. Professionals from a variety of disciplines love to opine on the subject, but the answer remains part of the elusive mystery of the universe. I don't find focusing on this existential question of purpose particularly useful for shedding light at the individual level. Often it leads only to overwhelm, a powerless sense that questions like that are unanswerable, or the subscription to a dogmatic belief system that attempts to answer the question for you.

As I define the term, *purpose* is really a collection of worthy, overarching goals and aims that provide direction in life, a reason for one's existence, and a "sense of engagement with life."[2] Purpose involves intention, motivation, planning, and action, as well as a mission that has meaning to us. As we pursue our life purposes, our actions are imbued with meaning. Our purposes are fueled by our primary concerns in life, including answers to questions about why we do what we do and why it is important. One's purpose is a consolidation of the underlying reasons for their immediate goals and the motives that account for most daily behavior.

Short-term desires come and go. A young person may desire a good grade on a test, a date to the prom, the latest PlayStation, a starting position on the basketball team, or admission to a prestigious college. These are desires; they reflect immediate aims that may or may not have longer-term significance. A purpose, by contrast, is an end in itself. When you are clear about your purpose(s), you are clearer about where you source meaning and what your beliefs and priorities are, making it easier to act in alignment with those truths. There is no higher way to live.

THE IMPORTANCE OF PURPOSE

It's well established in scientific literature that living purposefully is associated with high levels of satisfaction and well-being. Feeling as though you have a purpose in this life is a cherished notion in our culture that most people yearn for but have no idea how to achieve. We all want to feel like our lives have significance and that our time here on earth matters beyond the mere fact that we are taking up oxygen and space. Purpose is the antidote to ward off one of our greatest existential fears: that our lives don't amount to anything meaningful. One of our study participants summed it up this way: "When you're not doing the work that you're supposed to do, you don't feel like you matter—and if you don't matter, then you're just a big bag of old water and bones, right?"[3]

What if we feel like we have no purpose? Many people in our culture keep their busy lives full to the brim so that they are distracted from confronting this question. Others suffer greatly from an acute awareness of feeling aimless, bored, and clueless about their purposes.

I had a boyfriend in college who felt lost and aimless in this regard. Hanging out in his dorm room (bored myself) while he was in class one day, I noticed a leather notebook sitting on his nightstand. I flipped it open, not exactly with the intention of snooping, but more with the curiosity of a teenage girl, thinking it was a little bit funny and adorable that he actually wrote in a journal. My eye caught the first sentence that said, "My life feels like I'm a painter who is holding a paintbrush, sitting in front of a canvas, who cannot decide what to paint, and who is waiting so long for the inspiration, that the paint has long since dried on his brush."

I realized I had just violated his privacy in a major way and slammed the book shut. But my heart ached for the anguish I knew it caused him to feel so paralyzed with uncertainty and disconnected from his purpose in life. I've always felt haunted by reading that line, and even now I feel that it is a perfect description of what lacking a sense of life purpose feels like. It's also a great example of the wrong way to go about finding a purpose—sitting around and waiting for it to come to you.

Dr. William Damon is a purpose researcher. In his work studying American youth since 2003, he found that those without a clear sense of purpose tend to fall into one of three categories: the disengaged, the dreamers, and the dabblers.[4] The disengaged are not passionate about anything beyond themselves and their own enjoyment and give no signs that they are interested in finding a purposeful pursuit. The dreamers have ideas about how they might find a life of meaning, but they haven't developed any practical, realistic plan to make those ideas a reality. The dabblers are engaged in activities that might be purposeful, but they jump from thing to thing without sustained commitment—an essential aspect of finding purpose.

In Damon's research, about 25 percent of youth were disengaged, 25 percent were dreamers, and 31 percent were dabblers. Only 20 percent were those who had found something meaningful to focus on, maintained that focus for a period of time, and were able to express what they were trying to accomplish and why—his definition of "purposeful." (Yes, that adds up to 101 percent, thanks to rounding.)

Too often that lost 80 percent won't pursue their dreams, find their passions, or make a needed change until the pain of not doing so becomes intolerable. To paraphase Joseph Campbell, this is the dull ache of the call unanswered.[5] Campbell describes that when the call is unanswered, you feel yourself drying up. The more pain you feel in this regard, the more likely it is that you are getting closer to answering the call.

The problem with the notion of a "purpose" is that it has been glamorized and romanticized over time to an unhelpful extent. Typically, when we try to summon examples of living with purpose, we think of people like Mother Teresa, Dr. Martin Luther King Jr., or Gandhi. The problem with these examples is that they are extreme and cause people to paint unrealistic pictures for themselves.

MYTHS ABOUT PURPOSE

Let's debunk a few of the most common misconceptions about what a purpose is or should be.

#1: A Purpose Is "Noble"

When I chat with people about purpose, I often find that they expect to be called to areas that are immensely important and noble—grand, world-changing endeavors—and they carry some degree of shame and guilt for not having realized their aspirations. This is probably what stymies people the most. The word *purpose* has a lot of baggage that comes with it.

The truth is that purpose can be found anywhere: in your volunteer work, caring for your children, being the best partner you can be, lovingly serving patrons a cup of coffee at the diner where you work. It depends on what's meaningful to you, not others.

Pursuing impressive careers or "important" causes that aren't personally meaningful to you will not give you the peaceful satisfaction that comes with following your true purpose. To paraphrase Jiddu Krishnamurti, through a wrong means, you can't achieve a right result.[6] Ego will never lead you to your purpose. You have to be careful to follow your heart—connecting to your true, honest self—no matter how humble your personal purpose may be.

I have a writer friend who was passionate about food and wine yet pursued a career as a lawyer because she wanted the societal legitimacy and paycheck of a professional occupation and figured she could do the job well enough. But she knew she would hate the work—the constant conflict and posturing, the lack of work-life balance, and the gut-clenching fear of making a mistake and causing irreparable harm to her clients' interests. She was right. It was misery for her.

Downsizing to a smaller, more relaxed firm that worked with wine and food clients helped but didn't solve the problem. So she transitioned to a part-time lawyer position and took on food and wine writing projects on the side—work that she loved wholeheartedly because of its creative, collaborative energy and subject matter. Interestingly, the disconnect between her legal career and her true passions became even more stark once she explored an area that suited her. Accolades for her legal work felt hollow and meaningless. It wasn't until she had quit practicing law entirely and was charting her own path as a full-time culinary and wine writer that she felt a true sense of accomplishment and success.

To her surprise, my writer friend makes a livable income as well as gained the priceless benefit of doing something she loves, controlling her own schedule and workload, and actually working *less*. She now spends around thirteen weeks a year doing things other than billable work—like traveling to the great wine regions of the world, eating her way through Southeast Asia, visiting relatives and friends, hosting dinner parties, and generally embracing life the way she wants to. Had she stuck with big-firm lawyering, my friend would be making probably six or seven times as much money—but she has no regrets. "You can't put a price tag on freedom, quality of life, or the satisfaction of working at something you love," she says. "Money is a renewable resource. You'll never get back the time you spend being miserable."

#2: A Purpose Is Singular

The second problem with the conventional view of purpose is the myth that each of us has just one distinct, overarching purpose in life. This notion puts needless pressure on us and can often make people give up on the idea of purpose altogether. In reality, nearly all of us have multiple purposes. We could and should have distinct purposes related to every large domain in our lives: a purpose related to the kind of parent we want to be, another related to the kind of work we want to dedicate ourselves to, yet another purpose to address the kind of life we want to lead, and so on. Consider a purpose to be similar to a brief mission statement for each of the important categories in your life, guiding your behaviors and beliefs.

#3: A Purpose Is Forever

The third problematic aspect of conventional thinking on "purpose" is that identifying one is your final destination. Human beings are in a constant cycle of budding, blooming, and withering away. Likewise, so are our many purposes. At any given moment, you can be living your current purpose, experiencing one fading away, or awakening a new purpose that is trying to emerge. Your job is to notice what's happening, taking inspired action to help it along.

As you seek your purpose, you may experience impatience and an unwillingness to yield to the natural unfolding process. But you cannot force the discovery of your purpose. It doesn't work that way. Impatience prevents us from exploring, following the clues, and taking the necessary baby steps that will lead to the next inspired action. We need to focus on the journey, not the end result.

LOOKING FOR YOUR PURPOSE

Seeking your purpose(s) is a deeply worthwhile pursuit and the ultimate way to feel supremely connected to yourself. Like the journey of self-connection, the exploration of your purpose begins by setting your intention and bringing mindful awareness to the question.

If you have already done this work and are living in alignment, then bravo! You are probably already living with great satisfaction. Remember to keep exploring within yourself, asking whether there is still more to be considered, more of you that wants to be expressed, more life within you that wants to be lived. If you haven't yet identified your purpose, I congratulate you also for taking this first step toward finding it.

Most of what is written about finding purpose focuses only on trying to discover what is untapped inside you—probably since that's the most exciting area. But it's equally important to pay attention to the other two areas: what is currently blooming in your life and what is fading away. Only with a holistic, 360-degree view of your life can you see what is calling you.

I find it useful to examine first what is currently in bloom, then move to what is declining, and finally to what is trying to bud.

Look at what is currently in full flower in your life to inventory the various ways you may already be living your purpose. The goal of discovering your purpose is not to negate what you are already devoting yourself to. Rather, it's to be brutally honest with yourself about the level of purpose and meaning behind your primary pursuits in life. We often regard everyday activities like raising children as not meaningful enough for a purpose because society doesn't value them as such, when in fact there is a profound purpose behind those activities. Any job or role can be a purpose or calling, depending on how *you* view it. As leading researchers in this area have concluded, "A physician who views the work as a job and is simply interested in making a good income does not have a calling, whereas a garbage collector who sees the work as making the world a cleaner, healthier place could have a calling."[7] Journaling can be incredibly helpful for identifying the meaning in our daily activities and, in my experience, it's the only way to really capture this frenetic territory of the mind and begin to see a cohesive picture emerge.

Richard Leider, a prolific author and entertaining writer on purpose, tells a charming story about a conversation he once had with a Boston cab driver, who said he only drove a cab to pay the bills. Nothing about it related to his true passion, which was coaching soccer. But when Leider asked him if he enjoyed any clients more than others, he admitted that he actually loved driving older ladies and came alive when they were in his cab.

"You've got a calling, then: giving care to older women through driving," Leider suggested to him. The man agreed: "You're right . . . I do. I come alive."[8] Pinpointing the aspects of your work that light you up can help you better understand what's meaningful and help clarify your purpose.

Next, focus on the purposes in your life that are fading away or declining. Remember that it's very important to bring an open, curious, nonjudgmental stance to this reflection process since otherwise your defenses might kick in and prevent you from finding the awareness you are seeking. Consider deeply which areas of your life no longer bring intense pleasure or have started to feel more like obligations. What areas of your life seem like they may have already peaked in terms of the meaning and satisfaction you derive from them?

For one of my clients, it was painful to admit that her purpose as a parent fell in this category. Her kids were in high school, and she found parenting teenagers was not as rewarding since they didn't need her as much. She was relieved to learn that, although one area of her life was in a natural state of decline, she didn't need to abandon it or feel she was a failure in that regard. For this client, her eventual answer was to recommit to her parenting and develop a passion around understanding and learning how to connect to and enjoy her teenagers, which brought renewed meaning and purpose to her life.

In other instances, the answer is to hasten the letting-go process when we are hanging on to declining areas of our lives. An important and powerful precursor to discovering our higher purpose is to let go of what is no longer serving us and thus creating the space necessary for something new to emerge.

So often, people want to hedge their bets and hold on to things that are meant to be fading away, such as a bad relationship, until a better replacement turns up. But life does not work best that way. You will only attract a similarly bad relationship that reflects your frustrated level of self-awareness. Letting go and creating true space involves a certain amount of fearlessness, courage, risk-taking, and faith. Those traits are synonymous with integrity and good character. When we act from a place of integrity and character, we are rewarded with higher consciousness and the evolution of spirit, enabling us to attract something or someone new into our lives that reflects our more enlightened, more conscious selves.

People often have the unrealistic fantasy that a new purpose (or new partner) will come and rescue them from their current miserable situation. But it's the other way around. You need to leave your bad situation, grieve its loss, grow from the experience . . . then spread your wings and take flight anew.

Considering what is trying to emerge inside of you or has yet to be discovered is the most exciting part of this exploration. At this stage, much of the work you've already done to become more familiar with how you source and cultivate meaning will be tremendously helpful. You'll still need to make the effort, pay attention, and take inspired action, though; you can't just sit around and wait for something to show up.

Following clues begins with creating opportunities for them to emerge. It's about opening up to a broader field of possibilities, expanding your field of awareness, asking empowered questions, having an open stance toward possibilities, embracing your unique gifts, and providing yourself ample opportunity to daydream, vision quest, and fantasize. Allow yourself to be deeply curious about each and every thing that gives you a heart surge or causes you to feel a burst of enthusiasm. For in these places, you will discover your greatest passions, hidden talents, deepest longings, desires, unmet needs, and true nature.

IDENTIFYING YOUR UNIQUE GIFTS

What are you naturally gifted at? The answers may help you find your purpose. Frequently, a person's highest purpose is one that puts their unique strengths to meaningful, productive use. If you're not clear on what special powers you have to offer the world, back up and take inventory of your obvious and not-so-obvious gifts.

Psychologist and former American Psychological Association president Dr. Martin Seligman has devoted his career to the positive psychology movement. He inspired our field to focus less on what is wrong with people and more on what is right with people—a shift that has shaped my passion and work. His website, authentichappiness.com, offers questionnaires and tests that you can take to discover more about yourself. The Strengths Test on his site is a great starting point to help identify and articulate your unique gifts.

What I appreciate most about the University of Pennsylvania and Dr. Seligman's questionnaires is that they were born out of academic rigor, according to the scientific method—unlike the slew of pop-psychology online questionnaires out there—with careful attention paid to internal and external validity of research results and interpretations. I strongly recommend them because of their proven reliability.

When I took Seligman's Strengths Test, I was surprised to discover that an appreciation for beauty and excellence, authenticity, and genuineness were my top strengths. Although I didn't see these qualities as part of my daily world, viewing them as my top strengths resonated with me, and a profound sense of rightness inspired me to seek areas in my life where I could honor and incorporate these elements more. I have no intention of becoming a designer or an artist, but I have taken a drawing class (which I found very fulfilling), and I've involved myself more intimately in the creative processes that are tangentially a part of my work, like web, book, and cover design or syllabus and workshop creation. These activities both indulge and amplify my strengths.

Dr. Seligman's research posits that we are healthier, happier beings when we use our natural strengths and talents. This makes intuitive sense to me, and I feel more complete as a human being since I started to highlight those areas of my life. When we are cut off from using our core strengths and gifts, we are not fully expressed and experience a latent, yet often imperceptible, grief related to those untapped passions. Doing, honoring, and expressing what you are naturally gifted at brings you effortlessly into closer connection to yourself.

Distinguish Your Gifts from Your Talents

One of my mentors cautions people not to confuse their gifts with their talents. He uses his wife, Amelia, as an example. She happens to be extremely good with numbers and has built a career as an accomplished accountant. Juggling numbers may be Amelia's talent, but it's not her passion, nor is it her real purpose.

Having known this lovely woman and worked side by side in an orphanage with her, I would have to agree that she has extraordinary gifts beyond mathematics. I watched Amelia become an immediate source of comfort, safety, and affection to a group of severely abused orphan girls in Peru. She had them laughing in no time and made them feel beautiful as she braided their hair, painted their nails, and let them do the same to her. More than anything, I noticed how Amelia radiated and seemed to come alive as she communed with these girls and helped them to feel like they mattered, even just for a moment. It was gratifying to see her in her element as she put her gifts to extraordinary use.

I myself excel at event planning, fundraising, and sales, and have engaged in many of those activities in my life. But these are not my true gifts . . . and in fact, they deplete my soul. I possess other gifts, real passions, that make me my best self, and those are at the forefront in the discovery of my purpose.

Our Weaknesses and Wounds Often Conceal Our Strengths

Interestingly, our true gifts are often related to our deepest wounds and to the qualities we are most embarrassed about. Fellow therapist, Ken Page, describes how he's "found that the very qualities we're most ashamed of, the ones we keep trying to reshape or hide, are, in fact, the key to finding real love. I call them 'core gifts'. . . . If we can name our own awkward, ardent gifts and extricate them from the shame and wounds that keep them buried, we'll find ourselves on a bullet train to deep, surprising, life-changing intimacy."[9]

I couldn't agree more with Ken and have had similar observations with my own psychotherapy clients. When a mother would admit to me her defeated, hopeless failings as a parent of a child with severe substance abuse issues, I could see her fierce commitment, unconditional devotion, and perseverance. When a teenage girl felt broken and tainted by her story of abuse, I saw a resilient, strong woman who knew how to survive and protect others. And when an elderly man admitted his lifelong struggle with loneliness and isolation, I saw his exquisite sensitivity and courageous vulnerability. My job as a therapist was to help these clients learn to see the strengths behind their painful experiences.

My friend and coach, Philip McKernan, believes that the greatest gifts we have to give this world often appear in our "story"—the tale of our struggles, pain, and life experiences that have shaped who we are. I recently had the privilege of organizing a TEDxYouth event about empowering and working with kids to help them articulate their stories and share them on the big stage in order to help and inspire others. I originally got involved as a way to contribute something meaningful to my boys' school other than bake sale items, and to have some fun working on a big project together as a family and with all of their friends. What I wasn't prepared for (and what has changed me forever) was the jaw-dropping impact of the kids' journeys. They had to dig deeply, uncover their own life stories and pain points, and take the huge emotional risk of acknowledging this vulnerability . . . not only to themselves, as they tried to piece together and bring coherence to their narratives, but also to a live audience of their peers and families.

Their courage was breathtaking. One young girl articulated the pain she felt from the social labels (and associated status) other kids had given her at school, spelling out how limiting, and even scarring, the experience was for her. She used her talk as both a call for compassion and as inspiration for other kids to ignore the confines of social labels and celebrate their complicated, many-faceted true selves.

Those of us who witnessed and participated in these kids' journeys were profoundly impacted by their metamorphosis from caterpillars into butterflies—not because they ultimately spoke in front of an audience of five hundred people, but because of their journey along the way, discovering their story and finding their voice to share it. Those young presenters found their true gifts to give the world, and they moved the audience to tears several times with the raw power and beauty of their stories.

So don't be afraid to look in dark corners for your gifts. Ask yourself where your pain points are and where your enthusiasm ignites. Likely, the answers will lead you to your gifts.

MINI-PURPOSES

In the quest for purpose, we tend to struggle with the fact that we have many significant domains of life, each deserving of a distinct mission statement or associated purpose. Creating a mini-purpose for each of these major areas is thus an easier way to get started.

For example, what is your purpose related to parenting? Romantic partnership? Work? Spirituality? In my parenting group, we discuss developing a parenting mission statement to help define one's purpose. People are often baffled at first and haven't given much thought to their ultimate concerns or guiding principles. Typically, they *do* know quite well, but they just don't have immediate access to the words that describe their beliefs because they have probably never been articulated before. After sharing ideas as a group, parents usually will say things like: "I want my children to be happy"; "Unlike my parents, I want to have as close a relationship as possible with my kids"; or "As best as I can, I want to avoid causing any harm." We then dig further so that they can revise or expand their purpose statements to a complete paragraph that captures the essence of what is most important to them. It takes some time and thought for parents to arrive at their ultimate driving concerns.

Journaling about the purpose of the main areas in your life can help. For example, in the romantic partnership area, ask yourself questions like, What kind of a romantic partner do I hope to be? What is my ultimate, highest, and best outcome in a romantic partnership? Karen Jones, a relationship coach and author of *The Heart Matters*, requires all of her clients to write a mission statement for what their vision of a fulfilling relationship looks like. She says that without that statement of purpose, it's unlikely she can be of much help. But once that statement is completed, her clients seem to manifest the relationship of their dreams, effortlessly and on their own.

Most people find it profoundly rewarding and grounding to create these statements of purpose around what they care most about. We yearn to understand our life purpose, but some of us expect the answer to arrive magically, through a crystal ball or tarot cards. You cannot understand your overarching life purpose until you are willing to create the individual pieces of the puzzle, thus contributing to a larger picture. Getting clear one-by-one on the mini-purposes of your life will help you to see overlapping themes and the larger mission statement of your life take shape.

We have a natural resistance to sitting quietly, asking ourselves these serious questions, and then reworking our answers until we are satisfied with the result. But the work must be done; in my experience, it's the only way to get there.

FOLLOWING YOUR DREAMS

Part of uncovering your true self and your purpose has to do with recognizing, honoring, and following your desires and dreams. Joseph Campbell wrote a beautiful book called *Pathways to Bliss*, in which he described how following what makes your heart leap is the pathway to finding bliss. We so often suppress our dreams before they've had a chance because we've prematurely decided they are unrealistic, inappropriate, or incompatible with the life we've chosen so far.

In a famous blog post entitled "Five Regrets of the Dying," Bronnie Ware described her work in a palliative care unit (a form of medical care that emphasizes quality of life and comfort for patients with life-threatening illnesses). In conversations where she questioned her patients about any regrets they had or things they would have done differently in life, she shared (consistent with my own experience) that the most common regret she heard was "I wish I'd had the courage to live a life true to myself, not the life others expected of me."

Ware goes on to say:

> When people realise that their life is almost over and look back clearly
> on it, it is easy to see how many dreams have gone unfulfilled. Most
> people had not honoured even a half of their dreams and had to die
> knowing that it was due to choices they had made, or not made. It is
> very important to try and honour at least some of your dreams along the
> way. From the moment that you lose your health, it is too late. Health
> brings a freedom very few realise, until they no longer have it.[10]

Following your dreams does not mean you must follow them to the bitter end. We tend to view our dreams in an all-or-nothing kind of way, yet we can satisfy different cravings in our lives even if we only get to first base. If you've always dreamed of being a musician or an artist, for example, or of owning your own bar, you don't have to quit your job to devote yourself to one of these pursuits wholly and completely. You might be able to satisfy your craving simply by taking guitar lessons or building a tiki bar in your backyard to host your friends on the weekends. There are typically many ways to enact or touch base with our dreams so that a deeply held desire doesn't go completely ignored. If you want to die with little to no regrets, start taking stock of all the things you once dreamed of or that you secretly wish you could do, and tick them off your list by taking action in some small way.

One of my therapy clients said he regretted never trying to become a professional baseball player when he had the chance. At age forty, he thought he was too old and saw no point in pursuing it further. But he agreed to reconsider after I asked if it might become a potential life regret and permanent disconnection from a part of his true self. When we resumed our sessions after a summer break, I was astonished to hear his story. He told me that over the summer he had hired a private coach to work with him weekly on his batting and fielding skills. And to his amazement, he loved his private lessons, increased them to four times a week, and was able to surpass his skill level from his peak years. He laughingly said that what he'd never realized was that he had something now he'd never had when he was younger: the financial freedom and the time to hire someone super talented to work with him.

"It's so much easier to learn when you're self-motivated and free from outside pressure," he said. "When you approach it that way, for the love of the playing and excelling, you can really accelerate your progress. It feels good to feel my strength again and spend time out there on the field." It turned out that this was all he truly craved. He wasn't compelled to join a team, quit his job, or take it any further; he was satisfied that he'd achieved what he'd wanted with his lessons and no longer felt like he was ignoring his cherished, long-held desire.

We all have natural gifts and talents, many of which will not get expressed to their fullest. In this one life we lead, there are several other lives we've had to forego. But sometimes we have dreams that do need to be pursued, if only just a little.

If you're not sure what those dreams might be, start by following your moments of bliss. Be on the lookout for anything that gives you a surge of excitement or vicarious joy. Envy can also be a clue. When you see someone else doing something you've always wanted to do, expand your mind and get curious about what you admire. Is it opera singing, raising butterflies, or writing a book? Or something more abstract like freedom to travel, a life of adventure, true self-expression, or deep connection with others? Be on the lookout for things that stir up a sense of longing inside you. While you may not want the whole package, there is likely some part of what you're seeing that speaks to a deeply held desire you could touch.

CONSIDERING A HIGHER PURPOSE

In the last few sections, we've discussed purpose(s)—the long-term endeavors you feel called to undertake—and how meaning, values, and priorities help clarify those endeavors. Now I want to turn to your *higher purpose* . . . a term that many people have thrown around and discussed in the context of finding supremely meaningful work, but one I think could use some further refinement. In my mind, a grand or higher purpose is the nobler calling that lies at the intersection of what you're good at, what you're passionate about, and what others need.

To give an example, Bill Gates's purpose may at one time have been revolutionizing computing through Microsoft, but as he describes in a TED talk with his wife Melinda, his higher purpose and sacred work emerged from dedicating himself to solving the world's biggest health, education, and community challenges through the Bill and Melinda Gates Foundation.

In a higher purpose, you are devoted to a cause that transcends your own immediate needs and gratification and that ultimately serves someone else, the greater community, or the world. This is often described as the highest form of enlightenment and contentment. The key distinction between a higher purpose and other purposes is that the higher purpose transcends the self's needs for a greater good.

Developmental psychologist Dr. Abraham Maslow described the now-famous concept of a hierarchy of human needs. The first, most basic level of needs are those related to bare survival (water, food, shelter). When those basic needs for survival are not met, there is little else we can focus on. As human beings master their needs for survival, however, they move on to higher-level needs, like safety, love, and esteem. When those are met, they move on to even more elevated needs, and so on, until all that remains is an essential imperative to fulfill the highest craving: self-actualization, which Maslow defined as "the desire for self-fulfillment . . . the tendency for [them] to become actualized in what [they are] potentially. This tendency might be phrased as the desire to become more and more what one is, to become everything that one is capable of becoming."[11] I think of a higher purpose as the highest point of self-actualization, at the very tip of the pyramid of needs.

As author David Brooks puts it, "You don't ask, What do I want from life? You ask a different set of questions: What does life want from me? What are my circumstances calling me to do?"[12] From this vantage point, your life's past difficulties and challenges feel like helpful lessons that prepared you for this noble undertaking. Your entire journey of life makes sense, as though it has all been in the service of this higher calling and destination. The late Wayne Dyer believed in this concept and joked during one of his talks that when God was laying out Wayne's life plan and realized how important resilience was going to be to his future destiny, he thought, "Well then, we'd better get your little ass into an orphanage."[13]

SELF-ACTUALIZATION

The highest level of the heirarchy, which includes personal growth and self-fulfillment.
These are only attainable once the lower tiers have been satisfied.

ESTEEM

Feelings of respect and achievement that are classified into two categoties:
the desire to respect yourself and the desire to have respect
from others within the community.

LOVE & BELONGING

The needs of humans to receive and give attention and be part of a community.

SAFETY

The fundamental needs of humans to feel safe, secure, stable, and
protected from natural elements and other potential threats.

PHYSIOLOGICAL NEEDS

The basic biological needs of humans to survive, such as food, air, and water.

Maslow's Hierarchy of Needs

In the same vein, I feel that one of my true gifts to share with the world is thinking, learning, researching, and writing about authentic connection—not because I am good at it but because I have always had a huge hole in my heart related to connection. I have yearned and struggled to feel more connected to myself and others more than anything else in this world. Sharing my struggle and lessons feels more like a higher calling than anything else I have ever known.

When you seek to identify your higher purpose, you're asking yourself how you can best serve the planet, how you can best be of service using your natural gifts, and above all, "Is what I am making or doing aligned with what people actually need?" While there is a growing movement toward social or purpose-driven businesses, many capitalistic ventures do not rise to the level of a higher purpose, typically because they cannot affirmatively answer that last question. Often, people work at a lower level of

Maslow's hierarchy, producing or selling a product based primarily on their own ego-driven and selfish needs—and too often at great cost to themselves, others, and the environment.

Your sacred work is as you define it and has nothing to do with scale of impact or income. Dr. William Damon put it beautifully in his book: "A mother caring for her child, a teacher instructing students, a doctor healing patients, a citizen campaigning for a candidate for the sake of improving society—all are pursuing noble purposes. So, too, are the legions of people who dedicate time, care, effort, and worldly goods to charity, to their friends and family, to their communities, and to God."[14]

A retired veterinary nurse I'll call "Ava" helps people care for their beloved pets during their final days so they can stay at home instead of at a veterinary facility. I doubt this job was very lucrative since Ava didn't charge much. But her commitment to her clients and their cherished animals was fierce. When my akita companion and friend of twelve years was at the end of her days, Ava was there for both of us. During the challenging period when our Lola couldn't walk and needed to be hand-fed and hydrated through injection, this woman was available to assist, day or night, and miraculously appeared whenever needed, in spite of her own busy life. More than just doing her job, Ava was personally invested. She seemed to love my dog as much as I did, and she genuinely cared about me as well. She gave her heart and soul to the effort, never seeming to grow tired or feel inconvenienced. It was clear Ava felt she was performing one of the most noble and important jobs that she was put on this earth to do. And she was.

I was moved to the core by how much Ava loved her role and her work. While the loss of my beloved companion was excruciating, the way this woman held my hand every step of the way, gazing lovingly at my dog in her final moments as I choked out my goodbye, was a profound gift that I will never forget. It was true compassion in action. The love and fulfillment Ava found in her work was palpable and enviable. At the time, I was feeling lost around my own purpose, and I remember thinking I would trade places with her in a second to have that kind of certainty—to know in my bones that I was providing a needed and important service that also filled my heart with joy.

Regardless of its economic or global impact, sacred work is using your greatest gifts and talents to be of service to others or the world, doing the most important work you can do, for a purpose that's greater than yourself.

EMPOWERING QUESTIONS AND EXERCISES TO GUIDE YOU

The questions we ask influence our quality of life. The same is true during the discovery process as we uncover our higher purpose and take inspired action. Asking what Dr. Michael Beckwith calls "empowering questions," without expecting or needing an answer right away, is one of the best ways to bring clarity.

Beckwith describes empowering questions as those that take us directly into the heart of our situation and open the door for us to progress. He encourages people to ask what qualities their current situations are urging them to activate and what ingrained patterns of thinking they need to release in order to shift their situations to the desired ones. "Such questions press the reset button within our mindsets and heart-sets, creating an opportunity for us to activate our more expansive, compassionate, joyous, and wise aspects of being"[15]—or, as I would put it, to reconnect to our true selves, letting our inner wisdom guide us where we want to go.

Asking these kinds of questions is akin to prayer—a powerful way to set an intention and allow the universe to help set the wheels in motion.

Here are some examples of empowering questions to consider, gathered from various thinkers in the field and from our own experiences:

Who am I when I'm at my best?

What activities make me feel the most alive and most like my best self?

If money, time, and life logistics were not an issue, how would I spend my time?

What do I love doing so much that I would pay someone to get to do it every day?

What do I love so much that I could talk about it all day without ever getting bored?

If I knew I couldn't fail, what would I try to do?

What would I want to keep doing even if I failed?

What exceptional talent or skill would I love to have?

There are a couple of effective brainstorming exercises we use in our workshops to help people generate their own empowering questions and stimulate creative thinking around their purpose. One of these techniques we borrow from Michael Gelb's book, *How to Think Like Leonardo da Vinci:*

Seven Steps to Genius Every Day. In it, Gelb describes how da Vinci was a huge question-lover who carried a journal with him everywhere to capture his ideas, thoughts, questions, and inspirations.

Da Vinci's belief in the power of questions inspired Gelb's "100 Questions Exercise," in which you jot down in a journal a list of a hundred questions that come to mind or that you find intriguing. It's important to do this all in one go. You want to be unrestricted in your writing and let yourself free-associate, jotting down whatever questions come to mind. The questions can range from the inconsequential, like "Why do we still use silent letters?" to "What really matters to me in this life?"

When we do this exercise as a group, participants write furiously at first, and the list grows quickly. Then they start to slow down somewhere around thirty or forty questions. There is often a temptation to quit when you run out of easy questions. It's important to push past these moments and keep going until you get to one hundred. You'll likely surprise yourself with the things you come up with. Once you hit a hundred questions, you go back over your list and jot down the central themes that emerge.

Gelb recommends picking out the ten questions that you find the most significant, rank ordering them from one (most meaningful) to ten (least). I do this in my workshops as well, but typically only after we have already done the work of identifying sources of meaning in participants' lives. I've found that doing basic meaning groundwork first makes it much easier to rank the questions generated by this exercise.

Another powerful but more heart-centered exercise inverts the technique and focuses on asking just one powerful question: "What's my true purpose in life?"[16] You then start writing your thoughts, letting the answers continue to flow until you write the answer that triggers a surge of emotion—or, as writer Steve Pavlina puts it, "until you write the answer that makes you cry. This is your purpose."[17]

He notes that it usually takes "fifteen to twenty minutes to clear your head of all the clutter and the social conditioning about what you think your purpose in life is. The false answers will come from your mind and your memories. But when the true answer finally arrives, it will feel like it's coming to you from a different source entirely."[18]

As with the 100 Questions exercise, don't get bogged down analyzing what you're writing or whether it's repetitive. Just keep writing nonstop until you get to the end. It's important to get through this in one shot, without any interruptions. When I did this exercise, it took me about thirty-five minutes, and I reached my final answer at number eighty-seven. My final answer was *To be awake—to live, love, and parent consciously, while working to empower and inspire others to do the same.*

What I love about these two particular exercises is their simplicity, short duration, and often profound results. The act of writing, without taking our normal processing time as we go, allows us to access deeper, less-inhibited areas of our brain and parts of our psyche that are more likely to surprise us and reveal truths we didn't know we had within us.

TAKING INSPIRED ACTION

Now that you're noticing and becoming more aware of all of the clues in your life that lead you to the path of discovering your higher purpose, it is equally critical to take inspired action from them. Because one clue leads to another, many major clues come only as a result of branching out and seeing what happens next, trying new things, and experimenting along the way.

I like to compare this process to the way my dad set up Easter egg hunts when I was a kid. Instead of your typical egg hunt, where eggs are hidden randomly in the backyard and frenzied kids run around at breakneck speed with the singular strategy of grabbing as much easy booty as possible, my dad created individual egg hunts that put our detective skills to the test. Each of us would get a different series of clues and riddles, starting with number one. We had to figure out the meaning of each clue in sequence to discover where the next clue and egg might be until eventually the final clue would lead to our personal Easter egg basket. Following the trail of clues to discover your higher purpose is basically just one of my dad's egg hunts, but for grown-ups.

Rather than trying to consider everything in front of you all at once, make an educated guess about which action you're inspired to take next, and take it. Once you've made a move, you have a new perspective and can reflect on what that action revealed for you. Be careful to distinguish your true self from your ego as you do this, and don't let the ego drive as you consider your course of action. Ego-driven actions simply lead to more busyness. You can never do enough to satisfy the ego. But actions inspired by your true self can have a lasting impact on your life and lead to the most profound type of existential contentment.

The key, though, is to *take action*. Don't wait to pinpoint your ultimate destination before you start walking; just get going in the direction you feel is calling you, and see what new signs are revealed along the way. Seemingly insignificant acts can turn out to be essential for recognizing and following your true path. Steve Jobs famously credits a random calligraphy class he audited for giving him the idea for the Mac's clean aesthetic and typeface.

Indecision and postponement fertilize fear, and ideas that go ignored will begin to stagnate within you, rotting from the inside out. Do not wait. Act.

Chapter 5

CONNECTING WITH YOUR PHYSICAL SELF

[T]o keep the body in good health is a duty, or otherwise you shall not be able to keep your mind strong and clear and have the lamp of wisdom burning.

BUDDHA[1]

Reestablishing a strong connection with your body is an essential part of experiencing connection to yourself. Physical, bodily connection promotes a sense of vitality and thriving.

Your body feels in balance, and you're able to sense your muscles, joints, veins, and lungs at work. You savor the joy of subtle (or intense) movement, experiencing the wonder of flexibility, coordination, strength, power, and grace. Our bodies evolved to be able to move in a mind-boggling variety of directions and actions—unlike most other animals. We run, we walk, we lift, we climb, we jump, we swim, we twist, we pull, we push, and we press. As Dr. John Ratey and Richard Manning put it in their book, *Go Wild*, "Humans are the Swiss Army knives of motion."[2] We're designed to move in all directions. Physical connection helps us acknowledge, honor, care for, and stay in touch with our most primal needs, and it leads to a rich and deep satisfaction. No matter what your state of body is and whether you are grossly out of shape, overweight, or ailing, we all crave and deserve to feel the powerfully connected feelings that come from experiencing our bodies in sublime motion. We honor our bodies instead of combating them.

As we've seen already in the course of this book, connection of any kind begets more connection. Cultivating connection in one area of your life will trickle over and catalyze spontaneous connection in other areas of your life; unfortunately, the same is true for disconnection. There is a colloquial saying in parenting that suggests, "You are only able to be as happy as your least happy child." That concept works similarly with connection—you are only as connected as the least connected part of yourself. It is difficult to connect deeply to yourself if you are neglecting major areas of self-care or if you ignore the self-destructive behaviors you engage in.

How often are you aware of your body and what it needs? Does your body need to rest or need to move? Most adults deny themselves proper self-care and pay the price both physically and emotionally. Check in multiple times a day with the original core question—*Am I feeling connected right now?*—and you will find yourself beginning to raise the *Titanic* from its cold, lonely depths.

You don't have to achieve mastery in all areas of self-care to be successful in experiencing deeper connection. But you do need to be awake to the holistic view of the many parts of yourself, scanning for your blind spots and bringing the intention to move the needle ever so slightly in each area of your life. With gentle persistence and a clear "why," you *can* turn around disconnection's ebbing tide and help connection flood into your life from all directions.

SENSORY AWARENESS

As we've gotten more into our own heads (and our screens) as a society, we engage our bodies and senses less and less. Whether we notice it or not, all human beings yearn to *feel* and have their physical senses engaged. The less we experience the sensory realities of being alive, the more we experience ourselves as detached and dulled. Often people don't realize how sensually deprived and starved they are, and they act out their need to "feel anything" in unhealthy ways, just to prove they are alive.

In an extreme example, one severely depressed girl, who was hospitalized for making several knife cuts on her arm, shared with me that her cutting was not a suicidal gesture, but rather an attempt to "feel something . . . something real . . . anything . . . to prove to myself that I was alive." It was an effort to feel something beyond the numbness she experienced day to day.

Heightening your sensory awareness doesn't require extreme or dangerous acts, however. It simply requires mindful awareness to amplify otherwise ordinary sensations so that they can become extraordinary experiences that leave you feeling vibrantly alive and connected.

In many ways, sensory experience is the original source of pure connection for all living beings. Visceral experiences like goose bumps, the hair standing up on the back of your neck, and the way your stomach drops on a roller coaster are all moments when we feel intensely alive and pulled into connection with ourselves and our bodies. But you don't have to wait for special circumstances or crises; you can intentionally seek out and use these kinds of bodily sensations to promote a more primal and deeply rooted connection to your body.

What exactly is sensory awareness? Dr. Russell T. Hurlburt and his colleagues have defined it as "the direct focus on some specific sensory aspect of the body or outer or inner environment."[3] It's a phenomenon of attentive experience, not mere perception. For example, if you hop absent-mindedly into a hot shower in order to get your day started, that is not sensory experience. But if you take a moment to pause and bring mindful awareness to the sensation of the warm water drenching your hair and face, noticing the pleasurable feelings and the motion of the water along your skin—that is sensory awareness.

Similarly, you are not using sensory awareness if you slip under your covers and focus on getting to sleep as quickly as possible. But if you pause to appreciate the softness of your sheets on your skin and the caress of the pillow on your cheek, you are experiencing it in full.

Or, if you are patting your dog's head and saying your hellos as you come in the door, but mostly making sure he's not jumping up and scratching you, that is not a sensory experience. But if you pause to gaze lovingly at him, intentionally stroking his head, marveling at the soft fur between your fingers and the tickle of his whiskers on your cheek as he tries to lick your face, that is a sensory experience.

Mindful awareness is, once again, the key difference in all of these examples—a mindful intention to amplify your awareness of the situation. Engaging your senses boosts your sense of vitality and makes you feel exquisitely alive. It is the magic fairy dust of experiencing true connection.

The sheer pleasure and joy that come from heightening and tuning in to our innate senses make this my favorite area of practice and what our workshop participants seem to enjoy the most. We are so often unaware of our bodies and our senses in our modern lifestyles. The practice of intentionally heightening our awareness to all of our senses (sight, hearing, touch, sound, and taste, to name a few) helps us fully inhabit our bodies.

The key is to pause and elongate the moment as much as you can in order to amplify and savor the experience. By attuning to your senses, you will notice them reawaken and become sharper. At the advanced level, you can even learn to modulate or resolve uncomfortable sensations, such as pain, by bringing a nonjudgmental, appreciative curiosity to the sensation.

Another way to activate sensory awareness is to seek out enhanced experiences. The wide array of health benefits of extremely cold water, for example—which includes neural regeneration, reduced inflammation, an increase in killer T cells, increased fat burning, and a more positive mood, among other highly desirable benefits—are becoming more widely understood and are fantastic bonuses to what most people would consider just a great way to deliver a turbocharge of sensation.[4] But jumping into any body of water, regardless of the temperature, with an intentional awareness of the tingling sensation, is an incredible way to experience yourself as completely alive.

In the modern age of first-world comforts, our bodies rarely get a jolt of sensory excitement because we all live within a narrow band of ambient temperature and unvarying experiences. Try getting outside of that safe and secure band. Go for a walk in the rain without an umbrella, feeling the youthful exuberance of getting soaking wet. Experiment with heat, and try a sauna or a sweat lodge. Research shows promising health benefits for regular activities of this kind in addition to the sensory thrill we experience.

THE FUNDAMENTALS OF SELF-CARE

As you embark on your journey toward deeper self-connection, you will experience much more dramatic and rapid progress if you pause to tend to your basic self-care needs. This is a critically important step. We each have our own top priority areas of self-care that we need to take care of in order to feel like we can function at our best. But for most people, these are the universal and profound needs of good nutrition, moderate exercise, adequate sleep, and hydration.

These areas of self-care are huge topics in our busy, modern culture because they are so often neglected. We cope with and rationalize our poor self-care by becoming disconnected from our bodies. We are oblivious to a myriad of signs and symptoms that our bodies communicate to us. We block them out, stop paying attention, and are unable to consistently differentiate our bodily needs. We often crave sugar, for example, when in fact we just need to catch up from a bad night's rest.

From a psychological perspective, it makes complete sense that diets fail, New Year's exercise initiatives fade, and in general we struggle to take good care of ourselves and make necessary positive changes. If we all had unlimited bandwidth, time, and resources, it might be easier to accomplish our goals. But what often prevents us from sticking with a healthier self-care regimen (besides our tendency to take on too many changes at once and become overwhelmed) is that we don't have a deeper "why"—a reason underlying the goal that is both intrinsically rewarding and self-sustaining.

As with so many other aspects of life, you will have a hard time overhauling your physical well-being unless you know what you stand for. If your "why" is weak, you are likely doing it for the wrong reasons, and your efforts will eventually peter out. You need to have your own system of beliefs around the various aspects of well-being and self-care, and if you don't already, you need to develop one. There's a worksheet in the appendix to help you articulate your "why."

Ask yourself, What really matters most when it comes to nutrition, movement, and sleep? Regardless of whether you think it's achievable or practical for your life circumstances, what do you truly believe about how we should eat, sleep, and move? How are you personally impacted by each of these domains? How does your body respond when you honor your beliefs? What does your body need to feel cared for and prioritized?

Having a belief system in these important areas enables us to create sustainable, positive lifestyle changes that are intrinsically rewarding to us. Taking action according to those beliefs then brings us the joy of knowing we are attending to and connecting with our most important needs—living in alignment with our truths.

WHAT'S *YOUR* ANGLE?

I failed to maintain any regular self-care regimens for most of my life. I also would have always described myself as a fairly healthy person who didn't have any major self-care deficiencies. Looking back, it's stunning for me to see how wrong I was.

During that time when I would have described myself as relatively healthy, I was mindlessly eating whatever I wanted, usually on the go, in the car or at a restaurant. I was helping myself to large, sugary Starbucks lattes every day, and alcohol was a routine part of meals. Dairy, gluten, and animal protein were usually included in each meal, and sugar was constant. Exercise was either my constant, guilty avoidance or a self-punitive, overbearing act. I didn't pay special attention to hydration and usually went to bed late every night, averaging about six hours of sleep.

This is a typical profile for most Americans, and since the human body can take a fair amount of abuse and keep functioning, most of us walk around thinking these habits are no big deal. Sure, I had the frequent bouts of low energy, headaches, difficulty concentrating, lack of motivation, allergies, and gut problems, but I heard most people complain of the same things and figured that it was all just part of being human and getting older.

It wasn't until I started looking at self-care through the lens of connection that I was personally able to find the motivation to make huge breakthroughs. Through a series of small, seemingly insignificant acts every day, I am able to send powerful messages to myself that I matter, that my needs are significant, and that I am worth the time and attention that is required to take good care of myself. It's an entirely different approach when you consider that being mindful of self-care is really an act of self-love and a way to be closer to yourself, more involved, more intimate, and ultimately more connected to yourself.

It's similar to how you build a relationship with any loved one or a child in your life—you communicate your love and devotion to them through many acts of service each day, letting them know nonverbally that they are worth your time, your attention, and your efforts. The only difference is that, in this case, *you* are the beloved, and you are forming this trusting, loving bond with yourself. Whenever you take the time to pay attention and do good deeds for yourself, no matter how small, it's a powerful symbolic gesture toward yourself that conveys the message that you are worth it. The deeper self-connection and improved health you get from proper self-care ultimately help you be the best parent, partner, sibling, and friend that you can be.

In short, properly tending to your body's basic needs is a fast-track way to repair and build up your sense of self-worth. And self-worth is one of the pillars that the house of self-connection is built upon.

Let's review the fundamental areas of self-care that most significantly impact our emotional and physical well-being.

NUTRITION: A SIMPLE APPROACH

Research at Cornell University's Food and Brand Lab suggests that we make about two hundred food choices a day, and most of them are unconscious.[5]

Do you feel connected to the food you eat? Do you know or care about where it comes from, what animals or environments might be harmed by its production? Are you thoughtful about how what you're eating might impact your body, for better or worse? Or, is it an unconscious process of total disconnection?

In order to answer these questions, ask yourself at your next meal: How connected am I to this meal and to the choices on my plate? Does it fit into my belief system? Do I have a belief system? If you don't have a belief system, it's hard to act in alignment. Knowing what your values are (what matters to you and what you care about) helps reintegrate these disconnected domains in our lives, converting them to a source of goodness and collaboration between you and your body. There is tremendous empowerment when you are connected to your food choices.

Discontentment is a normal part of the human condition. When we feel that way, we often turn to food as a numbing technique. Next time you notice this, ask yourself instead what you're really hungry for. Is it love, nurturance, understanding, relaxation, alone time, an apology?

The Perils of Eating in the US

In today's culture, it's not easy to feel good about our food choices. The United States' food system is dangerously dysfunctional. We as a nation, and as individuals, are largely oblivious to where our food comes from, how it's made, what's in it, and how to interpret unintelligible ingredient lists. We are more often than not oblivious to what's served to us at restaurants and to what we are putting into our mouths. At the same time, the biggest players in the food industry operate like every other big business—spending countless dollars on lobbyists and marketing campaigns to ensure a healthy bottom line for themselves rather than a healthy product for healthy consumers.

"Big Food" feeds the nation (and the world) with low-cost, mass-produced products with reduced healthful properties and often incompletely tested, hazardous additives to enhance texture, flavor, and profitability.[6] Although awareness is certainly building and momentum is gaining (at least in some parts of the country), a new food system has yet to be built, and it's still a daunting challenge for even the savviest consumers to find and feed themselves healthy, nutrient-rich foods on a consistent basis.

We are inundated with contradictory information and often go to great effort and expense to buy organic foods and create or find healthy meals for ourselves. It's no wonder that most people take an "ignorance is bliss" approach and ignore what they are eating or rationalize to themselves, as I did, that they're doing the best they can and things really aren't *that* bad.

But the standard American diet (SAD) is, indeed, very sad. While there is vast disagreement and debate among nutritionists and experts about what the ideal diet or best approach is (another reason for mass confusion), the one thing all experts agree on is that the human body is highly adaptable and able to accommodate many different diets—*except* the standard American diet, which consists of lots of animal protein, carbs, and sugar.[7] Most nutritionists seem to agree (other than the sugar industry nutrition experts) that sugar is poison. And virtually all experts agree that the chronic diseases that now afflict and kill most of us—cancer, heart disease, diabetes, obesity—are directly linked with adoption of the standard American diet.[8]

In fact, the gut is now being recognized as essentially a second brain, with an enormous impact on mental as well as physical health. Research shows that digestive irritations in this second brain—also known as the enteric nervous system (ENS)—can trigger significant mood changes and are linked to anxiety and depression disorders. Though much is still unknown about how the ENS works, it is now proven beyond a doubt that the food we eat plays an important role in both our health and happiness.[9]

A Simple Approach to Eating Better

Michael Pollan put together a simple, seven-word prescription for good nutrition that, I think, offers the best commonsense solution for our dietary confusion: "Eat food. Not too much. Mostly plants."[10]

In this model, we should ideally load up on a wide variety of leafy greens and eat healthy fats like olive oil, avocado, nuts, fish, and coconut oil. Instead of placing animal protein and saturated animal fats at the center of meals, we should minimize our consumption by treating them as condiments, or "condi-meats" as Dr. Mark Hyman calls them.[11] You should also minimize foods that contain alcohol and caffeine, or those that tend to aggravate your system. For some people that includes dairy and gluten. Because most restaurant meals fail on all of these measures, simply cooking more meals at home from whole foods can dramatically improve our nutrition.

Competing narratives about proper nutrition and the disconnect between "healthy" foods and the choices that are convenient for day-to-day living made it difficult for me to make strides in this area of my life for many years. I knew I was ignorant about and disconnected from my food choices; I could barely even remember what I ate on any given day. I knew that this was a hold-out area for me and that if I wanted to open all of the floodgates of connection, I couldn't ignore this aspect of my life any longer.

At some point, I decided I would be willing to at least look at and consider my own food choices, whether or not I was willing to ultimately make any changes. I resolved to take a picture of what I was eating at mealtimes to find out what my diet really looked like.

This small act led to a lot of fascinating discoveries for me. At first, I had some fun documenting the clearly unhealthy, on-the-go type foods I was eating and took pictures of myself eating them in defiant poses. But then many interesting things started happening. Just the act of acknowledging each meal made me want to be more thoughtful and consider alternative choices. I noticed a reluctance to eat things that I would not be excited to photograph, followed closely by efforts to select foods that I would feel proud about snapping a photo of. Eventually, I found myself making several small, good (or better) choices each day for the right reasons—I was feeling much more awake, aware, and intentionally loving and connected to myself with each one I made. The payoff was huge. And for the first time in my life, I'd found the right "why," so the "how" was easy.

The start of the day is a great time to set intentions for many people. Take just a few moments to consider and visualize, in broad strokes, what you'd like your food choices to look like for the day. Think about how your vision compares to your values and belief system around eating. By mindfully connecting with your goals of eating at the start, you are more likely to make subtle changes throughout your day to conform to your ideals.

Nutritional deficiencies come on slowly, a death by a thousand mindless acts. But cultivating healthy and sustainable eating patterns is achieved the same way—with a thousand small, seemingly insignificant choices that add up over time. Throughout your day, as best you can, try to inject a moment of mindfulness when you are choosing what to eat (staring at a menu, standing in front of an open refrigerator), and ask yourself whether the choice you are about to make fits with your vision and whether there might not be a slightly better option.

Sometimes, the gains are on the periphery. When your entrée is indulgent (and hopefully you are fully savoring it—guilt free), you may decide to lessen the load on your body by skipping the bread, having water instead of wine, or skipping dessert. These little wins can also be sources of pride and encouragement. Noticing how good choices bring you a sense of joy and satisfaction helps you ride a wave of naturally reinforcing behaviors that's fueled by the right motivations. Learning how to stay neutral and gentle with yourself when you aren't able to make good choices is also essential. By maintaining connection to yourself, you make it easier to get back in the right gear when you are ready.

The end goal here is to develop the habit of staying mindful of your choices, being careful to support your choices whatever they may be, and maintaining self-connection as you develop a more intimate, healthy relationship with your food.

Because things like diet, food choices, and body image can be such huge shame triggers for people (and women especially), it's important to ease into these areas slowly. Stay curious and open to possibilities as much as you can, and try to avoid laying big guilt trips on yourself or imposing unrealistic goals in a heavy-handed way.

A woman whose passion is to teach fitness and nutrition to plus-size women has an approach that I really admire. "Rhonda" encourages her clients to eat more, rather than less. She boasts that she doesn't care about the bad foods, and instead of food elimination, she teaches clients how to begin to love and nurture their bodies at each meal by choosing something green and nutrient dense, no matter how little, as an act of self-love.

Rhonda believes that getting people to care about themselves and to associate nutritious food choices with self-love leads to a natural progression of the good foods nudging out the bad choices over time, in a way that bypasses resistance. A client who orders a green drink at breakfast, for example, is free to chase it down with a donut if they want. But often, the sense of personal pride and self-love they feel from choosing the green drink makes the donut seem less appealing afterward. Rhonda's goal is to get her clients absorbing more nutrients more often to increase their energy levels, thus moving the ship in the right direction.

Our relationship to food is an enormous, complicated topic that most people struggle with on some level. Many battle with serious behaviors such as bingeing, purging, and starving themselves literally to death. It's much easier said than done to heighten our awareness and connection to our food. As we'll find with physical activity in the next section, the best way to forge our way through this vast territory is to set aside the decades of baggage and preconceived ideas and set an intention to simply be more curious—curious about how you define healthy eating, about what you are really hungry for, about how your body feels after you make a bad choice, about the kinds of nutritious eating that excite you, about the relationship between what you eat and how you feel afterward. Curiosity is a neutral state that resembles a beginner's mind. It shifts you into an open-minded perspective that allows you to stay connected to yourself and to your observations.

When you approach a new area with cautious optimism and no expectations, you open the door for natural motivation to occur and creative spontaneous solutions to emerge. Ideas and solutions that are born from this place of ease and self-acceptance are generally more congruent with your true nature and are far more likely to succeed. Use your food as a source of energy, nourishment, and self-honoring rather than an immediate, short-term comfort. When you are not able to move past prioritizing convenience or comfort, forgive yourself and be compassionate; no one is perfect.

Nourishing and honoring your body in this way boosts not only your health and physical ability to function, but also your connection to yourself.

MOVEMENT

At my connected parenting groups for mothers, I like to start by asking the moms to participate in an intensive self-care regimen for several weeks before we begin discussing parenting techniques. Mothers are notorious for sacrificing their own self-care in the service of others and, in order to be present for more closeness in any relationship, your own tank needs to be full first.

The first time I started a group this way, it was striking to hear how each and every mother felt unfulfilled by, unhappy with, or out of touch with her own body. Most of them had grown to accept this condition as normal over time. Their feelings weren't necessarily related to the size and shape of their bodies. This was more about their own physical satisfaction.

Some tried to joke about it, chalking it up to age, "use it or lose it," or having "mom-bod." But the poignancy of the grief these moms felt around this issue struck a chord with me and inspired me to want to understand how we can become so easily disconnected from our bodies without even realizing it. It also challenged me to explore the truth of my own relationship to my body more deeply.

The more I honestly reflected, the more I realized that I was also disconnected from my body and its movement; I was in no position to teach other people how to connect to their bodies until I solved my own issues first. The only intentional movement I did was some form of chore-like exercise, which I had to push myself uphill to perform and which I therefore did not do on any regular basis.

There was nowhere to go but up.

Movement Versus Exercise

I titled this discussion "Movement," rather than "Exercise," because I don't think exercise is necessarily the way back to connection with our bodies. While exercise certainly has its place, I would argue that movement is the better way to mediate reconnecting with our bodies.

Movement can include exercise, but is much broader in its interpretation, motivations, and scope. Movement is an expression of what it means to be alive and something that we fundamentally need and crave, whether or not we are conscious of that need. Movement in some capacity is available to nearly every human being, regardless of age, weight, body type, or condition.

The idea of movement fosters greater connection to our bodies, tapping into the natural joy and physical desires we have to experience our bodies as flexible, coordinated, powerful, weightless, graceful, and sensual. In contrast, we often equate exercise with extrinsic goals such as losing weight, having a better body, looking good, gaining strength and flexibility, living longer, attracting a mate, and so forth. This is why movement offers us a greater chance of success.

Intrinsic and Extrinsic Motivation

The numerous mental and physical benefits of exercise are well established in the scientific literature and have been for some time.[12] Yet, we are still a largely sedentary society, and many people report being unable to maintain a regular routine of staying active. According to the Centers for Disease Control and Prevention's 2009 research, 50 percent of American men and 60 percent of American women never engage in any vigorous physical activity lasting more than ten minutes per week.[13] The 2017 report from the CDC found that only 24.4 percent of US adults meet the government's official physical activity recommended levels of aerobic and strength-training activity.[14] How and why is this the case?

From various psychological studies on theories of motivation, we understand that there are important distinctions between extrinsic and intrinsic motivation. Extrinsic motivation, which is the predominant motivating force in our culture, arises from things outside of yourself and is not necessarily aligned with your passions or sense of self. We are conditioned as a society to look to extrinsic motivators and often have to push ourselves to achieve those goals. Not surprisingly, research shows that extrinsic motivations generally tend to result in less well-being than intrinsic motivations do.[15]

Intrinsic motivation is different. We often don't have to push ourselves at all to achieve goals that are intrinsically motivated because they are inherently joyful and rewarding experiences for us—typically because the behaviors are aligned with our deepest beliefs. Consider someone who paints a picture of something because they find it beautiful or enjoyable compared to someone who paints to collect a fee. Intrinsic goals are usually anchored to a higher purpose, whereas extrinsic goals tend to have less meaningful aims, like earning more money to get a bigger TV or the latest electronic toy that everyone else seems to have. Intrinsic goals are clear of the usual resistances that show up with extrinsic goals (procrastination, stop and start, quitting, ambivalence, need to recommit) and require little perceived effort, since the experience of being engaged in these activities is usually pleasurable and therefore self-reinforcing, requiring much less effort to sustain.

For most people, exercise is not a naturally occurring activity since it is extrinsically motivated. Unfortunately, when we are sedentary, we go back to being cut off from the neck down (alienating 92 percent of the entire mass of our beings) and losing connection with our bodies as a whole. It is a devastating price to pay, and the effort of staying mentally connected to ourselves is negated by the effects of being disconnected from our bodies. We are primal, physical beings, first and foremost. Being out of tune with our bodies can lead to devastating health consequences and extreme levels of disconnection. Think of the heavy drinker who slowly develops cirrhosis of the liver or the workaholic who collapses from a heart attack caused by lack of physical activity.

The scholarly data on the benefits of exercise are vast. Among other things we know about, it prevents or minimizes all kinds of illness; improves memory and brain function; relieves and prevents depression and anxiety; improves overall mood, sexual functioning, and relationships; enhances creativity; makes detoxification more efficient; improves metabolism and insulin regulation; and increases production of mood-enhancing neurotransmitters such as dopamine and serotonin.[16] A massive, long-term study published in 2018 found that lack of exercise is far more likely to kill you than smoking, diabetes, and heart disease.[17]

What remains less clear is how much we should exercise and which forms are the most beneficial. Claims and fads by the exercise industry promote all kinds of unrealistic regimens that may be preventing many of us from finding our own true north when it comes to moving and relating to our bodies.

Four Essentials of Connected Movement

There are four essentials to cultivating healthy movement practice: (1) finding your "why," or your intrinsic motivation; (2) developing a repertoire of frequent micro-movements throughout your day; (3) prioritizing consistency over intensity; and (4) cultivating your own natural love and passion for movement.

Finding Your Why

Tapping into your "why" reveals the intrinsic motivations to move your body—the ones that are aligned with your deepest values. As we discussed previously in the context of taking a stand for your values, begin by asking yourself what you believe when it comes to movement. If you don't know, then work on developing a guiding principle that is your truth, not someone else's. Once you identify or develop your belief system, decide whether your "why" feels important and powerful enough to make you get up and move. If it's not powerful enough, then keep digging deeper until you get to a more robust conclusion.

More powerful "whys" generally sound something like: "to have some quality alone time with myself" or "in order for me to get out of my head and into my humanity" or "to celebrate my innate masculinity/femininity" or "to honor myself and my body with proper care" or "to forge physical connection with my body each day."

When the "why" is more profound, the "how" becomes much more creative and flexible. There is a wide variety of options for connecting to yourself through movement each day, from simply stretching before bed; to enjoying a slow, meditative breaststroke back and forth in a pool; to a crazy, sweaty game of racquetball with a friend. These possibilities stretch far beyond the usual narrow options for an extrinsic goal like needing to burn three hundred calories each day.

A 2011 study asked a sample of university office workers why they exercised.[18] Seventy-five percent of participants stated they did it for weight loss and/or better health; the remaining 25 percent stated they did it to enhance the quality of their daily lives. After following them for a year, the researchers found that the group intent on improving quality of life exercised 34 percent more than those who exercised to lose weight or improve their appearance and 25 percent more than those who exercised for health reasons. The authors attributed this significant result to the intrinsic-extrinsic differences between something a person does for herself (quality of life) versus something she does because her doctor or society tells her she should. Their conclusion, which I wholeheartedly agree with, is that people need to stop thinking of exercise as an extrinsic, health-related necessity and start viewing it as their ticket to a subjectively better, more personally rewarding quality of life.

When you think of movement as something that enriches your life in a way you value, you're far more likely to do it. But it's just as critical that you choose a type of movement that works for you . . . one that you enjoy and that doesn't feel like a chore. This might be different for each person. Don't worry that your preferred form of movement is not "ideal" for health. The physical movement you do regularly is always more effective than the optimal exercise regimen you abandon after a week. And, more and more, research is finding that vastly different forms, types, and frequencies of exercise can have comparably positive impacts on health. Short bursts of high-intensity interval training a few times a week, for example, are now considered just as viable a form of exercise as several hours of traditional aerobic exercise like jogging.[19] For one anxiety-prone teenaged client, movement became a daily commitment to help even out her moods, reduce some of the cortisol in her body, and improve the quality of her sleep. Those reasons were easier for her to embrace and avoided the up-and-down emotional roller coaster of trying to exercise to have the perfect body.

What matters most is that you move your body regularly, in a way you enjoy, for reasons that matter to you and that align with your personal priorities. The following sections discuss some lesser known forms of healthy movement that may (or may not) resonate with you. Check them out and see what you think.

Frequent Micro-Movements

Recent research shows that moving frequently throughout the day may be more beneficial than moving vigorously for one longer period of time. In her book, *Don't Just Sit There*, international biomechanics expert Katy Bowman reviews the facts about prolonged sitting and sedentary lifestyles and explains why limiting exercise to one single period of the day is not, in fact, healthy. Bowman describes how sedentary, static positioning in our cars, at our desks, in front of our computers, or on the couch at home is the real culprit. While Bowman disagrees that sitting is as bad as smoking (because unlike cigarettes, sitting itself is harmless, if done in small doses), she also disagrees that standing all day at your workstation is the answer because it's simply trading one static position for another.

Research shows that repetitive static positioning (remaining in the same position for long periods of time each day) changes the cellular makeup of our muscles, reduces our range of motion, and leads to stiffening of arterial walls within those muscles.[20] Extended sitting also deforms fat cells in your buttocks, which over time can cause them to produce lipids at a faster rate.[21]

Bowman argues that the best solution is incorporating movement frequently throughout your day in small ways that flex muscles and help protect your natural range of motion.

She makes a compelling case for rediscovering how movement is available to us throughout our day . . . whether it's deciding to take the stairs, park farther away, go for a brisk two-minute walk, or just stretch discreetly under our desks. Her ideas are both practical and boundless in terms of creativity, and I highly recommend *Don't Just Sit There* to help open your mind to the many ways you can swap long bouts of static positioning for dynamic movement.

Nowadays, several of the popular activity trackers on the market can buzz your wrist to remind you to stand up from your desk, pace back and forth during a conference call, or do a few jumping jacks. This is a great way to stay mindful of long periods of inactivity and to ensure we don't forget to move.

Outer space research has also helped us understand the detrimental effects of remaining still. Dr. Joan Vernikos, the former director of NASA's

Life Sciences division, shares groundbreaking medical research from her work with astronauts in the book *Sitting Kills, Moving Heals: How Everyday Movement Will Prevent Pain, Illness, and Early Death—And Exercise Alone Won't*. In a nutshell, that research reveals how vital continuous, low-intensity, gravity-defying movements are to optimal health, adequate bone density, weight management, and illness prevention. Her thirty years at NASA researching the biological effects of space confirmed that the antigravity conditions of space were responsible for astronauts' dramatic loss of bone density, loss of muscle mass, slower reaction time, impaired balance and physical coordination, reduced stamina, reduced senses of taste and hearing, reduced sensitivity to insulin, less restful sleep, slower and less effective gut performance, delayed healing, and suppressed immune functioning—the same pattern of symptoms we typically associate with aging. But NASA's rehabilitation programs proved that people were able to reverse these changes and regain their prior levels of functioning simply by intentionally and naturally interacting with the forces of gravity back on Earth—irrespective of age. Vernikos and her fellow researchers concluded that aging is not actually the cause of these age-associated changes—that in fact they're "a direct consequence of the sedentary lifestyles we tend to adopt as we get older."[22]

This theory is supported by the increasing prevalence of spaceflight-like symptoms among ever-younger Americans on Earth. Vernikos points the finger squarely at the static, sedentary modern lifestyle of the twenty-first century, which involves far less daily motion than life one hundred or two hundred years ago. She notes that both children and adults are far less active than they used to be due to advances in technology. She sounds the clarion call for a major intervention, arguing that it is never too late to turn back the clock on these symptoms. Her book urges people to adopt frequent gravity-challenging movements as part of their everyday activities (something she calls G-habits) and offers a plethora of activities to help.

As Vernikos notes, research suggests that even a shift in attitude about movement can provide big health benefits. A study by Dr. Ellen Langer at Harvard University compared the blood pressure and body weight of two groups of hotel housekeepers who performed the same tasks: changing sheets and cleaning hotel rooms.[23] One group was told they should think of their work as exercise, and they were informed of the number of calories their common activities burned; the other group was told nothing about health benefits of their work. After four weeks, the health-informed group had on average lowered their blood pressure by 10 percent and lost two pounds and 0.5 percent body fat.

Both Bowman and Vernikos also stress the importance of good posture, which affects the function of your internal organs and blood circulation as well as your muscles and spine. Vernikos offers as one of her G-habits the old-fashioned but highly effective exercise of placing a book on top of your head to improve both posture and balance while typing on the computer.[24]

Posture expert and creator of the Gokhale Method, Esther Gokhale, has described the ideal sitting position in helpful detail:

> [I]n our stack sitting method (which is really healthy sitting, primal sitting, if you will), you have your behind out behind, but not exaggeratedly. That's very important. Then your bones stack well and the muscles alongside your spine are able to relax. . . . Now when you breathe, your whole spine lengthens and settles, lengthens and settles. There's this movement which stimulates circulation and allows natural healing to be going on as you sit. If you sit poorly, whether relaxed and slumped or upright and tense, you've lost all of that. So do we want to blame [all the adverse health effects] on sitting, or do we want to blame it on the poor sitting form? That's my question.[25]

Consistency over Intensity

Just as frequent movements are more beneficial than intense ones, consistent movements—the ones you do regularly over longer periods of time—are more important than the ones you do haphazardly or seasonally. Remember, it's always the diet or exercise program that you can stick to that works the best, even if other programs may theoretically be "better."

My "whys" with regard to movement increased my awareness of my muscles, my joints, and their motion—I became more attuned and sensitized to my body every day. I wanted to get reacquainted with my physical self and foster a positive relationship with my body so I could more easily hear and understand its messages. In short, I wanted to feel connected to my physical body. With that clear goal in mind, a couple of strategies made all the difference for me. I used to aim to do a twenty- or thirty-minute run on my treadmill, but that rarely happened. And when it did, I often experienced the event as slightly negative. Now, I commit only to a small daily goal that is easily achievable: I will walk two miles a day, each and every day, on the treadmill. I prioritized consistency over intensity.

My current goal doesn't cause me to break into a sweat, and sometimes I'm going so slowly that I don't think my heart rate even changes. But what I do know is that I'm guaranteed to walk sixty more miles a month than I normally would—which is huge. Although my goal was not to lose weight, after just eight weeks of implementing this routine, I lost five pounds without changing a thing about my eating.

A key element to walking every day was that I ritualized it. I made myself walk two miles at the same time every morning, no ifs, ands, or buts. The ritual helped it become an ingrained habit, requiring zero effort or thought to perpetuate. Sometimes my workout organically extends to five miles or over an hour if I am engrossed in my emails, and sometimes I kick it up to the pace of a run when I'm feeling it. These are not the goals though. I've created a win-win scenario where I can easily be successful and feel good about myself because I've achieved my small two-mile goal, and I will continue to achieve it every day.

By developing a daily movement ritual that sets a low bar, you are virtually guaranteeing that you will get the job done and feel good about yourself each day. Pick an activity that works for your life and personality, and start today.

Cultivating a Natural Love and Passion for Movement

Before I revisited movement with an eye on improving my self-connection, I couldn't remember the last time I had experienced the joy of movement just for movement's sake. I had no idea what kind of movement my body enjoyed or was good at. I couldn't say for sure how much movement was too much, too little, or too intense for me. I showed up to exercise classes and let the instructors define the experience for me, while I watched the clock the whole time. I'd been relating to my body from a distance for decades and never knew any other way.

I panicked a little when I realized I had no self-knowledge in this area and no idea how to turn things around. But natural wisdom exists inside of us if we ask the right questions and create the space to really listen for the answer. I decided to break out my trusty strategy of following clues with mindful awareness and begin my Easter egg hunt in the misty memories of my childhood.

When I was a kid, movement came spontaneously and naturally. During elementary school, I was constantly in motion, cruising around on my Big Wheel, selling Girl Scout cookies on my roller skates, owning the four-square court, trying to master a cherry drop on the horizontal bars, climbing big trees, or playing handball by myself. Movement was a complete joy and celebration of my body back then, something that just happened naturally. I didn't have to think about it. My body and I were in complete harmony.

After reflecting on how much connection I'd lost since those happy childhood years, I dedicated an entire year to rebuilding my relationship with my own body and figuring out how to enjoy it again. My intent was to bring a beginner's mind and curiosity to movement, to try every type of movement that seemed like it might help me rediscover myself.

I suspected that my elementary school glory years were the likeliest place to offer clues and started by asking myself about the last movement activity that I had absolutely *loved*. The answer that came to me was ice skating—a surprise, since I'd almost forgotten I had briefly taken lessons. The moment the idea occurred to me, I felt a surge of excitement, and then the usual voices of resistance started chattering inside my head—you're too old, it's not real exercise, it's too inconvenient, what's the point, it's for young girls, it's a waste of time, you will fall and crack your skull. I pushed past the voices and signed up for weekly group lessons at a nearby rink. I was nervous at first, but soon the sensation of gliding and moving across the ice had me giddy and feeling like a kid again. I started hitting the rink three times a week and found that I looked forward to skating more than anything else in my week.

I tried not to let myself focus on comparisons with other people or get too concerned with learning fancy moves. Instead, I allowed myself to follow what was most enjoyable to me, which was simply the feeling of gliding; using graceful, feminine movements; and experiencing my body as balanced and coordinated. So I mastered the basics of long forward and backward crossover strokes to move across the ice, paying particular attention to form and extension. This was the first time in my adult life I had allowed myself to pursue a movement experience just for the joy of it, without a particular purpose or goal in mind. I kept up my skating for the entire year, and even though tricks weren't my goal, in that short period of time, I conquered three different jumps and even learned to spin. The learning, I noticed, happened so naturally and effortlessly because this activity was inspired from a place of joy and freedom from pressure.

My ice-skating experiment spawned a wave of more experimentation. Now that I knew I was drawn to experiencing my body in a graceful and feminine way, I scanned the other options in my county that might bring the same sensation. I settled on belly dancing and hula dancing. *Bullseye.* I don't think I ever broke out into a sweat during any of the classes, but I was blissful at the fluidity of movement and the feeling that I was channeling an inner goddess. Particularly in hula dancing class, I was struck by how all the women, no matter their age or size, looked so beautiful and self-possessed while engaged in this slow, deliberate, spiritual dance.

I went on to explore movements that prompted different sensations, like the feelings of power (indoor rock climbing and taiko drumming) and fun—

something I'd long ago abandoned as a kid. I enlisted the help of a girlfriend for the fun quest, and we replaced our usual suburban dinner and wine evenings out for playful activities—trampoline dodgeball, drop-in volleyball at the Y, competitive ping-pong, country line dancing, and fierce games of air hockey at the arcade. Our friendship bloomed with this new approach because we were sharing hilarious new experiences and laughing so hard together instead of just sitting around drinking chardonnay and kvetching about mundane life.

Playful movement was addicting to me, and I started bringing it everywhere I could. I ran to grab my own swing when the kids and I hit the playground, instead of doing my usual stand-back-and-watch routine. I started cannon-balling into pools and dunking myself into the ocean instead of hanging back, trying not to get my hair wet. My partner joined in on the action, and he and I started hitting dive bars on date nights to play shuffleboard and pool together—anything that involved movement and play. We dropped in on a square-dancing session at the community center and joined a co-ed softball league, which was both pathetic and hilarious at the same time. In many ways, we were reliving the wholesome aspects of our youth.

I even volunteered to coach my boys' basketball and baseball teams, though I'd never played those sports and knew nothing about them. It was good to reconnect with the simple pleasures of throwing and catching a ball or making a basket—activities I had long ago stepped away from in my serious adult mom role.

Through all of this experimentation, I began to know myself physically and learned a great deal about my likes, my dislikes, my capabilities, what brings me joy, what makes me feel alive. Movement and I were back together again, as we were in my youth—full of variety and reckless abandon, anchored in fun and joy, free from pressure and goals. I had rediscovered something that left me feeling totally in tune with and connected to my body from head to toe.

My friends and readers who are accomplished athletes may feel that a revival or exploration such as this isn't necessary. But I invite you to ask yourself whether the physical track that you are on is wide enough for you and if there are any blocked areas that need unblocking. Is your repertoire of movement large enough that you are regularly exploring and discovering new capabilities? Is there enough pleasure and playfulness in your activities? Are you as physically curious and experimental as you were as a kid, or have you prematurely thrown in the towel on many activities?

After my year of experimenting with motion, I realized that there is a whole other universe of physical expression and connection available to me. This process of awakening the layers of physicality within me and connecting more deeply to my body has transformed my life and my relationships more than any other aspect of my quest for authentic connection.

Tips for Connecting with Movement

The best first step is to set an intention to connect to your body more deeply before the movement. During the activity, try to bring a loving awareness to usual movements in order to notice and appreciate how it feels to move your body. Slowing down and elongating movements can turn ordinary motions (such as reaching for your toes during a stretch) into an extraordinary heart-opening experience.

Try using this technique, along with sensory awareness, to appreciate tiny miracles of your body's ability to flex, cooperate with your wishes, and breathe in the throes of vigorous exercise. Becoming curious and tuning into these ordinary sensations can bring an aliveness, meaning, and transcendence to an ordinary workout—as if you've just had a spiritual encounter with yourself.

Suspending self-judgment, again, is essential here. Let yourself fully inhabit your physical body and savor the sensations of exertion without guilt or shame. For many people, learning to embrace the joy of movement in this way can also improve intimacy with their partners—a healthy side effect that further promotes connection. All the more reason to stop depriving ourselves of these richly rewarding, primal pleasures.

A note on prolonged sedentary periods: These are often the times people abuse themselves the most, both mentally and physically. There's an underlying assumption (based on a common cognitive error called "all-or-nothing" thinking) that goes something like, "Because I haven't worked out in ages, I might as well not do anything else that would be healthy or physically engaging for my body." We build up an internal resistance to movement and become more permissive about choices that are destructive to the body. This creates a powerful downward spiral, typically reinforced with self-loathing, that feels nearly impossible to break.

The best way through and out of these periods, I have found, is to work on your mental attitude. First, try to normalize the experience by reminding yourself that some sedentary periods are natural, and even necessary at times. Any farmer knows the benefit of letting a field lie fallow. Sedentary periods are instinctive during various times of year such as cold winters or during times of stress, transition, or busyness. If it's been years or even a lifetime since you were physically active, acceptance and compassionate self-talk can help to reduce feelings of shame—the nefarious force that locks us into our descending spiral. From a place of emotional neutrality, you will be able to see the possibility of reengaging physically, without all the baggage associated with your past behaviors.

Having that open, non-self-critical attitude toward moving is the key to feeling and staying connected to your physical self. Even if you are not engaging in physical activity, the neutral (and therefore nonnegative) stance helps you maintain self-connection and more easily determine your body's wants and needs. This small shift in perspective, though it may not immediately prompt action, can have a powerful impact.

The key question to ask yourself in this area is about the quality of your relationship (or connection) to movement: Is it positive or negative? Do you feel guilt-ridden, pressure-filled, and perpetually inadequate, laden with unrealistic expectations and fantasies of the ideal body? Or do you have a lighthearted willingness to lean into opportunities for motion and to creatively explore ways to combine joy and fun with movement in your life, no matter the condition of your body? Do you have a commitment to let go of critical self-talk and not berate yourself, regardless of how long you go without "working out"?

I would argue that the quality of your relationship to movement has a huge impact on your connection to your body overall and sense of self in general. My clients have reported that just committing to stop self-judgment and negative self-talk related to "exercising" was effective. That switch enabled them to reengage and tiptoe back into various types of movement, creating an entirely new and rewarding relationship with moving their bodies. Even if they were in a prolonged sedentary period, they were always able to work on their attitude, replacing tense insistence with a spacious, easygoing attitude toward movement.

Whether you are a hard-core athlete, a couch potato, or an on-again–off-again exerciser like the majority of people, I invite you to (re)consider the nature of your relationship with movement . . . and whether that relationship could be revisited and revitalized. I think you'll find that there are, indeed, more satisfying, meaningful ways to move and feel connected to your body.

SLEEP: BEST PRACTICES

During my nine years as a hospital-based psychologist, I had the opportunity to observe and work with nearly every type of psychiatric disorder, usually in combination with severe medical illnesses. It was a wild ride that often felt like I was drinking from the firehose of knowledge every day. I was lucky enough to be part of some of the brightest and most effective multidisciplinary treatment teams I'd ever encountered.

Each morning, we would conduct rounds on our in-patients together and have lengthy team meetings afterward where we would discuss their diagnoses and the best approaches to treatment. The beauty of these multidisciplinary teams was that we often had up to twelve uniquely trained specialists in the room, all comparing notes from their specific areas of expertise. Whether we were discussing a dual-diagnosis organ-transplant patient, a mother with postpartum psychosis, a schizophrenic who thought he was the lord Jesus Christ, or a depressed teenage girl who was cutting herself, it never ceased to amaze me how important and predictive quality sleep was for each and every person's recovery or stabilization.

It was often the first question we asked people when visiting their room: "How was your sleep?" If a patient's sleep was not stabilized, we often had difficulty pinpointing what was going on since poor sleep can mimic so many other problematic conditions.

The same is true for human beings who aren't in psychiatric hospitals. If we don't get adequate sleep, all bets are off. Well-being and good health literally start and end with sleep.

USC Medical Center's Dr. David Agus is widely considered one of the most brilliant medical minds of our time. Although controversial, his refreshing and disrupting approach to modern medicine has people like Al Gore, Dr. Dean Ornish, Marc Benioff, and many Fortune 500 CEOs backing him. His unrelenting quest to cure cancer and conquer proteomics (the study of human proteins, their purpose, structure, and partnerships to better understand cellular processes, which may be the key to ending all illness), puts Agus at the forefront of breakthrough medical advances.

At a lecture promoting his book *A Short Guide to a Long Life*, Agus discussed the key health habits that can drastically reduce your chances of contracting common major illnesses and give you the best odds of exceeding the standard life expectancy. One of the biggest keys is sleep.

In his book *The End of Illness*, he writes:

Both laboratory and clinical studies have shown that virtually every system in the body is affected by the quality and amount of sleep we get a night. Among the proven benefits: sleep can dictate how much we eat, how fast our metabolisms run, how fat or thin we get, whether we can fight off infections, how creative and insightful we can be, how well we can cope with stress, how quickly we can process information and learn new things, and how well we can organize and store memories. Losing as few as one and a half hours that our body needs for just one night can reduce daytime alertness by about a third.[26]

While Dr. Agus agrees with most other experts on commonsense ways to protect your sleep, his unique area of discovery was the primary importance of keeping to a regular schedule of sleeping and waking time. It's not as essential to focus on how much sleep you get, since we are all different in the ideal amount of sleep we need (although most adults need seven to nine hours each night). It's more important that your sleep time is regular, seven days a week. His studies have shown that our bodies are incredible at self-regulating, and that within a few days of being consistent with your bedtime and wake time, your body's natural circadian rhythms will adjust to and crave that rhythm, leading to quicker onset of sleep and higher quality and duration of sleep.

In the Department of Behavioral Medicine at Harvard Medical School's Cambridge Hospital, I taught sleep hygiene techniques to medical patients and medical students. Not every sleep hygiene tool is equally impactful for each person . . . but I recommend trying them all to give yourself the greatest odds for successful sleep. Over time, you will come to know which ones are the most important for you:

1. A strict regular schedule, particularly at bedtime, is huge. Pick a bedtime and stick to it. Smartphone apps make this easier now and can alert you as bedtime draws near. One of the top two predictors of poor sleep is going to bed later than usual. (The other is stress; see number 8, below.)

2. Reduce or eliminate caffeine. If you must have it, restrict it to morning times.

3. Reduce or eliminate alcohol. As little as one drink can negatively affect your sleep quality. According to Dr. Michael Breus, one of the country's foremost sleep researchers, "the effects of alcohol in the body are what are known as *biphasic*, meaning 'in two phases.' When first consumed, alcohol has a stimulating effect. Later, after

alcohol has been in the system for a period [of] time, its effects are sedating. But as this new research indicates, the effects of alcohol—particularly the stimulating effects—are magnified during certain periods of the body's 24-hour circadian cycle"—specifically the evening, when most people typically consume alcohol.[27]

4. Make sure that your bedroom is cool and completely dark and that all electronics and glowing lights are removed. If you can't sleep without your phone in the room, put it in airplane mode. You want to reduce the number of electromagnetic waves floating in the atmosphere and make sure your room is a sacred sleep sanctuary.

5. Get plenty of exposure to natural sunlight each day. Remove your sunglasses in the sun and let your eyeballs take it in. Sunlight helps your body register that it's daytime in a way that home and office lights do not, thereby reinforcing an accurate circadian rhythm in your body, which helps to regulate your hormones, and sleep hormones, specifically.

6. Stop looking at any screens (TV, phone, computer, etc.) at least one hour before bedtime. Blue light in these screens blocks the secretion of the sleep hormone melatonin, keeping you up past your natural schedule.

7. Cultivate a nonstimulating wind-down routine thirty minutes before bedtime, such as journaling, reading (something not too stimulating), listening to an audiobook set to a timer, practicing yoga, stretching, or meditating.

8. Try to reduce and resolve stress; develop coping skills (like meditation or breathing exercises), and engage in at least twenty minutes of cardio exercise each day to lower and burn off the stress hormone cortisol.

9. Avoid using your bed for anything except sleep and sex. You want to create a strong behavioral association between your bed and falling asleep. If you can't fall asleep after a reasonable period of time, get out of bed and do something nonactivating (like stretching or yoga) and don't get back in bed until you feel tired again.

10. See your doctor and get a full blood panel to make sure there isn't an underlying medical issue at play, such as being hormonally out of balance (thyroid in particular) or being low in a key vitamin (such as vitamin D).

11. Avoid sleeping medications except on the rare occasion when trying to adjust to a new time zone. Sleeping medications are psychologically addictive, decreasing your confidence and increasing your anxiety related to your own ability to achieve sleep. They also tend to interfere with achieving sufficient deep sleep, preventing the important restorative and healing functions that need to occur each night.

12. Consult an integrative medical expert about how supplements that support the body's natural ability to relax and produce sleep hormones might benefit you (such as magnesium, melatonin, L-tryptophan, and GABA).

It was ironic that I was tasked with teaching sleep hygiene techniques since I myself suffered from horrible, debilitating insomnia for years. In my case, none of the usual hygiene techniques were helping me break through it. It wasn't until I had my hormone levels checked that I discovered a thyroid imbalance (common in women) and a significant progesterone deficiency, both of which can manifest as sleep disturbance. Once I started taking bioidentical hormone supplements, my sleep improved. But it wasn't until I started keeping a strict bedtime schedule (which for me was before 10:00 p.m., since a frightening second wind usually kicks in for me after that witching hour) and shutting down electronics an hour beforehand that my sleep became amazing.

Now I sleep eight and a half to nine blissful hours a night without fail and feel like the bionic woman when I wake up each day. The only nights I ever have trouble falling asleep are when I break my rule and keep working on my computer right until lights-out time.

It never ceases to amaze me how utterly transformative a beautiful night's sleep can be. My mood, my outlook on life, my motivation—they are all elevated to epic proportions. After a good night's sleep, I typically wake up feeling a surge of natural connectedness to myself, my priorities, others, and the world around me. Sleep is the connection wonder drug, if you ask me.

HYDRATION

Hydration is something we tend to forget about on a regular basis—a common example of how we lose touch with ourselves on the most primal level. Yet it's also one of the easiest ways to reconnect with ourselves and boost health in virtually every area. This simple, one-minute act can turn around days and weeks of disconnected self-neglect. I've found that in times of chaos, when I've allowed disconnection to creep back into every area of my life, reaching for a glass of water is one of the most powerful micro-actions I can take to plug back into myself. No matter how hopeless the rest of it is, all is not lost. I can still tend to my body in this one small, essential way.

Medical research has determined that water is basically a health elixir and that chronic dehydration can contribute to a host of illnesses as well as to weight gain, low energy, and mood problems. Since water makes up 60 percent of our bodies and 76 percent of our brains, drinking fluids is critical for every system we've got. Fluids carry nutrients to cells, flush them clean, clear bacteria from the bladder, and prevent constipation. Water is used for the breakdown of substances, as a medium for chemical reactions, and for the diffusion and osmosis of substances across membranes and cells.

But studies show that 60 to 70 percent of the population is chronically dehydrated. Warning signs include weakness, low blood pressure, dizziness, confusion, and dark urine, with fatigue often the first symptom to manifest.

Dr. Julian Seifter, a kidney specialist and associate professor of medicine at Harvard Medical School, says that healthy people should drink between 30 and 50 ounces (1 to 1.5 liters) of water each day to ward off dehydration.[28] It's important to stay hydrated gradually, throughout the day, rather than trying to drink your daily allowance all at once. Seifter recommends eating water-rich foods like salads, fruit, and applesauce, and making sure you're getting fluids at meals, with medicine, and when visiting with others.

I've known dehydration is bad for health pretty much my whole life, but it wasn't enough to get me to drink up. We often ignore some of the most obviously helpful health recommendations simply because the "why" is not powerful enough or immediately tangible to us.

For me, the turning point was actually a "peak performance" seminar I attended with Tony Robbins, the well-known motivational coach and speaker.[29] I love listening to Tony for many reasons, and it's amazing how his messaging (and client list) has evolved over the years from his infomercial beginnings. Tony is passionate about the fundamentals of self-care as a building block to achieve optimum peak performance in love, life, and work, and in this six-hour seminar about peak performance, he devoted *one entire hour* to the importance of water. That got my attention. This was an area I never considered to be a problem for me, since I'm rarely thirsty. Tony was the first person to tell me that the primary symptom of dehydration is *not* being thirsty. If we're feeling thirsty, he said, it's too late—we're already dehydrated.

He challenged us in that seminar to super-hydrate, drinking at least half of our body weight in ounces each day. For me, this was more than quadrupling my normal water intake, but I decided to finally give it a shot. As with most behavioral changes, all I needed to do was to nurture a new habit until it took root and started to bloom on its own.

My new habit, per Tony's recommendation, was to drink thirty-two ounces of water in the morning, when we are most dehydrated, then refill and carry that thirty-two-ounce container for the rest of the day to sip on as much as I could. I also started a mealtime ritual of finishing off a tall glass of water before starting to eat. This increases the body's ability to hydrate and makes you feel fuller, and thus less likely to overeat. These methods got me to my daily recommended intake pretty easily.

I was surprised to notice that the more water I drank, the more I craved it. Either I was finally tuning into my true levels for the first time, or I was increasing my body's appetite for water. Either way, it was a good thing. It was amazing to see the correlation between on-track hydration and overall health. When I'm hydrated, I sleep better, I think better, and I have fewer headaches and better energy.

But most importantly, I feel like I'm rewarding myself. Tuning in with and connecting to my body brought a warm and self-loving spirit to the humdrum act of drinking water and helped to spark other spontaneous moments of awareness. Hydration helped me tap into how my body was really feeling, and to identify how I should make my next good choice.

I now use drinking water as my anchor activity for connection. Since it happens frequently throughout the day, it gives me an excuse to pause for a moment, take a sip, and check in with my body and how I'm connected to it.

Turning a banal activity like hydration into a richly rewarding ritual of self-love and pride paves the way to reconnecting with your truest self.

Hydrating with Other Fluids

Some people claim they don't like water and that they can get all the liquid they need from other beverages and foods. It's true that you can hydrate with other fluids to some extent, but it's not the same. Stick to water and unsweetened, noncaffeinated, nonalcoholic, nonacidic water-based drinks as much as possible. Caffeinated and alcoholic beverages can act as diuretics, and acidic liquids require you to drink even more water to flush out the acid.

A study published in the *Journal of Human Nutrition and Dietetics* provides additional evidence to support the commonsense notion that plain water is the best beverage choice for health.[30] In this study, researchers from the University of Illinois analyzed data on the eating and drinking habits of 18,311 adults, as recorded in National Health and Nutrition Examination Surveys between 2005 and 2012. The researchers found that participants who drank the most plain water in their daily regimen also consumed fewer total calories, drank fewer sweetened beverages, and took in less total fat, saturated fat, sugar, salt, and cholesterol. They also noted that increasing plain water consumption by one to three cups each day could decrease daily calorie intake by 68 to 205 calories. That adds up to a lot fewer calories over time, facilitating significant weight loss.

If you *really* hate water, or find it impossibly boring, try adding a squeeze of lemon or a splash of apple cider vinegar, or invest in some noncaffeinated tea. There are countless varieties in stores today. You can also make your own rehydrating tea just by steeping a little fresh ginger or lemongrass—traditional digestive aids in many Asian cultures—in hot water. Just be sure to skip the sweetener.

Keeping tabs on the little things that mean a lot—like how much water we've had and how our bodies are feeling on the most basic level—is the essence of connection. To paraphrase the poet Julia Carney, little drops of water make the mighty ocean.[31]

PHYSICAL SELF-CARE PAVES THE WAY FOR EMOTIONAL CONNECTION

Philip McKernan is fond of saying, "we give ourselves what we feel we deserve."[32] If you truly want to change your self-care habits for the better, you must first value yourself and believe that you deserve those improvements. That's why tending to your fundamentals is a lifeline for finding your way back into connection after periods of feeling lost or uncertain where to begin again.

When our physical needs for nourishment, hydration, rest, and movement are reasonably met, we can focus on our lives with unmatched clarity. We can quiet our thoughts, summon reserves of energy, and open up our imaginations. Physical self-care gives us a solid foundation of connection from which to tackle the really tough stuff—like our emotions. That's because our bodies and emotions are inextricably bound together, like dance partners locked in a hold. When we feel emotional conflict, our muscles tighten. When we're tired, we feel irritable. After enjoying a great meal, we feel satisfied. The link between body and mind can't be underestimated.

When we neglect physical self-care, we neglect ourselves. Physical disconnection feeds upon itself and leads to disconnection in other aspects of life. We slide more easily into negative, even harmful, behaviors—poor self-image, runaway addictions, and chronic guilt, to name a few. What may start out as a small moment of unkindness toward ourselves or our bodies quickly becomes a destructive habit. If these habits take root, they send us spiraling downward even further. We act out against our bodies, deepening our disconnection and creating a vicious cycle of unhappy thoughts, emotions, and experiences.

If we want authentic, enduring, and sustainable well-being, we can't ignore the physical side. Connection theory encourages us to nurture an intimate, gentle, positive relationship with our bodies every day through small acts of self-care. Putting self-care at the top of our list, rather than the bottom, and creating simple, daily habits that move us in positive directions is the first step down the path of true satisfaction.

One client, a woman who had fluctuated her entire life between morbid obesity and being unhealthily underweight, shared with me that the simple act of drinking water every morning before breakfast started her on a positive path for the rest of the day. She had one mugful while she made her coffee. It was a ridiculously simple goal, but for someone who had continually abused her body with food on one end of the spectrum or starvation and exercise on the other, it signaled that she was capable of self-care. The one cup of water grew to a cup again before lunch. Soon, she added a few more daily habits. She set a specific bedtime and (most of the time) turned off her electronics an hour beforehand. She took the first few minutes of the morning, while her fiancé showered, to listen to her own breathing. None of these new habits had anything to do with food, but she reported that she no longer relied on willpower, shame, or guilt to regulate her eating. She wasn't on a "diet and exercise regimen" that could flame out as intensely as it started. She began to identify the emotional triggers that led her to over- and under-eat and to "renegotiate the terms" with those feelings. As she focused on trying to reconnect with her body a little more each day, my client got more energy to try a new ritual, setting up a positive cycle where before there had only been a destructive one.

As this client's behavior shows, self-care doesn't have to be an overwhelming, never-ending list of "shoulds." It can be as simple as stopping to take a deep breath and listen to the physical cues your body is giving you at that moment.

YOUR NONNEGOTIABLE SELF-CARE FUNDAMENTALS

The multiple areas of self-care discussed so far may seem overwhelming and more like "nice ideas" to implement rather than practical realities. Our best chance of success at making positive changes in multiple areas simultaneously is to use an organizing belief system that incorporates our own personally non-negotiable elements of self-care.

It begins by committing to your own personal why . . . why *you* want to tend to your own self-care. Hopefully, you've already written this out in the worksheet provided in the appendix. Next, decide what your minimum daily requirements are to feel you're caring for your physical self in ways that matter to your why. These fundamental touchpoints will become your self-care nonnegotiables. Write them down (there's an appendix worksheet to guide you) and post a copy of them somewhere you will see them in the course of the day. In the past, I used an errand app on my smartphone to track my nonnegotiables so that I could have the visual reward of checking them off each day.

How do you decide what your core areas of self-care are? Five common contributors to physical wellness have been discussed so far—sensory awareness, nutrition, movement, sleep, and hydration. Take a few minutes to consider and journal about which activities in these realms, when done regularly, make you feel more whole, grounded, and cared for. My early-stage fundamentals were eight hours of sleep each night, a large glass of lemon water in the morning and before dinner, three food choices that I felt proud of, and ten minutes of aerobic activity. For one of my clients, it was getting his blood pumping by doing a two-minute series of burpees first thing in the morning, followed by a big glass of water. For another, it was it was engaging in a morning stretching routine to relieve back tension and taking the time for a skin-care regimen.

It doesn't matter how small or insignificant your touchstones of self-care might seem from an objective standpoint. Just a symbolic gesture of jumping on the treadmill for two minutes when there simply isn't time for more can contribute meaningfully to greater self-connection. The most important thing is developing a habit of staying mindfully connected to these areas of your self-care and never letting them fade too far away from your awareness.

Physical Self-Care

SLEEP
SENSATION
HYDRATION
MOVEMENT
NUTRITION

By connecting with your body every day, you nourish the most primal form of connection there is, opening the door to healthier connection with your emotions, other people, and the rest of the world.

Chapter 6

CONNECTING WITH YOUR EMOTIONAL SELF

We cannot tell what may happen to us in the strange medley of life. But we can decide what happens in us—how we take it, what we do with it—and that is what really counts in the end.

JOSEPH FORT NEWTON[1]

The field of psychology has traditionally divided the brain into three broad processing centers: cognitive (or intellectual), affective (or emotional), and motivational. Until recently, intellectual testing and definitions of intelligence were only interested in cognitive processing—ignoring the other equally powerful processing modes of the brain. But in recent decades, the theory of emotional intelligence has exploded onto the scene, touted as the edge people can use to get ahead in business and life. Today, having a high emotional intelligence quotient (EQ) is considered a kind of X factor for success.

At its most basic level, EQ measures a person's ability to accurately label and identify emotions, to stay open to those that are both pleasant and unpleasant, to understand what information or meaning the emotions convey, to distinguish between helpful and unhelpful emotions (as well as accurate and inaccurate emotions), and to accurately express their emotions and personal needs related to those emotions. As you've probably guessed, living in tune with your emotional world in this way is a critically important part of becoming more connected to yourself. People with a high EQ tend to find it easier to connect to their own emotions and to recognize and appropriately respond to the emotions of others.

Fortunately, since a person's EQ level is a product of both nature *and* nurture, there is much we can do to incline our minds toward greater emotional intelligence and the greater levels of connection that it offers.

Achieving accurate self-awareness of our emotions can be a challenging, lifelong pursuit. Our emotions can be a soupy mess of ever-changing mercurial tricksters that lead us astray or even block us from achieving insight. People usually find themselves at varying levels of emotional connectedness, depending on their EQ, what's going on in their lives currently, their emotional coping styles, and how accepting or unaccepting of their own emotional reactions they are. Some simple mindful practices can help us learn to corral our emotions into coherent groupings, to spot patterns, and to better understand how we typically respond in any given situation.

Setting out to boost EQ and connect with our emotional landscape is not something most of us are in the habit of doing. But it turns out to be much easier to accomplish than you'd expect, and—even better—it doesn't require an excavation of your entire childhood to do it.

There's nothing more powerful than connecting with your emotions, understanding what sets you off and how you really feel about things. It truly is a superpower.

THE NEUTRAL, CURIOUS OBSERVER

The first step to connecting with your true feelings is to get better acquainted with them. Be curious, and check in with yourself frequently throughout the day on how you are feeling as you engage with others or perform various tasks. As a starting place, it's helpful to note where and when you feel at ease versus where and when you don't. Be honest in your observations. You can't discover your "real truth" or your "true self" until you're willing to accept how you really feel about things, rather than how you think you should feel.

Take a moment to reflect—in the middle of a conversation with someone or some other context—and bring a mindful awareness to how you are feeling. Notice whether you are relaxed or uptight, feeling authentic or inauthentic, truly enjoying yourself or just going through the motions. The purpose of gathering these clues is not to indict whomever or whatever you are engaging with. It's simply to shed light on *you* and what tends to move your needle left, right, or center.

We are typically not in the habit of tracking our reactions to the people and activities that we spend time and energy on. Extreme positive or negative reactions are easy to spot and react to, but it's the subtler feelings that we are after.

These hold a wealth of information for us. I discovered that I feel anxious in large groups, am bored around certain people, and tend to daydream in positive ways while taking the ferry, but I feel more agitated when commuting in the car. I found that I am exhilarated when working with my research partners and experience vicarious joy when watching my parents interact with my kids. I also noticed how much I laugh during phone calls with my sister.

Handwritten exercises that track thoughts and feelings are the most common homework assignment I give my clients. I'll often recommend that people set aside a few minutes each evening to journal about the high and low points of their day—jotting down what happened as well as the thoughts and feelings they were experiencing at those moments. What story were you telling yourself when you started yelling at your partner/kids/ the driver who cut you off? The results never cease to amaze and delight. I can almost guarantee you will discover something surprising about yourself. This technique leads to far more impactful insights than just talking to a therapist could ever produce.

While some of the conclusions you reach may just confirm what you already know, there is a surprising benefit to that knowledge. The positive experiences/ emotions amplify the benefits you receive and remind you to repeat those actions more often. Tracking your feelings throughout the day can sometimes contradict your assumed truths as well. Noticing moments where you are surprisingly off-center or feel disconnected helps you become more curious about the root issue and the potential solution.

Regularly taking stock of how you feel enables you to become more in tune with your emotions, which empowers you to make better choices about how you spend your time or to realize a stuck area in a relationship that needs to be addressed. After just a few days of tracking feelings, workshop participants who had previously described themselves as having zero emotional awareness were able to report with surprising, granular detail many emotional nuances and subtleties that led to important realizations.

DON'T JUDGE EMOTIONS

We waste an enormous amount of energy and create a lot of self-suffering when we react to our reactions. A Buddhist parable teaches that our reaction to the "arrow" of negative experiences is really a second arrow in itself— something just as painful as the first that can double our suffering, if we let it. Unlike the first arrow, which is prompted by external forces, this second one is within our control. We can dodge it if we want to. But too often we don't, and we wind up piling more suffering on top of the existing suffering by reacting to our reactions.

If you believe you aren't supposed to have a certain feeling or reaction, you may deny its existence, making it harder to learn from. Or, worse, if you feel shame about a certain emotion (such as jealousy), you will be blocked from the lessons that are there to be learned. If you commit to radical acceptance of any and all emotions as a starting point, you will find it is easier to learn from and about your feelings. Accept that all reactions are fair game and okay for you to have. Your job is to bring an open and curious beginner's mind to your feelings in order to learn from them.

Psychologist Dr. Kristin Neff's theory of self-compassion views acceptance as the key to self-esteem and a healthy relationship with ourselves. She writes that we must learn to "*stop judging and evaluating ourselves altogether.* To stop trying to label ourselves as 'good' or 'bad' and simply accept ourselves with an open heart."[2]

Neff theorizes that self-esteem is elusive in our ultra-competitive modern society because "we need to feel *special and above average* to feel worthy. Anything else seems like a failure. . . . The problem is that by definition, it's impossible for *everyone* to be above average at the same time." As she aptly points out, "there is always someone smarter, prettier, more successful."[3]

According to Neff, the only way to escape this never-ending cycle of self-delusion, disappointment, and self-loathing is with self-compassion. We must strive to "accept ourselves with an open heart. To treat ourselves with the same kindness, caring, and compassion we would show to a good friend."[4]

Neff's theory helpfully breaks down self-compassion into three main components, which can help restore our connection to ourselves and our emotions:

1. Noticing. We must pay attention to what we are experiencing without fighting it. We simply notice and accept. We can be in touch with difficult emotions without letting them run away with the story.

2. Kindness. We must take a warm, understanding stance toward ourselves, showing kindness as we would for a cherished friend who is suffering. Support and validate yourself, saying things like, "Wow, this is really hard feeling these emotions and having these thoughts right now." Then ask yourself, "What do I need in this moment?" Above all, acknowledge, accept, and forgive your innate imperfection and humanness.

3. Common humanity. We often feel that whatever unpleasant thing is happening shouldn't be happening, at least not to us—when actually, this is what it means to be human. Failing or making mistakes doesn't isolate you from others; it's exactly what unites us with others. By recognizing this, we can stop judging ourselves as isolated, abnormal freaks and embrace our fate as simple humans bound together in our shared imperfection.

As Dr. Deepak Chopra emphasizes, self-judgment is one of the greatest reasons that people feel stuck. If you think you are unworthy, you close off possibilities for yourself and keep expectations low. You stay in the unchallenging job instead of going for what you want. You shut the door to positive emotions, abundance, and actions that could lead to greater fulfillment. People who are self-compassionate, however, are more likely to take risks because they are able to forgive failure as a natural part of living. They're also more likely to take responsibility when they harm someone else and apologize or make amends.

Self-compassion is one of those qualities that sounds good to everyone and is hard to disagree with. But in reality, self-compassion is *not* a given for most people and must be examined, understood, cultivated, and made a habit in order to reap its amazing rewards. Regularly cultivating self-compassion is essential to emotional connection, as we'll discuss in more detail below.

PARSING MANY FEELINGS AT ONCE

Positive emotions like joy or appreciation feel straightforward, but other emotions—particularly ones around loaded subjects—can be quite complicated, layered, multifaceted, and even clashing. We often experience many different emotional reactions simultaneously. Instead of letting the loudest or strongest emotion dominate your awareness, it's helpful to break down the various emotional viewpoints you are having and see each of them as valid and valuable in terms of the information it can provide.

As an example, I once found myself feeling very emotional while listening to a sex therapist's lecture. In fact, I was so disturbed that I had to leave the room. Once I was alone, I had the chance to self-compassionately reflect, think through, and break down all the different ways in which my emotions had been triggered. I used a visualization technique to help, trying to picture each of my varied emotional reactions as a "different passenger on the bus."

Through this visual exercise, I was able to identify the little old lady on my bus who was feeling extremely conservative and judgmental and who resented this former sex worker's seemingly reckless and permissive attitudes. I was also able to identify the professional psychologist on the bus who was horrified at the speaker's lack of formal training and concerned for the harm she may have inadvertently caused the public by holding herself out as an expert.

Another passenger on my bus was a young girl in her twenties, who was intrigued and admiring of this woman's fearlessness and free-spirited nature. A little girl in the back of the bus, whose parents came of age during the late '60s, was reminded of the insecurity she felt around loose boundaries like these.

Yet another passenger on my bus was a middle-aged woman who envied the speaker's disassociation from the scientific community and lack of regulation by an ethics committee or a licensing board. There was also a college-aged feminist who was angry at this woman for claiming to empower women, when she really seemed to disempower women, dressing it up as "therapy" to make it more acceptable. Other passengers were on my bus, too, but these were the loudest voices.

While I had walked out of that seminar with a head full of steam, I was able to rejoin the end of the talk with a clear, calm, and self-assured sense of where my reactions were coming from. Without taking the time to break down the different sides of myself and my emotional viewpoints, it would have been impossible to discern all the nuances of these various, equally valid viewpoints, and instead I would have just been dominated by the strongest emotion in my head—anger—leaving me with very little information and hardly any ability to articulate my views. Once I regained my composure and rejoined the group, I was able to raise questions to the speaker and share some of my emotional reactions with the group. The "nonemotional" expression of my reactions sparked a rich, rewarding discussion between the group participants that helped me further resolve my feelings.

To change your relationship with your emotions, you must change your attitude toward them. Endeavor to become more familiar, more accepting, more curious, and more connected to your emotions, and you will discover that a previously unavailable world of wisdom, choice, and ease opens up to you.

HANDLING NEGATIVE EMOTIONS

We've all been there at some point: furiously ranting and ruminating to ourselves about a setback that was perpetrated by evil, thoughtless, stupid, useless, sadistic people. We repeat the same negative thoughts and stories over and over in our heads, blinded and blocked by our angry, negative feelings. We operate with tunnel vision, emotionally disconnected from our true selves and deeper feelings, unable to access true wisdom.

Anger is the classic default (often referred to as the "iceberg emotion") most people experience when displeased. Unfortunately, anger itself is not a very illuminating emotion and often blocks true awareness and insight from occurring. The key is to consider anger as an important clue that sits on the superficial surface of your problem. Catch yourself mid-rant, dig deeper, and get more honest with yourself about the tender, vulnerable feelings underneath the self-righteousness. It's easy to stay stuck in the armor of righteous indignation—and in fact, many people make a lifetime habit of it. But if we fail to question surface emotions like anger, we gain very little insight. We are blocked from "processing," or moving through the underlying emotions.

In these situations, we must humble ourselves enough to admit that underneath all our powerful arguments against the thing that's enraged us, we are actually deeply disappointed, sad, heartbroken, grieving, terrified, or in some other vulnerable state. These deeper emotions—concealed by our surface emotions—are the more meaningful, poignant ones we can really learn from. Surface emotions like anger tend to be repetitive and keep our worldview narrow or obscured. Deeper emotions feel fresh, are sincere, expand our worldview, offer clarity, and often lead to sudden tears when we access them.

Anger is a defensive emotion, used to inflate our egos, make us feel powerful, and defend against the more vulnerable tender feelings underneath. Recognizing it as such can help us learn to be suspicious of our angry internal rants and to become a fearless investigator of what lies beneath. Usually it's as simple as asking yourself, *What am I really feeling besides anger?* Or asking, *I wonder if I'm also feeling hurt or afraid somehow?* I find that when I ask my clients these kinds of questions, there is almost always a huge sigh of relief as they spot the true source of the wound. You'll know when you've touched on the right underlying feelings—there is an immediate internal softening, and your iron grip on your point of view will start to relax a little. Often, recognizing the deeper emotion underneath is all that is needed for natural self-compassion to emerge and for the laying down of weapons to begin.

A client recounted the shock of walking in on her then-teenage son during a lewd sex act. She was disgusted, ashamed, full of anger, and she spent most of the session venting her outrage. When we dug a bit deeper though, she was surprised to discover tender feelings of real loss: loss of the image of her son as young and innocent, loss of control over the decisions he was making, and grief that her little boy had turned into a grown man without her realizing it.

Once you've uncovered the deeper feelings that lie beneath, adding a dose of self-compassion to the equation is extremely effective in terms of promoting healing, emotional digestion, and clarity. Dr. Kristin Neff has articulated several key phrases that can help awaken much-needed self-compassion during such times. Repeating these to yourself can help you open your heart and move forward in a productive direction:

- This is a moment of suffering.
- Suffering is part of life.
- May I be kind to myself in this moment.
- May I give myself the compassion I need.[5]

Know Your Triggers

Becoming familiar with what makes you feel angry or emotional is hugely valuable information that you miss if you're not paying attention. Think of the repercussions when we fail to examine the cause and effect of our emotions: we fire off highly charged email or text replies or spew poor parenting responses when we are running late for work. Our behavior and access to wisdom are often severely impaired while we are under the influence of an emotional reaction. We aren't taught how to become familiar with our own reactionary tendencies, so we most often imitate emotional tendencies without being fully conscious of it. We have to make the effort to learn, as adults, what sets us off.

If we put our minds to it, we can all create a long list of topics, circumstances, people, and feelings that tend to reliably trigger us. Don't make yourself right or wrong for your reactions, just notice them and approach them with a neutral curiosity. It's enormously empowering and illuminating to create a mental or actual list and add to it over time. You will begin to understand what your "kryptonite" is.

Many environmental conditions predispose our brains toward negative emotional states. Some of the most common are poor sleep, alcohol consumption, and stress. Being mindful of when those conditions are present, and understanding what other unique conditions light the kindling for emotional fires, can make a world of difference. Whether it's certain people, places, or situations that always seem to get you stewing on negative emotional ground, try to notice the trends. Ask yourself if your emotional response feels familiar and what it is about this type of person or situation that gets your goat so badly.

When you step out of the immediate reaction, you can see your patterns or hot buttons more clearly. Recognizing your triggers makes it easier to tell the difference between valuable emotional reactions and useless noise in your head.

It is also helpful to learn your own unique emotional patterns—how certain emotions tend to cluster together in your mind. For example, many people feel anger, followed by shame, which all too often results in disconnection. We are more likely to judge ourselves harshly for feeling certain negative emotions, and we often bundle them together subconsciously as unacceptable: jealousy, rage, rejection, loneliness, failure, and inadequacy are a few prime examples.

By observing which of my feelings tend to get paired with others, I know that when I catch a whiff of feeling rejected, I tend to jump the gun, feel begrudgingly toward others, and reject them before they can reject me. Being left out is a big trigger for me and tends to prompt all kinds of other difficult feelings such as sadness, fear, worry, and even paranoia. While rejection never feels good, I don't take it as seriously anymore since I understand it's one of my tender areas of vulnerability and probably has more to do with experiences from my past than what's happening present-day. Recognizing this emotional pattern has helped me realize ways in which I unknowingly push people away—or disconnect.

One of our research participants shared that when someone challenges her work—whether it be the quality of her work or the timing of her deliverables— she feels immediately defensive. This prompts her to disconnect and ultimately sabotage the client relationship. While there was much more to unravel about the emotions behind her reactions, recognizing this recurring trigger-response combination was a first step in learning how to stay connected to herself and her clients for a better resolution of the situation.

When you find that the thoughts and emotions you're experiencing are not useful, the popular cognitive behavioral therapy technique called "thought stopping" can help you get back on track. Try visualizing a stop sign, or saying out loud to yourself "STOP," to rip the needle off the record and reset.

How Do I Resemble What Bothers Me?

As imperfect mortals, we tend to project onto others things that are true and that we don't like about ourselves. Put another way, we are most repelled by behavior that reminds us of our own failings. Embracing this very common human tendency can teach you so much about yourself in the heat of triggering moments.

Next time you find yourself judging someone or having a strong negative reaction to them (particularly if it feels disproportionate), get curious and ask yourself how you might resemble what you are criticizing. As an example, if you get irritated or threatened by someone's primping or other efforts to show off their looks, it may be that you've placed too much emphasis on your own external appearance. Just as the kindness within you allows you to see the kindness in others, it's easy to spot your own negative traits in others.

There isn't always a direct link, however. Despising someone for being rude doesn't necessarily mean that you yourself are rude. Sometimes the link is indirect, as when you have history with a rude person and are therefore oversensitized to rudeness in others. The point is to get curious any time you have a strong negative reaction to someone. You usually don't have to look far to discover something worth knowing about yourself.

When you find the point of commonality with a person who triggers you, your condemnation of that person naturally tends to soften. Compassion comes next, as you acknowledge that "it takes one to know one." Ideally, you then go on to extend forgiveness to the other person and to yourself for struggling with this difficult trait.

Habitually deconstructing why certain people trigger you is an excellent way to stay in connection with yourself and with others. Even if the connection to that person is only inside your own head, it's still valuable to experience yourself as part of a shared humanity—particularly when you would otherwise be consumed by silent disconnection.

Examination of your emotions is one of the best ways to get acquainted with your shadow, the darker sides of yourself that may be outside of your usual awareness. Bringing more parts of yourself into the fold (the good, the bad, and the ugly) helps to expand your connection to yourself.

It also helps keep you connected to the world around you. Next time you're consumed with fury about some "terrible injustice," ask yourself whether the culprit's behavior seems so intolerable because you yourself have done something similar. Can you perhaps relate to those all-too-human tendencies? If you miss these opportunities for self-acceptance and forgiveness and stay mired in your contempt for someone else's bad behavior, you remain yourself "a hater," disconnected from that other person because of your judgment, and disconnected from the darker parts of yourself that you are unwilling to acknowledge or accept. I call this a double dose of disconnection.

Pay Attention to How Thoughts Connect to Feelings

People vary in their ability to see the connection between their thoughts and feelings, and EQ research is now helping us to understand how valuable (and trainable) this skill really is. Studies show that people who were good at connecting thoughts to their feelings are better able to "hear" the implications of their thoughts and to better understand other people's emotions.[6]

Cognitive behavioral therapy, which is based upon learning the connection between our thoughts and feelings, has a successful technique we utilized with some of the most disturbed individuals at Harvard's Cambridge Hospital. These patients had seemingly intractable negative beliefs, ranging from severe paranoia and delusions to feelings of shame and rage, which caused them to want to harm themselves and others. With such severe cases, I was initially quite dubious that simply considering how certain thoughts led to certain feelings could break the spell that bound them and allow clear thinking to enter. But it almost always worked.

In our therapy sessions, the patients would write down their upsetting thoughts and beliefs in one column, then list in the column opposite how they felt when they had those thoughts—making the connection explicit. Then they were asked to write down the factual evidence for and against each of their beliefs. After looking at their list of evidence, they could create a more accurate belief to replace the irrational one and sidestep the emotional trigger that had been upsetting them. I've included a worksheet for doing this in the appendix.

This exercise is helpful for people like you and me who *don't* suffer from clinical paranoia or delusions. If you notice a pattern of thoughts prompting negative emotions, take a hard look at them and challenge yourself to find a more accurate view of the situation with a more positive emotional result.

Pay Attention to How Certain Feeling States Lead to Others

While our emotions and thoughts may reveal important information to us, we can't always rely upon them. Often our brains are simply on autopilot rehashing old material out of habit. It's critical to learn to recognize which scenario we are in.

First, understand that negative thoughts and feelings lead to more of the same. Many negative emotions we experience in the course of a day are actually just echoes of a negative emotion we felt before. Often we ruminate about something we've already gotten to the bottom of or that is simply incongruous with our surroundings or mood state.

I challenge you to observe the next time you are in the shower, commuting to work, or just daydreaming, what happens when negative thoughts and emotions start brewing. When the first negative thought or feeling occurs, your mind is far more likely to leapfrog to another negative emotional lily pad issue, and then on to another, and another, until you wake up and realize these emotions are just a function of the negative momentum you've created and not truly reflective of how you currently feel about those issues.

When I have a bad feeling brewing inside of me, I've learned to pause and ask myself what I was just thinking about before the negative thoughts (let's say a long-ago fight I had with my sister) popped into my head. Usually, I can trace the emotion back to something earlier in the day, like a less-than-pleasant goodbye with the kids on the way to school that morning. It is more useful to dive into why I feel guilty and inadequate as a mother when the kids and I say goodbye on a bad note than it is to rehash some old fight with my sister. It's fascinating when you start to notice how one negative thought-emotion combo leads to another. Like a skipping stone, your mind can race from one bad feeling or subject to the next, leaving a residue of confusing, apparently unresolved emotions behind.

It's not realistic to reflect on your emotions or pursue the deeper meaning behind them at all times. But remembering to consider feelings as clues, even once or twice a day, can help bring you closer to your true self.

Befriending Difficult Emotions

We can't become truly connected to ourselves until we are willing to embrace the entire spectrum of our emotional world. *All* emotions deserve respect. It's a false assumption of modern society that the goal is to feel mostly positive emotions. We are wired for the full spectrum of emotions, and life is a full-spectrum experience.

The problem is our greediness and preference for pleasant-feeling states and our intolerance of unpleasant emotional states. In reality, there are no good or bad emotions. Once we do away with that made-up dichotomy, it is much easier to accept all of our emotional experiences—and accept ourselves.

It's typical and *normal* for people to have challenging areas in their lives. Whether it's chronic clashing with your in-laws, grappling with a physical ailment, an unreasonable boss, complications of a divorce, financial struggles, or the legacy of a difficult childhood, we all have areas that challenge us— sometimes temporarily and sometimes chronically.

A large part of what makes these areas problematic is our attitude toward them. Unless we've managed to make peace with our chronic challenges, we tend to hate them and go to battle with them on a regular basis—a rinse-and-repeat dynamic that springs up every time we get triggered in these areas.

People often hold underlying beliefs that *This shouldn't be happening* or *This shouldn't be happening to me* or *I shouldn't have to be struggling like this*. It's our resistance to accepting reality that leads to most of our suffering. For my end-of-life patients at the hospital, those who accepted their situations found their state of grace, while those who remained in conflict or resisted what was happening to them suffered the most.

We tend to massively disconnect from ourselves, from others, and from our clarity and wisdom when we resist reality. The best first step toward reconnecting is to accept and even embrace the fact that "unsolvable problems" are a normal and ongoing part of life. Simply normalizing your experiences releases an enormous amount of pent-up steam related to the issue. Even more importantly, it can help you move from anger and resentment to the deeper feelings of sadness and loss. Those deeper feelings, in turn, allow you to access self-compassion, or even forgiveness, and ease the emotional gridlock. Regardless of whether the original problem gets solved, this relief allows self-healing and connection to begin.

As Buddhist tradition teaches, mindfulness and meditation practice can also offer relief from painful emotions, helping us to take responsibility for our mind states and change them for the better. Accepting responsibility is the only real solution for the anxiety, fear, sorrow, and emotional confusion of the human condition.

When You Need to, Surrender (for a While)

There are times when it seems like no matter what you do, you're unable to lift yourself out of a negative emotional state. When this happens, try *not* resisting for a while. Surrender to the experience, and let yourself feel it. Often, once you've sat with and processed the emotion, you can let it go and move on—typically with a new understanding because of the experience. As we've been discussing, negative emotions are an inevitable and natural part of life, and allowing yourself to really feel them can provide a new level of self-connection.

Let's say, for example, that the sixth or seventh time you play back a fight you recently had with a good friend, you finally realize that what you're really feeling underneath it all is betrayal, sadness, and profound disappointment. Don't challenge the feelings; just lay it on thick with the self-compassion and begin to silently say soothing self-statements such as *Wow, it is so hard to feel this way, especially about someone I've loved for so long* or *It makes complete sense that I would be feeling so hurt* or *I am so sorry that this has happened to me*.

Through this self-compassion, you give yourself the necessary sympathy, affirmation, validation, acknowledgment, and permission around the *real* feelings underneath. When you validate the experience of those real emotions, it feels incredibly good and may prompt a new release of emotion. This is where the important stage of processing, moving through, digesting, and understanding our reactions (or our true selves) happens. It's a step that is rarely achieved and often skipped over, but it is truly where all the magic happens.

It's a tall order for many of us, myself included, to always bring a curious, compassionate, nonjudgmental stance to difficult emotions. But on the occasions when I am able to remember and successfully practice this position, I am rewarded with palpable relief and mental ease as I access a deeper, wiser part of myself.

CONNECTING PRACTICES

There are a number of practices that can help promote the level of connection in our day-to-day lives. While you don't have to adopt all of these to live a connected life, the more you can do, the richer your existence is likely to be.

The Power of Time Alone

In the first class of my very first day of psychology graduate school, I remember our professor—who was somewhat of a rock star for developing the most widely recognized personality test of our time (the MMPI-2)—handed out a paperback book to all of us and said, "Here, take this. It's my gift to you. Read it before you read any of your textbooks. It may be the most important book you'll ever read during your five years here." That book was *Care of the Soul* by Dr. Thomas Moore. We were all a little surprised that this bespectacled clinical research titan would be concerned with matters of the soul. But I dove in and devoured the book. Needless to say, he was right.

In his thoughtful, incisive way, Moore—a former Catholic monk—confronts how and why it is so hard for us as individuals to slow down. He has brought his message to mainstream media as well: "We seem to have a complex about busyness in our culture. Most of us do have time in our days that we could devote to simple relaxation, but we convince ourselves that we don't. . . we don't get a lot of support in this culture for doing nothing. If we aren't accomplishing something, we feel that we're wasting time."[7]

In our culture, being busy is considered a badge of honor. Even those of us who don't buy the folly of that credo still feel self-conscious about stealing time just for ourselves—or worse, sitting around doing nothing. We have lost the art of sitting on a park bench, picking daisies, and lying in the grass staring up at the sky. Most of us are so used to being scheduled that it actually feels uncomfortable to have unstructured time, and we are quick to fill the void out of habit.

We fill our time with chores, errands, or our trusty smartphones. We're afraid of being left alone with ourselves because we're afraid of discovering who we are. And in this fast-paced digital age of FOMO (fear of missing out), we're desperately afraid of being left behind as the rest of the world careens into the future.

While time alone is often discussed anecdotally as a good idea or helpful for well-being in pop-psychology forums, it is absolutely essential for people who want to live more authentically connected lives. Research shows that we overestimate how much we need people and underestimate the value of solitary experiences. It's true. Quality alone time leads to valuable personal enrichment.

Living a more authentically connected life requires us to be more aware and awake than the average bear when it comes to our day-to-day internal and external experiences. We learn to pause regularly to check in with ourselves to see if any course corrections are needed, typically while surrounded by people and the hustle and bustle of life. But despite this, carving out and protecting precious alone time remains a necessity.

Quality time by yourself is more than simply being alone because you allow yourself to appreciate and benefit from the experience. It doesn't matter if the time you're enjoying is a by-product of a carefully laid-out plan and intention (such as going on a long bike ride by yourself) or something that occurred by chance (finding yourself alone on a subway car or browsing the shelves of a bookstore). What matters is the quality of attention you bring to the alone time, no matter how brief or unexpected it is. The moment you bring a keen awareness to it and savor how good it feels to be having a very private personal moment with yourself, you will likely experience a deep exhalation and drop in blood pressure and find yourself in an altered state, free to reflect, your spirit soaring and unfettered.

The Benefits of Being Alone

Alone time allows you to slow down and collect your thoughts. Slowing down is necessary to hear yourself, to get beyond everyday reactivity, and to discover your real truth. In solitude, we think more clearly, which leads to gaining more clarity—critical prerequisites to feeling more connected to our truths and ourselves.

Time alone also allows you important, but sadly infrequent, opportunities for self-expression, autonomy, and freedom of choice. You can move at your own pace and follow your own urges. The relaxation we often experience during quality alone time also helps us to clear our heads, empty our thoughts, and recharge our batteries. When we pause and take time out, we momentarily stop chasing. We slow down and signal to ourselves that we are enough—this moment is enough—and all that we need.

Solitude also allows us to access fresh, creative, and inspired thoughts. While group-think and brainstorming strategies have long been the favored strategy of corporations, research confirms that we are far more productive and creative on our own. Group brainstorming causes people to be shy, to conform to other's ideas, or to underinvest in the process. Susan Cain, former attorney and author of the book *Quiet*, states that "solitude is a crucial (and underrated) ingredient for creativity."[8]

In our modern culture, it is even more important that we learn to balance the demands of our external world with the needs of our internal one. The doorway to accessing our internal world, and all we hold sacred, is through spending time alone. Whether it be meditating, praying, browsing in an art gallery, going for a hike, feeding the ducks, or reading a book, time for ourselves is how we recover, rejuvenate, refresh, and reconnect.

Making Time for Yourself

The best way to maximize your time alone is to schedule it as a priority and take advantage of the spontaneously occurring opportunities for solitude throughout your day. Exceptionally grounded individuals all seem to understand the importance of alone time, whether they are extroverts or introverts. They prize it, protect it fiercely, and schedule it as if it were on par with other top priorities in their lives. They may differ in their activities, but you'll often hear these people saying things like, "That's my time" or "I'm taking time out for me" or "That's when I get to be with myself" or "That's my sanity break."

For some people, alone time is best experienced in nature; for others, it revolves around some kind of exercise, such as a ritualized stroll home from the bus each day or taking the dog on a walk. It could be sitting in a coffee shop, reading the paper. The activity isn't important; what matters is that you preserve this time for yourself first and foremost. Schedule it in stone. What gets scheduled gets done.

Prioritizing and scheduling some alone time each day is a way to communicate to yourself that you matter: your needs, your feelings, and your sanity all matter. It's a powerful act of self-love and self-care. Finding ways to spend small, medium, and large amounts of alone time on a regular basis is important; in my experience, larger periods of time alone allow for even greater rewards.

But scheduling me-time is only part of the solution. We often find ourselves alone many times throughout our day (in the car, at our desks, in our homes, in an elevator, waiting in a doctor's office, doing errands) and are totally unaware of the solitude. In these moments, we are usually elsewhere, completely distracted, caught up in the story lines in our heads or consumed with our to-dos and our devices. This is not quality alone time—it's continuing to rush around our day. Again, the goal is not to be 100 percent connected all the time, but we should be mindful of the huge chunks of time that are largely unconscious and unconnected. In those moments, it only takes a single deep breath and intentional moment of awareness to bring you back into your body and enable you to momentarily access a bigger perspective of life.

These naturally occurring moments of solitude are wonderful opportunities to intentionally recapture and embrace unexpected moments of quality alone time. If you pay attention to how you are typically operating during these distracted solitary moments, you might start to notice certain conditions that help create a quality moment, as well as the conditions that block it.

For example, does listening to music you love in the car tend to be more conducive to mental soaring than listening to talk radio or news? If you commute on public transportation, you might find that looking out the window, rather than at your devices or a newspaper, has the same effect. Scan your environment for the conditions that help you to wake up and savor unscheduled moments with yourself. I try to steal moments for myself like this as much as possible. Something as simple as plunking down on a random bench for a few minutes and watching the world go by has a way of plugging you back into yourself and your environment.

If you're not used to taking solitary timeouts, it can be awkward and uncomfortable at first. Clients have reported that it can feel boring, anxiety producing, lonely, or like a waste of time. If you've spent a majority of your time outer-referencing and looking to others for how to think or feel about yourself, this is a completely natural reaction. But it could be an indication that you're still in the process of learning to enjoy your own company. Some people will give up at the first indication of feeling uncomfortable when alone. Don't make this mistake. Developing a comfortable relationship with yourself is well worth the journey and, once achieved, can be life changing. Most people who have cultivated the art of quality time alone describe the practice as something they deeply cherish. Take it slow, but stick with it, and try a variety of different ways to hang out with yourself.

Longer solo voyages can be particularly life altering and are associated with profound transformation (consider spiritual pilgrimages such as the Camino de Santiago pilgrimage in France and Spain, or Cheryl Strayed's journey on the Pacific Crest Trail). During these classic heroic journeys, individuals are challenged to grow, to face their fears, and to discover sides of themselves they never knew existed. This is why in many cultures rites of passage for young people involve spending a significant period of time alone, usually in nature. Even in our culture, troubled youth can experience dramatic epiphanies and self-empowerment after participating in an Outward Bound expedition where they must fend for themselves in the wild. The time-honored, transformative potential of quality alone time, natural surroundings, and a sense of self-sufficiency is acknowledged by organizations, religions, and wisdom traditions around the world.

But you don't need to embark on a solo trek through the hinterlands to bring the daily benefits of alone time into your life. A simple two-minute walk around your block can do wonders to clear your head and reconnect you to yourself and the world around you.

Thomas Moore reminds us that "We live in an extremely externalized culture. . . . We are constantly pulled outside ourselves—by other people, by the media, by the demands of daily life. Nothing in our culture or in our education teaches us how to go inward, how to steady the mind and calm our attention. As a consequence, we tend to devote very little time to the life of the soul, the life of the spirit."[9] Alone time helps us bridge that gap.

MEDITATION

Meditation has taken the world by storm. Or at least that's the case in my corner of the world in the San Francisco Bay Area. Long gone are the days when meditation was largely relegated to the domain of crunchy granola people, Zen centers, or Buddhist monks. Thanks to the curiosity of many and of the scientific community, in particular, we have hundreds of empirical studies that show astounding emotional and physical benefits from meditation, regardless of age or circumstance.

Meditation has even become quite fashionable and is being practiced in the most unlikely places—such as preschool classrooms, high-tech companies, veterans' groups, and even stodgy old law firms. Among seekers of higher consciousness and enlightenment, it is considered the *numero uno* practice—as part of that community, you would be seen as an ignoramus if you did not meditate daily.

Just to be clear, let's take a brief look at the physical and emotional benefits of meditation. Western clinical studies as far back as the 1990s have shown that adopting meditation practices for just eight weeks can help reduce stress. This is probably the best-known benefit, and it's a huge one. A recent (and quite rigorous) review of the hundreds of meditation studies out there concluded from reliable evidence that the hype is real: meditation reduces clinical anxiety and negative mood *comparable with what would be expected from the use of an antidepressant*—but without, of course, the associated toxicities, unwanted side effects, and expense.[10]

And studies every day are expanding the list of known benefits and exceeding expectations of what we thought meditation could do, whether it's related to battling cancer, substance abuse, chronic pain, psychological trauma, menopausal symptoms, or just improving cardiovascular health.[11] Studies in a variety of contexts have found meditation associated with higher emotional intelligence, superior attention skills, enhanced cognition, and less negative reactivity to emotional challenges.[12] In short, meditation can have a huge positive impact on your mind—and life.

My approach to meditation is very simple and doesn't follow any particular dogma. I simply lie down on my back, take a couple of nice, big clearing breaths, and then just relax, gently tuning into and following the rhythm of my breath as it goes in and out. Thoughts come and go, and I try to be a neutral observer. If I get lost in my thoughts and forget that I'm meditating for a bit, I gently bring my attention back to the breath and repeat. That's it.

Often, my meditation feels like nothing is happening other than a relaxing opportunity to take a moment with myself before the mayhem in my house starts. Sometimes I feel spontaneous bursts of bliss and well-being or increased sensory awareness as I tune into the sounds of the birds outside my window. Occasionally, it feels annoying and like I'm itching to be done. Other times, it is sublime and revelatory, and I may sense true clarity and wisdom emerging. There are times when my two minutes organically expand into twenty minutes, and I don't want it to end.

The point is, it doesn't really matter what happens while I'm meditating. What *does* matter is that I'm showing up with the intention to meditate, day after day. According to the gurus, the benefits occur later and throughout your day, not typically during your practice. So, let go of any expectations of how it should be, feel, or look, and just rest assured that the payoff is forthcoming.

Like brushing my teeth, meditation is now an ingrained habit that I don't have to put any thought or energy toward. I do it every day, it's generally enjoyable, and I feel confident that it is good for me. I'm sure a traditionalist would be horrified at my dumbed-down version of meditation. But it works for me. I show up for it every day. The best technique won't make a darn bit of difference if you don't do it faithfully.

If you don't already meditate, I suggest you start with a laughably small goal, as I did, to set it up as an easy win for yourself. Think of it as a no-fail exercise that you can't screw up even if you try to! In a worst-case scenario, you spend a couple minutes relaxing quietly by yourself. What do you have to lose?

The starting point is connecting with the breath. But ultimately, meditation is about connecting with the self. Before I began my daily practice, self-connection could disappear from my life for days, weeks, even years. Now there is always this one small anchor in my day, where I prioritize being with myself and tuning in to the life-force of my breath. The result is that, as long as I keep up with my meditation practice, I never stray too far away from the core of my being. That's a pretty big payoff for only two minutes a day.

If you're still wary of the do-it-yourself approach I describe, consider trying my favorite guided meditation. Dr. Deepak Chopra and Oprah Winfrey have collaborated to produce a series of twenty-one-day meditations that you can listen to at your leisure from your phone or computer. They do an absolutely stunning job in this series, and their guided meditations are a complete joy to listen to. Chopra puts it beautifully:

> In meditation we disrupt the unconscious progression of thoughts and emotions by focusing on a new object of attention, whether that is a mantra— like the ones we use in our 21-Day Meditation Experience—our breath, or an image. Meditation is one of the best ways to loosen the grip of sticky emotions and connect to our true self, which isn't limited, angry, or fearful, but is infinite, pure consciousness. Meditation brings us home to the peace of present-moment awareness and gives us an experience of profound relaxation that dissolves fatigue and long-standing stresses.[13]

GRATITUDE

Gratitude and forgiveness open your heart and mind, enabling connection to occur more naturally. Gratitude might actually be the ultimate way to kick-start feeling connected to yourself, to others, and to the world around you. It warms your heart and opens the floodgates of naturally occurring connection between you, others, the present moment, the universe, and life. It makes you stop and savor the blessings in your life instead of just letting them pass by unnoticed.

Nearly every religion and wisdom tradition embraces the individual, interpersonal, and societal benefits of giving thanks, being aware of your blessings, and appreciating that which has been given to you. An awareness of your blessings is associated with a state of grace and facilitates a connection with your concept of the divine. In *Ask and It Is Given*, Esther and Jerry Hicks concur that appreciation of others and self "are the closest vibrational matches to Source Energy of anything we have ever witnessed anywhere in this Universe."[14]

In connection theory, gratitude practice is a cornerstone habit used to incline our minds toward the positive flow of energy while experiencing a sense of oneness. There are many positive forces at work when we experience gratitude. When we are in a state of thankfulness, the goodness inside us can see and appreciate the goodness in others. In other words, our ability to see beauty is a direct reflection of the beauty we ourselves possess. So feeling appreciative is one of the most effective ways to experience ourselves as good and loving—we grow fonder of, closer to, and more connected to ourselves each and every time we think, feel, or express gratitude. We are proud of ourselves and feel closely connected to our inner beings through gratitude— which is why it is the fast track to greater self-connection.

Empirical data confirm the benefits of even miniscule levels of gratitude practice. Dr. Robert Emmons of the University of California, Davis and Dr. Michael McCullough of the University of Miami report that participants who kept gratitude journals and practiced self-guided gratitude exercises improved their sleep, exercised more, made faster progress toward their goals, had more positive emotions, and helped others more frequently.[15]

Gratitude helps us understand what we consider meaningful in life. Brother David Steindl-Rast, a Benedictine monk, has said: "Gratefulness is the inner gesture of *giving* meaning to our life by *receiving* life as a gift."[16] By recognizing the incredible gift of our own existence, we see its value more clearly.

One of my greatest heroes and mentors, the late Dr. Angeles Arrien, helped guide and illuminate the lives of thousands of students on their paths to personal enlightenment with her gratitude-centered work. I adopted her elegant, simple approach as part of my daily personal practice, with incredibly powerful results.

Arrien recommends keeping beside your bed a journal that is specifically dedicated to gratitude. Each night, make a brief entry that answers the following questions:

- What touched me today?

- Who or what inspired me?
- What lessons did I learn today?

It takes five minutes of your day.

I love this approach because it encourages us to reflect on blessings, gifts, and appreciation—the good things we encounter each day—as well as difficulties we experience. This is great practice for learning to reframe some of our life struggles and helping us to lean in and feel more connected to the unsavory parts of our lives that we typically push away.

As with any new habit, at first I had to push myself and fake it till I made it. But over time, it has become such a cherished, tiny ritual in my day that I feel off-balance if I skip a night or two. After a couple of weeks answering these questions, you may feel that your journal is a treasure trove of precious memories and wisdom.

From the literature, there are several things we know about cultivating gratitude that help make it even more successful.[17] The first thing is to go for variety in your subject matter. Writing that you're grateful for your children, your health, and the roof over your head can get pretty rote and even meaningless if you do it every time. The goal is to begin noticing a wider variety of tiny daily miracles in your world, from spotting a hummingbird, to something that made you laugh out loud, to appreciating a thoughtful gesture by a friend.

Secondly, vary the ways you express gratitude. Although it's critical to have a ritualized approach (such as journaling), to cultivate regular practice and build muscle, you can and should also experiment with other forms—sending an unexpected card to dear friends, writing a glowing Yelp review, leaving a waiter a note of thanks or extra-large tip, verbally expressing yourself to others, and the like.

One group participant sent an email once a week to someone she appreciated. After just a few weeks, she reported huge ripple effects from this twenty-minute exercise. Not only did it bring her closer to many people, including workmates, family members, and colleagues, but she also reported feeling a transcendent bliss as she reflected on her positive encounters and made her weekly selections.

If you want to attract more good into your life and feel more aware of, tuned in to, and connected to that good, then you should use your mindful awareness skills to intentionally notice, celebrate, and appreciate that which you cherish. The psychology community often says that the measure of one's mental health is the ability to see the good in everything. Perception is the key.

SPIRITUAL PRACTICE

I have always loved the clean, quantifiable measures of scientific research. I abandoned my longer-term Freudian training and jumped headfirst into the cognitive behavioral therapy (CBT) revolution as it was taking the field by storm. Instead of spending years dissecting childhood wounds to find the source of distress, CBT focuses on the desired solution—helping people stop their harmful thoughts and behaviors as soon as possible. With CBT, a therapist encourages patients to challenge inaccurate beliefs or perceptions and break chronic patterns of thought, behavior, and emotion. This evidence-based approach to mental health treatment seemed limitless in terms of whom it could benefit and how far it could reach—from eating disorders and trauma to depression, anxiety, suicidality, psychosis, delusion, and substance abuse.

Under the CBT umbrella, therapists were able to help chronically disturbed clients resolve issues, which, in the past, were deemed hopeless. Thanks to the swift, consistent, and stable positive outcomes of these therapies, mental health treatment was finally legitimized by insurance companies, in hospital settings and institutions where longer-term, open-ended therapies had never previously been welcome.

I still wholeheartedly believe the CBT approach is the gold standard for achieving lasting behavior change across a variety of conditions, and I pledge allegiance to the fundamental tenet that behavior wags the tail of emotion. But for all its success, there's one significant problem with CBT therapies: they are spiritually dead. So my slavish obsession with CBT and natural proclivity to only believe in things that could be seen and measured meant that I was spiritually dead too.

It wasn't until my marriage was crumbling and our second child was nearly to term that I realized nothing I'd learned in graduate school or as a clinician could help me prevent, understand, or make sense of what was happening in my own life. To make matters more difficult, this dissolution sent shock waves through my entire social system, and many key family members and friends were unable to offer the kind of support I needed; in many cases, they only made things worse. This was particularly hard because family meant everything to me. I found my own belief system was now being shattered—or, more accurately, I came face-to-face with the fact that I didn't have a belief system.

While I was able to lean heavily on my beloved cognitive behavioral therapy techniques to keep myself out of severe depression, the truth was that all of CBT's horses and all CBT's men couldn't put me back together again. I was missing something more fundamental. Because something more fundamental was missing from my perspective.

I ended up resigning from my position as director of the health psychology and postdoctoral training programs to take some time, find myself again, and figure out what that missing component was. I was desperate to expand my worldview, so I decided to expose myself to everything *but* the familiar tried and true. My journey led me from Buddhist temples to indigenous shamans in the Amazon jungle, from churches to astrologers and mystery schools, from meditation groups to ecstatic dance. It was a real stretch for me at first, and I remember nearly laughing out loud at my first-ever psychic reading—the woman requested a moment of silence while she invited my "guides" into the room.

What I uncovered throughout this circuitous journey was a profound reverence for the exquisite, mysterious forces that exist in the universe. More importantly, I was reminded that I am not the center of the universe. In essence, I discovered my own spirituality.

The Value of Spirituality

Whether you call it God, Jesus, Mohammed, Buddha, Allah, a higher power, the spirit realm, the universe, or something else, faith in a force greater than ourselves is what pushes us to transcend our existence and appreciate a bigger-picture view. As we discussed earlier, transcendence is the top of the pyramid on Abraham Maslow's famous hierarchy of human needs. It's the highest, final need that human beings crave when all our other, lesser needs have been met.

Historically, many psychology researchers have been at odds with religion and spirituality, and therefore reluctant to study them. But that tide is starting to turn, and there is now an increased interest in the unique emotional and social benefits of a faith-based practice.

Renowned psychiatrist Dr. George Vaillant, best known for his study of ego defense mechanisms, turned to more happiness-related work in his later career. In his book *Spiritual Evolution*, he wrote, "The absence of faith is nihilism, not atheism." Faith means having "basic trust that the world has meaning and that lovingkindness exists."[18] Without faith, there is no meaning in life.

It's important to note that faith may include religious or spiritual beliefs, but it doesn't have to. Faith can also be what we hold most true and dear when we operate from a place of pure clarity and wisdom. I have personally come to appreciate the beauty of many different spiritual belief systems, and most importantly, I have learned to have an open mind that seeks the interconnected nature of all things.

Most of the religious and wisdom traditions of the world emphasize the importance of integrity and good character, so it's not surprising that many of the most common virtues urged by religion tend to promote well-being in and of themselves. Humility and surrender are two of these.

Drs. William Damon and Anne Colby formulated a definition of humility based on their studies of moral leaders. In their view, humility is best described as the state of having:

1. a low degree of self-seeking or focus on the self;

2. a sense of perspective on the self (such as by having a sense of humor about yourself, not viewing yourself as superior relative to others, and not showing off special status with material or symbolic trappings of power, wealth, etc.);

3. an awareness of one's limitations (including efforts to avoid overestimating or overstating abilities, the welcoming of constructive criticism, and reluctance to judge others);

4. open-mindedness.[19]

Humility is the antidote for solipsism and self-absorption, helping us look beyond our own egos to see what we believe is most important and to move toward faith.

Faith traditions also teach and encourage the idea of surrender. One of my dearest college friends and fellow therapist, Julie, reminds me often that "what you resist will persist." So much of our distress, and I would argue disconnection, comes from our refusal to accept what is happening to us, refusing to allow things to "be" and unfold as they are meant to, and instead trying to force them in a certain direction. Trying to combat reality is a fruitless endeavor that blocks connection to ourselves.

But surrender is not a position of defeat or giving up—quite the contrary. It's more about feeling your feelings, setting a strong wish/intention/desire for things to be different, and then letting it go. One of my interns shared a story about her client, a ninth-grade boy, who was struggling with being brutally "dropped" by his group of long-time elementary school friends when they transitioned into their freshman year. She remarked that although it was clearly very painful for him, he was not depressed or ruminating, and he seemed to be coping well. He said: "It hurts, and I don't get it, but I just decided to pray and let God take it from there."

He had identified his emotions, acknowledged them, and moved on. Surrendering responsibility to a higher power made it easier to accept his own powerlessness over the situation—which freed him to focus his attention on other matters, instead of fretting, ruminating, or beating himself up.

Oneness

The Buddhist monk and philosopher Thich Nhat Hanh teaches, "We are here to awaken from our illusion of separateness."[20] That sense of oneness may be the most profound and sublime state a human being can ever achieve. In this blissful experience, we are overcome with joy and multidirectional feelings of intense connection. Oneness is truly the pinnacle of connection, in every sense of the word.

In essence, oneness is a feeling of interconnectedness and transcendence of boundaries or dividers. It is usually experienced as an intense heart-opening where one is consumed with love, incoming and outgoing, radiating in every direction. It is often accompanied by an awareness of the inherent goodness of all beings and an ability to see beauty everywhere. From that state of mind, it is easy to imagine a pathway to end all human conflict and pain.

Though the name for it may differ, the concept of oneness is a cornerstone of most major religions, wisdom traditions, and spiritual pathways—and it's even discussed in quantum physics. *Oneness* is sometimes used as a synonym for God or spirit, and in spiritual terms, it is the optimal state of enlightenment and transcendence often used to describe a communion with God. Much of what is written about the experience of oneness is very abstract, obtuse, and metaphysical. There are many different interpretations of what oneness means—often articulated with arcane words like *duality, inter-being, non-self,* and *pure consciousness*—which can make the concept confusing or feel out of reach for many. But in plain language, oneness is simply feeling that you are not a separate living creature, but rather part of a single, loving consciousness.

In the context of connection theory, we think of oneness as the experience of feeling love, closeness, and unity to all that surrounds you in a single moment. It might be as simple as a sudden burst of love, gratitude, and interconnectedness when you look around a dinner table of dear friends. It might be the awe you feel gazing up at the stars. It can be a momentary wave of feeling and awareness that passes over you or something far more impactful and life-altering where you suddenly see the truth of everything, all at once.

Oneness can be experienced on a micro-level, where the boundaries between you and another being dissolve, or more broadly, as when you feel united with all creation. Environmental philosopher Dr. Glenn Albrecht describes oneness with nature as the feeling "where the boundaries between self and the rest of nature are obliterated and a deep sense of peace and connectedness pervades consciousness."[21]

Oneness is the polar opposite of the illusion of separateness, which certain belief systems hold to be the root of much, if not all, human suffering. The illusion of separateness is literally the false assumption that you are separate and distinct from everyone and everything in the universe. More figuratively, it is the notion of separateness that promotes many of the ills of humanity—the "us versus them" mentality, and in-group/out-group thinking that promote conflict and war. On an individual scale, a mentality of separateness leads to painful isolation, feeling like you are an island incomprehensible to others and that your struggles are unique and yours alone. This form of alienation from the rest of humanity is one of the most profound and painful forms of discon- nection that we can ever experience.

In the intriguing book *The Illusion of Separateness: Exploring the Cause of Our Current Crises*, Giles Hutchins argues the inherent interdependence, fluid connection, and harmony of the natural world, and notes that much of modern day sociopolitical and environmental issues can all be traced back to the illusion of separateness that human minds tend to create. But the simple awareness of our interdependence, shared humanity, and the interrelatedness of all beings is what begins to shatter that illusion and help us rediscover wholeness.

Human beings tend to live in an illusion of separateness as we go about our day-to-day lives, but we can tap into oneness when we are open to greater awareness. We have likely all had some experiences of this kind but may not have thought about them this way, or used this terminology. Consider the rap- turous, overwhelming love that a mother might experience when holding her newborn child for the first time; the exultant, I-can-walk-on-water feelings of a new romantic connection; the profound humility and peace of being alone in an unspoiled wilderness; or the euphoria and freedom that can result from some mind-altering drugs.

Some individuals' experiences of oneness are so powerful that they are per- manently life altering. This is frequently the case with people who have had a near-death experience.

Cardiac rehabilitation patients, for example, have by definition experienced some kind of near-death or revival-from-death event. This type of experience typically has such a lasting emotional impact that the hospital I worked for developed a weekly support group to help these patients process the meaning of their experiences and how it changed their worldviews. These patients were fascinating individuals who seemed to be brimming with wisdom and clarity, as if they had been struck by lightning.

It was amazing to hear them recount having their lives flash before their eyes, understanding the meaning of life and everything in the universe all at once. The common threads in many of their stories were how interconnected we are and how peaceful and love-filled their experiences were while (technically) dead.

They were talking about oneness, even if they were not using that word. For many of these patients, that experience inspired them to make radical changes in their lives to recapture those perfectly connected moments.

Cultivating Oneness

Too often a concept like oneness gets claimed by organized religions, spiritual seekers, or new age devotees, making something that is free and easily available to everyone seem like something you need to qualify for spiritually in order to experience. The truth is, spirituality is *not* an exclusive club with members-only privileges. You don't have to have a near-death experience or adopt any particular belief system to experience a state of oneness. This beautiful state of mind can occur as a spontaneous response to ordinary life events, like a walk through the woods or a heartfelt conversation. It's simply a matter of recognizing oneness for what it is and inclining your mind toward it.

I find it useful to think about oneness as a practice—something we stay open to and intentionally strive to cultivate. Experiences of oneness are profoundly heart opening and transcendent moments on your journey to more connected living. Oneness illuminates natural wisdom that makes it far easier to see what matters in life and what doesn't. It enables us to bask in our inherent sense of worthiness, belonging, and beauty.

The experience of oneness comes in many different shapes and sizes. Some of the best descriptions of oneness have come from my interviews with nonspiritual and lay people:

"a connection to all humans, to our planet, and to a higher power"

"that there is a link . . . that everything is linked . . . that everything we do has an effect"

"I sensed a connection to the world outside of the one I'm living in."

"a realization of the miracle of what's been created . . . and feeling tiny in it . . . feeling insignificant, in a good way" "an intuitive understanding of the purpose of existence, and all life, that brought peace, calm, and utter simplicity"

"overwhelmed in reverence, and a connection to the universe"

"Ecstasy!"

Experiences of oneness often happen when we are alone and frequently occur in nature. (Here is yet another reason to prioritize both!) My favorite description of oneness comes from a woman who happened upon an ancient Jain cave while hiking during a trip to India and encountered a sudden flurry of wild birds, peacocks, and monkeys. As she sat down on a rock to pause and take it all in, she described it this way:

> *This very calm and very beautiful feeling started to spread over me . . . it felt like being in sync with the breathing of the world. It was a strange feeling of complete harmony with the universe, where I was neither wanting nor needing anything, and also not missing anything. I suddenly felt in sync with my life, no longer craving an answer to anything. Every breeze was caressing my face . . . the texture of the rock I was sitting on felt perfect . . . things smelled better, more fragrant, colors seemed brighter. I felt like I could see the molecules of life. They were beautiful . . . and so was I. After I left that cave, I knew everything was going to be fine in the next phase of my life and that I didn't need to have a big plan . . . there was this beautiful sense that all is well.*[22]

But oneness can also happen in the company of others. It may be a silent, sudden awareness, for example, that the people on the subway, who seemed like strangers just a moment ago, are really your brothers and sisters on this shared journey of life and have many of the same dreams and heartaches that you have.

Certain emotions such as love, appreciation, and peace tend to accompany oneness and can provide clues that you are entering into an ultra-connected state. Your only job is to try to become more aware of these moments, to linger with them longer, to savor and allow them to amplify. Take note when you feel your mind and heart opening simultaneously, and don't be afraid to be over-inclusive in your personal definition and experiences of oneness. More is merrier when it comes to oneness. The more you think about experiencing oneness, the more you are alert to noticing it, and the more connecting experiences you are likely to have.

CREATIVE ENDEAVORS

Over the last decade, the scientific, business, and personal growth communities have increasingly emphasized the importance of regular creative expression. A quick search on Amazon.com offers more than 5,000 books about creativity published within the last thirty days alone. More and more, our society views creative expression as a birthright, an important part of what it means to be a whole person, a necessary competitive edge in business, and an instinctive need for all rather than the exclusive domain of the naturally "gifted" and talented.

I concur. Creative expression is a primal need that helps us connect to our true selves. As Julia Cameron put it in her classic book, *The Artist's Way*, "Creativity is a natural life-force that all can experience in one form or another."[23]

Yet there are still myths that linger in our culture around creativity. These include that you're either born with a unique talent or not; only people born with a unique talent should pursue it; creativity is a waste of time, self-indulgent, or something you do when you retire; creativity is for kids or flakey, irresponsible people who have too much time on their hands; it's more for girls, not manly, and not worth doing if you're not good at it; and that you should be embarrassed if your creative work is not up to par.

In addition to weighing us down with the cultural baggage of myths like these, the creative process often prompts uncomfortable feelings of uncertainty, anxiety, and fear—even as it asks us to surrender, have faith, and allow the process to unfold. Not surprisingly, the prospect of creating something or being artistic can trigger tremendous shame and vulnerability. *Don't* be one of those people who shy away from the endeavor with the deflecting chant, "I'm not the creative type." That reaction closes your mind to an entire world of creative potential and talent that exists within you.

What you may not realize is that it is precisely that uncomfortable grappling with vulnerability and anxiety that makes the creative process so worthwhile. Creativity requires us to stretch, grow, and activate untapped areas of our minds. We feel immensely satisfied, alive, and proud of ourselves as a result. Intentionally seeking out opportunities to be creative helps us learn to overcome fear and anxiety, which translates into valuable personal growth and symbolic significance.

Engaging in creative expression has an enormously positive effect on your sense of self. It brings you into direct contact and connection with your true nature. It doesn't matter if you are sketching a still-life scene, cooking a new recipe, making a music playlist, snapping pictures on your smartphone, decorating your bedroom, or picking out a special outfit for yourself—you are expressing yourself, your uniqueness, your preferences, your originality, and your version of beauty. It's through self-expression that we experience and discover our completely unique gifts and contributions to the world that cannot be replicated. It's the closest we can come to experiencing the preciousness of our own humanity, which naturally nurtures greater connection to ourselves.

It's through creative expression that we become more familiar, in touch, and in love with the essence of our beings. When a human being makes something that is an expression of their soul, it has a uniquely precious beauty, regardless of its presentation. In a world of almost eight billion people, where we often struggle to feel that our contributions have significance, daily creative expression is the simplest and most reliable way to remind ourselves of our own unique and irreplaceable gifts.

Psychological research has discovered that creating with our hands has another important benefit. Neuroscientist Dr. Kelly Lambert spent years researching the connection between old-fashioned handwork and reduced levels of depression, which led her to theorize that our brains are actually hardwired to reward physical efforts that produce tangible, visible, and meaningful results.[24] Lambert's research noted that the brain's reward center (the nucleus accumbens) is located between the area responsible for motor control (striatum) and the structures involved in emotion and learning (the limbic system). The links between the motor and emotional systems extend to the prefrontal cortex, where we do our planning and strategic decision making. Every symptom of depression originates in this network of links, which Lambert calls the effort-driven rewards system.

Patient, diligent, old-fashioned work with our hands to create an outcome we value and look forward to causes the cells in this network to secrete dopamine and serotonin—neurotransmitters involved in boosting our mood and sense of satisfaction.[25] It also strengthens neural connections and likely prompts the development of new brain cells (neurogenesis), which may be an important factor in recovering from depression.

Modern conveniences that remove the physical challenges of our existence (cars, supermarkets, restaurants, washing machines, etc.) also remove the opportunity for these hugely positive effects. Not surprisingly, researchers have found that depression is virtually nonexistent in traditional Amish communities where members still perform most of life's essential tasks by hand.[26]

Lambert and others theorize that the decline in handcrafting is a significant contributor to the rise in depression over the last century.[27] But we don't really need scientific research to confirm what we already instinctively know to be true. Consider how satisfying it is to fix, build, mold, stitch, whittle, or create something with your own hands. Even mundane chores, such as cleaning your car by hand, can leave you with a unique sense of well-being, pride, and satisfaction as you step back to admire your results.

The intuitive truths and research underlying these concepts have led some schools to institute knitting as a mandatory activity, to help kids achieve a calm, creative mind state that soothes and refreshes them—making academic learning easier. The Waldorf schools, well-known for their holistic approach to intellectual, practical, and artistic development (and their primary goal of fostering imagination in learning), teach knitting and similar handwork from first grade on and, by some accounts, have included it in their curriculum for at least ninety years.[28]

Unfortunately, many art classes in mainstream American elementary and high schools are more focused on achieving certain consensus standards than they are on nurturing a true creative process. Programs that impose a rigid value rating on art, exalting the select few who demonstrate early aptitude for established styles, can actually have the opposite of the intended effect: teaching kids to dislike art and conclude prematurely that they aren't creative or good at it.

My own experience volunteering in my sons' art classes involved an extremely stressed-out teacher and classroom of kids commanded to copy a famous Monet painting in twenty minutes so their work could be displayed in the glass case of the school lobby for parents and administrators to oooh and aaah over. My job was to go around to each student and hurry them along. As I made my way around the room, I heard the familiar moans and groans of disaffected students. A few of them said outright: "I don't understand why we can't just paint whatever we want." The class was focused solely on achieving proscribed results, not on learning the process or the joy of artistic expression. I suspect many of the kids in that class came away from the experience thinking, *Art is not my thing.*

Alonzo King is an exciting and visionary ballet choreographer in San Francisco who disrupts and reinterprets traditional ballet, imbuing it with explosive new expression by collaborating with all kinds of visual artists, composers, and musicians from around the world. King gave a poignant and humorous interview on National Public Radio where he articulated his view of what it means to be creative. Asked what he thinks about people who say they are not creative, he responded:

I think it's akin to someone saying "I'm a sinner." It's a cruelty, you know. People can be so cruel to themselves. No, you're not a sinner! Everyone is meant to be creative; that is our legacy, that is our heritage. So if that [creativity]'s not employed, something's not working. . . . And so what is that addressing? The educational system that robs children and restricts them from acknowledging what they already know. Because intuition in children is very loud, and it becomes shrunk through those restrictive kinds of educations. Because everyone, regardless of what discipline, regardless of what choices you've made, whether that's raising children or agriculture, if art is not a part of it, then it's poorly done.[29]

I wanted to applaud King for his deep knowing and astute awareness that creativity is not primarily the domain of the uber-talented, such as himself and his dance company, but rather an essential life-force that exists within all of us and desperately needs to be invoked. To do anything well, it must be done creatively.

Researcher Dr. Brené Brown emphasizes that "the only unique contribution that we will ever make in this world will be born of our creativity."[30] Our creativity reminds us that what we bring to the world is completely unique. It offers us some of the richest opportunities we have to create meaning and, thus, achieve greater connection to ourselves.

Best Practices for Cultivating Creativity

I've put together this list of what I found to be the most helpful things to keep in mind as you cultivate your own connection to creativity. But ultimately, the only thing you really have to remember is: get creative.

1. Expand your definition of creativity to include all facets of life. Get yourself out of your well-worn creative paths, and push yourself into uncharted territory.

2. Bring intention and mindful awareness to your creative activities, savoring the process and connection to your higher consciousness. Stay present, and really inhabit the experience of what you're doing.

3. Become familiar with typical blocks to creativity. Stay away from comparison, self-judgment, and good-bad dichotomies. Trust that everyone and every piece has an ugly stage—stick with it through that phase.

4. Schedule time for creativity. Creative time is seldom viewed as an urgent need, but it is crucially important. Make time and space for it to happen regularly on your calendar. What gets scheduled gets done!

Creating something with my hands is one of my favorite ways to recharge and reconnect after long, difficult, or draining periods of disconnection. At one recent large extended-family gathering, where I couldn't plug in and be present given the tense family dynamics and hostile undertones happening that day, I decided to whip out my sketchbook and work on a tiny watercolor at the kitchen table. Even though the act was born out of a quiet desperation and a desire to be anywhere in the world except in that kitchen with my family, the act of beginning to work on a painting pulled me into a quiet, peaceful, centered place. My vibration shifted to a higher note that was more available for connection. I started to feel like I was coming back into my body. Even though at first it felt like a loner escapist activity, it actually had the opposite effect. I noticed others being drawn to me in curiosity and affection as they observed what I was doing. One of my boys even came and leaned on my leg to get a front-row view.

This experience reminded me of a comment my art teacher made to me recently when he was showing the class some photos of his work. In one picture, his young daughter was sitting on his lap, staring at his painting, while he painted with one arm reaching over her shoulder to the canvas, and the other arm around her. He remarked, "I get an enormous amount of affection from people when I am creating."

It's really true. We humans instinctively admire and feel a sense of closeness toward total strangers when we witness expressions from their souls. Like sharing vulnerability, sharing artistic expression is endearing and draws us closer into connection. Whether we spy a series of careful rock piles along the shore, discover an evocative rainbow of sidewalk chalk, or stumble upon somebody's elaborate sandcastle at the beach, it is always arresting to us. On some fundamental level, we instinctively recognize and appreciate the true value, meaning, and beauty of creative expression.

For all of these reasons, discovering, amplifying, and cultivating your own inherent creativity is one of the most important pathways for connecting deeply with your own spirit while also opening yourself up for more connection with others. As a tool for cultivating more connection in a variety of contexts, creative expression is hard to beat.

LOOKING FOR THE BEAUTY OF EVERY DAY

Another highly effective way to incline your brain toward greater connection is to take advantage of the moments in your day that offer a heightened awareness through beauty. Noticing beauty is an undeveloped skill because of what psychologists and neuroscientists refer to as negativity bias—the brain's evolutionary adaptation to notice and remember threats in our environment (or anything negative, displeasing, or nonpleasurable) far more than we notice, register, or even remember positive experiences and stimuli.

More often than not, we go about our day with a semiconscious background commentary that applies negative judgments to many of the things we see or experience. Whenever we are in judgment, we are disconnecting from ourselves, our surroundings, and usually from others in subtle ways that we don't notice.

On days when I forget to prioritize connection, I rarely notice the naturally occurring moments of beauty around me and am far more likely to have a negative mental chatter running through my head about the unpleasant things I see, such as rush hour traffic or graffiti on the side of buildings. On days when I remember to look for connection, I'm more likely to marvel at the technological brilliance of the comfortable automobiles we ride in or the vibrant colors and artistic expression behind the spray-painted walls. Everyday negative observations are replaced by an awareness that beauty abounds, and I am flooded with opportunities to notice, savor, and connect with beauty throughout the day.

Heightening our sensitivity to beauty and to feeling love is an enormously powerful tool because these emotions are a superhighway to a natural sense of connection. Reconnection in a harried day can be as simple as looking up from whatever you are doing and focusing your attention on the environment around you. Stop and linger longer than you usually might on whatever it is you find beautiful—the particular shape of a cloud formation, a sleeping child, the sound of a songbird, a satisfying and collaborative work call, the view from your office window, strangers whose looks appeal to you, an act of kindness, the way the sun reflects on the water, and, in particular, nature of any kind. Nature is full of beauty; it's low-hanging fruit when you're looking to catalyze connection.

Try to admire and feel grateful for what you see. Usually within the span of a few short seconds, colors seem brighter, shapes become more interesting, people look more human, and everything seems to have a more palpable presence. This is the beginning of what feeling connected feels like—you are suddenly awake, alert, and engaged with your surroundings.

It's essential that you not let yourself engage in comparative or judgmental thoughts about yourself or your own life, as that will block your connection immediately. The key is to admire *appreciatively*. You may notice a warm-heartedness and a softening occurring—often a deep breath of relaxation, where the shoulders drop. This means you are on the right track.

You can also use the breath to amplify this exercise. Your breathing almost always slows as you contemplate something beautiful. Go with this natural tendency, and take a series of gentle, long, slow breaths inward, followed by slow exhalations. Intentionally breathing in this way during times of reconnection tends to increase the feelings of closeness and emotional warmth. It also makes the experience feel more reciprocal, where you are giving and getting connection in the same exchange: breathing in the beauty and closeness you witness between a mother and her child, for example, and breathing out your connected feeling to them on the exhale.

Feelings of exchange and closeness morph easily into feelings of love or loving admiration. Love is a natural tendency of the brain when we open ourselves up to giving our admiring attention to anything and stay with it long enough. This feeling catalyzes the most abundant and powerful feelings of connection possible, washing over you and becoming the lens through which you look at everything else. It leaves you feeling intimately connected to that which you behold, even if only in your mind.

I've seen this fascinating (and quite endearing) human tendency in action many times in workshops, where participants pair up with complete strangers in the group and try to maintain eye contact in close physical proximity for several minutes. While at first the exercise makes people squirm, participants report afterward a natural progression: moving past initial judgmental thoughts of self and other, to being able to see the person behind the eyes, to finally experiencing warm feelings toward the other person that often progress into something that feels very much like love.

If warm, loving feelings can naturally arise toward a stranger in only a few minutes, think of the untapped potential we all have for experiencing more love in our lives. We normally associate and reserve feelings of "love" for our most intimate circle and other narrowly defined objects. Learning to expand our definition of what is love-worthy opens up a larger world of possibility and allows us to fill our emotional cup from a variety of sources.

Collecting and savoring beautiful moments allows you to feel more of your own humanity and a closer, more loving relationship to the world you inhabit. Conveniently, your attention to beauty is an easy muscle to tone—if you invoke it, you'll likely feel results on day one. It only requires setting a small intention and putting a value on the benefit of seeing, savoring, and sinking into beauty.

LEARNING, EVOLVING, AND GROWING

In a keynote talk to thousands of employees of Salesforce.com in San Francisco, Tony Robbins boldly asserted that to feel alive, you have to grow. I can't think of a truer statement. Tony frequently emphasizes that what makes us happy is who we are becoming. The process of learning and growing is one of life's great sources of pleasure as well as an essential key to brain health. Pioneering neuroscientist Marian Diamond identified "challenge" and "newness" as two of the five essential things our brains need regularly in order to be healthy.[31]

Learning and growing connect us to our life-force. Whenever we are learning, we are evolving and growing. The only thing that is required for learning is curiosity. It doesn't matter what you are learning about, whether it's learning a new language or skill, trying a new recipe, reading historical fiction, or simply watching a documentary film. Learning broadens our perspective, causing us to reexamine our beliefs, promoting empathy and understanding as well as self-awareness, self-confidence, and mastery. Often, learning challenges us to rise to a new level of skill or to stretch our comfort zone.

The further we push outside of our comfort zone to try new things, the more we are rewarded with an expanded sense of self, strength, courage, and confidence. It is a time-honored wisdom that it is good for human beings to muster up courage as often as they can, pushing to do the things that they think they cannot do. Maya Angelou and many others have recommended that we should do one thing that scares us each and every day.[32] For nothing makes us feel more self-pride and greater self-worth than when we act courageously and break our own belief barriers.

The sweet spot for summoning courage is to seek out challenges that are just beyond the edge of our capabilities, but not so far beyond that edge that we feel overwhelmed and stressed. Said differently, aim to push yourself to try things that are a little foreign and cause a little discomfort, but are not so uncomfortable that they scare you and cause you to shut down.

We are stimulated by learning even the smallest of new things, like a new term or phrase we didn't know before. As we discover the prospect of creating or doing something new, enthusiasm surges within us. Enthusiasm is one of my favorite words and states of mind. The word traces its origins to the Greek words *enthousiasmos*, meaning divine inspiration, and *enthousiazein*, which means to "be inspired or possessed by a god, be rapt, be in ecstasy."[33] When we are enthusiastic, we feel connected to rapturous joy. Continually exposing yourself to new things helps you discover what turns your enthusiasm on (or off) and is an important way to take inspired action. It's also essential for a sense of aliveness and vitality.

A friend of mine who studies learning for a living uses art museums as an example to illustrate why it is so important. When we wander around with no prior knowledge or context for what we are looking at, we get a one-dimensional impression of the artwork, evaluating it primarily for its aesthetic value. If we had instead invested some time to read about the artist and their work, as well as the social and historical relevance, we would experience the art in a much more meaningful way. Likewise, the more we take time to learn about the culture or language of a country we visit, the more likely we will be to interact with its people more meaningfully and recognize significance in the sites and experiences.

Contextualizing tends to bring things to life and make them more meaningful to us. Understanding more about a person, place, or topic gives you many more possibilities to connect them with something that's meaningful to you. So make the effort to learn more about the people or the subjects that you normally ignore or find less meaningful. Broaden your horizons beyond your current repertoire, follow your enthusiasm, and ask yourself: What is capturing your imagination lately?

Whenever we learn, grow, or challenge ourselves, we are likely to feel completely connected. Drs. Anders Ericsson and Robert Pool argue that "we humans are most human when we're improving ourselves. We, unlike any other animal, can consciously change ourselves to improve ourselves in ways we choose. This distinguishes us from every other species alive today and, as far as we know, from every other species that has ever lived."[34]

Embrace learning as a lifelong activity. It is one of the simplest ways to renew and expand your possibilities for finding greater meaning and connection in life.

FLOW

When was the last time you got so caught up in a project or activity that you forgot about everything else? It might have been at work, while playing a game, or even while cooking. This state of total absorption and engaged enjoyment is known in positive psychology circles as "flow." The lead researcher on this peculiar human state, Dr. Mihaly Csikszentmihalyi, chose the name "flow" because so many of his subjects described the experience like they were being carried by a current of water. Other disciplines call it different things—"the zone" in sports, "wired in" in computer coding—but the phenomenon is the same: intense, absolute, and energized focus on the activity of the present, to the exclusion of everything else.

When you're in a state of flow, you feel in control of what you're doing and confident in your ability to succeed at it. You feel outside your everyday reality, free of self-consciousness and other limiting thoughts. You are so thoroughly engrossed in the task at hand that your awareness of other needs—and your sense of time—become skewed.[35] As one Millennial self-help author puts it, you "forget to eat and poop."[36] You are single-mindedly focused on what you are doing, not because of some eventual goal, but for the sheer joy of doing whatever it is that you're doing.

Besides being an enjoyable and inherently rewarding experience, flow is also an ideal mental state for connection. It's a place of complete engagement where your mind has shut out every other distraction. You are doing something you enjoy doing without reservation, self-consciousness, or self-doubt. It's the ultimate expression of alignment.

Finding Flow

The obvious questions are: How do we achieve this nirvana? What kinds of activities will get us there? What kind won't? Csikszentmihalyi has been studying this for forty years, and he's got a few pointers. Here are three of the most important things to look for.

1. There is a clear object of your focus (a goal or set of goals) and immediate feedback as you work toward it. Csikszentmihalyi's studies reveal that flow tends to occur when we face a clear set of goals that require appropriate responses. Games—chess, tennis, poker, and even some video games—tend to be good examples because they have "goals and rules that make it possible for the player to act without questioning what should be done, and how."[37] Unlike a lot of situations in real life, these kinds of activities offer total focus on goals that are clear and provide immediate feedback on how we're doing. Activities like rock climbing or performing music are the same—you know immediately whether you're still on the cliff or in key. There is instant or near-instant feedback for everything you do.

According to Csikszentmihalyi's analysis, flow typically happens during someone's favorite activity—like cooking, playing music, talking to friends, driving, or gardening. His studies found that flow occurs surprisingly often while working. In contrast, passive leisure time activities (like watching television or internet cat videos) seldom result in flow. You need an activity that you actively engage in—where your actions have a clear and immediate impact on what happens.

2. Your skill set is well-matched to the challenge presented. Flow also tends to occur when we confront tasks that challenge our skills but don't defeat them. Really easy activities typically don't have the same appeal—we get bored and disengage/disconnect from what we're doing. But tasks that are too hard for us, or ones that require a skill set we simply don't have, also hinder flow. We can't find our groove in something we don't know how to engage with.

The best activities are ones that provide enough challenge to pique our interest but enough familiarity that we can actually do them without over-whelming anxiety and stress.

3. The activity is its own reward. The Greek word *autotelic* means something that is its own reward—an act you do simply because you like doing it, not because you're invested in its outcome. The value lies in the activity itself and not in the result.

The benefit of flow is the control you gain over your attention—rather like the benefit of meditation. You connect with yourself to the exclusion of other distractions. The more often we experience this immersive experience, the more satisfied we are with our lives, and the more connected we feel. Ideally, then, we should be finding ways of turning mundane events and actions into a series of autotelic moments throughout the day.

One of my most powerful experiences of flow came during an art lesson. I'd decided to challenge the story I'd grown up telling myself about how I couldn't draw and wasn't the artistic type. I enrolled in a weekly painting class to see if maybe I had that assumption wrong—like so many other beliefs and assumptions I had never bothered to test this until midlife. I was pleasantly surprised to learn that drawing and painting were skills that could be learned, and there were a substantial number of tricks, tips, and shortcuts that made me look like I knew what I was doing in a short amount of time. But what surprised me the most about the activity was how inexplicably enjoyable it was.

My relationship to time completely changed. I had no concept of it during class, and three hours seemed to go by in a snap. I would have gladly continued for another eight if I could have, each and every time. It was bliss for me to be able to focus on a singular task so totally and without distraction. I could get completely lost and absorbed in the activity. I looked forward to this experience more than anything in my week—not because I loved mushing colored oils

Emotional Self-Care

around on a canvas, but because I cherished that prolonged state of singular focus. I found it more relaxing than anything else I'd ever tried, in spite of the feelings of anxiety and self-consciousness that sometimes came along with it.

My fellow class participants all laughed and nodded in agreement. This sense of flow was the best part about creating art for them too. One student compared the experience to religious reverie. To me, it was the incredible feeling of connection I felt to myself, my surroundings, and to my life during a state of flow, and afterward.

Experiment with the activities you find interesting or engrossing, and set aside time to "lose yourself" in them. In a paradoxical way, the experience will actually help you find yourself . . . and reconnect.

Chapter 7

CREATING TIME AND SPACE TO CONNECT

*[A] life of integrity is the most fundamental source of personal worth. . . .
Peace of mind comes when your life is in harmony with true
principles and values and in no other way.*

STEPHEN COVEY[1]

S o far, we've talked about what self-connection is, why we need it, and how we can achieve it by tapping into our best physical, emotional, and principled selves. What we haven't talked much about yet is how to carve out the time and energy we need for living connected lives. Those wondering how on earth you're going to be able to make all these important changes in your habits, this section is for you.

PRIORITIES AND TIME MANAGEMENT

Once you have taken stock of your values and prioritized what is most important to you, you are ready to start aligning your life activities with those priorities. If you don't have a sense of the order of your priorities, there's no way you'll be able to properly allocate your time. You might spend most of your time on your third and fourth biggest priorities in life while giving short shrift to your first and second most coveted priorities. This was true for me.

Take a good hard look at how you spend your time. Not how you *think* you spend your time, but what you actually do each day.

Failure to really examine my time allocation stalled me on my own journey for years. I had done my work figuring out where I sourced meaning, and I had a good inventory of my values and priorities. I was more in tune with my own needs and truths, and overall I was feeling more connected and happier with my life. But I had hit a plateau because my behaviors were not aligned with my values. It seemed that there wasn't enough time in a day to handle my responsibilities *and* attend to my highest priorities. But then I realized my problem wasn't a lack of time; it was that I wasted so much time on things that were not my highest priorities. I had never fully audited my time nor completed an honest account of where the time went each day.

Dr. Rick Hanson taught me a valuable lesson in this area. Rick is a huge proponent of being fiercely intentional and scrutinizing how you spend your time for the sake of psychological well-being. He inspired me to track my time hourly for one week and then, at the end of the week, to analyze what I'd done and how much time I'd spent on each type of activity.

Before this exercise, I never paid much attention to time management "techniques" and chalked them up to being more relevant to corporate life, when you're looking to sell more widgets in less time for less cost. I never related time management as a factor in reaching my higher consciousness or helping me spiritually connect. I couldn't have been more wrong.

When I looked at the results of my week, I found that I had spent tons of time doing things that had never even made it into my awareness when I estimated my own time allocation. It turns out that after I factored out sleeping, eating, and grooming, the majority of my weekday time was spent on the following:

1. Driving (this was a shocker since I mostly work from home!)

2. Responding to random emails and texting

3. Conference calls

4. Personal and professional appointments

5. Grocery shopping

It was truly eye opening to realize that the majority of my time was spent doing things *that were not even on my priority list*, let alone something I thought had meaning. This wake-up call led me to brainstorm how I could reclaim this wasted time and take back my life.

Prioritizing for the Win

My first step was to prioritize my priorities each day. Prioritizing is an energy-consuming activity for the brain, so it's best to do it early in the day when your mind is fresh and the fuel tank is full. You don't want to squander your chance to drive somewhere important by using up too much gas driving around on stupid little errands. So, start with the big questions; the rest can follow.

Dr. David Rock compares the brain's processing ability to a toy helicopter: "Once Dad gets the helicopter off the ground a few times, it won't get off the ground again because the power is too low. It gets close, rising a few inches off, and then collapses back down. And the more you try, the less energy there is."[2]

Rock has concluded from research that just ten minutes of emailing will blow through the power you need to prioritize effectively. So make it easy on your brain—prioritize your day first thing in the morning, before the countless demands for your attention eat up your ability to get it done properly.

URGENT VS. IMPORTANT

In *The 7 Habits of Highly Effective People*, Stephen Covey broke our lives into four distinct quadrants: quadrant 1 (upper left corner) is the time we spend on urgent and important deadlines; quadrant 2 (upper right corner) is for nonurgent, but important, longer-term strategizing and development; quadrant 3 (bottom left corner) is for urgent distractions that aren't important but still need to get done ASAP; quadrant 4 (lower right corner) is for nonurgent, nonimportant activities—the things we commonly do during our breaks from urgent and important obligations.

If you are like most people, you probably spend most of your time in quadrants 1, 3, and 4. But nearly all the good stuff happens in quadrant 2. This is where self-care lives, alongside long-term goals such as writing a book, recreation, and play. Also in this category, we find elusive but desirable things like nurturing your relationships, journaling, spending time in nature, doing your sacred work, volunteering, and the like. You have to work both tactically and strategically on matters such as these. Quadrant 2 is where you want to spend your time—on the things that are not urgent, but are important.

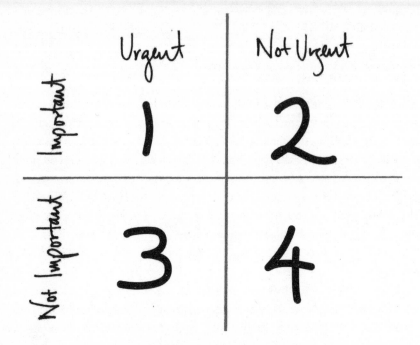

Stephen Covey's Four Quadrants

Of course, some things in the not-important category need to get done. But think about ways you might be able to minimize or delegate these and preserve your own precious time. Many items we think of as urgent, aren't—at least most of the time. Texts, voicemails, and emails don't typically need an immediate response—we just think they do.

Recent research shows that the busier we are, the more likely we are to address "urgent" things first, regardless of their importance.[3] We tend to choose tasks because they are urgent, rather than because of their actual payoff or value to us. As one journalist aptly described the findings, "time stops being a means to an end, and becomes the end itself."[4]

Don't let false urgency interrupt the truly important things you should be doing, like spending time with the kids without your devices, calling your family to chat, writing that book, planning for retirement. Block out time in your calendar for the truly important things, and honor that commitment by ignoring the countless interruptions and distractions the digital age affords us. There are many tools to make this easier, from the simple "do not disturb" function on cell phones to software that will block alerts (and even access to the internet) on your computer.

I like Covey's quadrant breakdown because it helps us see more clearly what we need to do. Delete things that aren't important and aren't urgent. Spend most of your time doing things that are important, but not urgent. Question whether something that is unimportant to you deserves priority, just because it is someone else's urgent request.

Before my personal time audit, I rarely visited quadrant 2 and felt the daily anguish of neglecting so many important needs. Now, it's shocking to see that I really am able to spend the majority of my time in quadrant 2, and yet it feels like there is plenty of time to do everything. I'm not rushed or stressed, and the way that I spend my time nourishes my soul and makes me glad. Time management is fundamental to living an awake, aware, and connected life. For me, it's the true definition of contentedness.

TECHNIQUES TO HELP

As we discussed, it is essential to parse (with ruthless honesty) which of your day-to-day activities feel important and related to a source of meaning and which do not. Once you've gotten the knack for mindful awareness and non-judgmental observing, you can start to overhaul your daily activities, moving toward meaningful ones and feelings of connection, and away from meaning-less activities that cause you to feel disconnected.

Taking Stock of How You Spend Your Time

Take an inventory: How are you spending your time each day? Notice what you're doing, for how long, and how meaningful those activities feel to you. Total up how much time you typically spend on the list of priorities and values that represent your inner truths, and then take stock of the big picture. Odds are, it isn't pretty.

Fortunately, there is a simple plan of attack to bring things into better alignment:

1. Cut out all the meaningless activities you can.

2. Create meaning for the activities that seem meaningless but cannot be avoided.

3. Do more of the activities you find meaningful.

You will be amazed at how many things you do or participate in each day are completely meaningless to you. Some of these, like watching TV, can be easily cut out of your schedule without any repercussions. Others—like commuting to work or doing laundry—can't. You'll need to decide whether to delete, delegate, or reframe your view of these meaningless gestures. This is the fun part—the time to get creative.

A lot of people struggle to admit that they find certain activities unrewarding. I've always felt uncomfortable chatting with mothers at my kids' elementary school during pickup and drop-off, for example, but I ignored my feelings and consistently pushed myself to keep it up each day because I believed I shouldn't have been feeling that way.

But after noticing that these chats consistently made me feel a physical unease, I decided to let myself off the hook from what I had considered obligatory chitchats. I gave myself a little pep talk about it, saying, "It's okay that it's not feeling comfortable and natural to be social. It's a mystery why this kind of socializing is unsettling for me, but that doesn't have to mean I'm a failure in any way." I tried not to blame myself or the other mothers for my feelings, and I just let it go and stopped trying to chat during those times.

To my surprise, it was a huge relief in my week to delete nearly ten instances of disconnection from my routine. The relief came immediately, but the insights and the self-awareness came down the road. Ultimately, I realized that my conscious attempts to connect with other mothers were ironically leading me to feel disconnected from them and from myself each day. I also realized that I don't enjoy time-pressured, idle chitchat. By pulling away from those situations, I became much more connected to myself because I honored my own needs and had renewed energy to discover alternative social outlets that were more in line with my true nature. I sought out less time-pressured activities like going on a hike or working at the book fair together. My relationship with the other school moms improved, and my levels of connection and meaning did too.

One of my clients, "Ed," felt that commuting to and from work was a completely meaningless activity that left him feeling either totally tuned out or in a perpetual state of agitation. He'd thought about taking public transportation before but calculated that it would be more hassle and time than it was worth; plus, he enjoyed the plush comfort of his car. When I asked him to reconsider this through the lens of prioritizing meaning and connection above all else, he agreed to experiment with getting to work in different ways.

At first Ed experimented with a carpool option, which was stimulating for him and brought a surprising amount of random interaction with strangers.

He agreed that this alternative was much more engaging and led him to feel more connected to the ride. But ultimately, the irregularity and lack of synchronicity in schedules and drop-off locations were too inconvenient. Ed was tempted to go back to old habits, but I urged him to keep questing in his search for what would be more meaningful.

He eventually discovered, to his surprise, that taking the ferry was a far more meaningful and connecting experience for him. Ed deeply enjoyed seeing the sunrise and sunset each day and described moments of deep exhilaration and even transcendence, observing the sparkles on the water and the wildlife sightings. While it was a three-part journey of taking a bus to the ferry and then a healthy walk to the office, he admitted that it was all worth it and that he even noticed feeling more fulfilled by the incidental human contact and conversation that spontaneously occurred on the bus or the boat. Ed's now a committed ferry commuter and looks forward to that part of his day. He even takes it one step further, listening to audiobooks on the days that he is required to bring his car to work because they hold him rapt. Now he eagerly looks forward to the journey, regardless of which transport he's using. By being willing to prioritize meaning and connection on his route to work, Ed discovered the wealth of options available to him.

You should notice results within days, a week at most, once you start actively scrutinizing and adjusting your activities—adding more of what naturally connects for you and deleting or minimizing what causes you to struggle or disconnect.

The Power of Intervention

Often the path to greater meaning and connection is as simple as avoiding the things that are not working for you, but obviously there are some things in life we simply can't avoid or replace. The real magic happens here, as you learn to apply what psychologists love to refer to as an "intervention" any time you notice yourself feeling disconnected.

Here's how it works: when you notice moments of disconnection (anytime you are not quite in your body or fully present to the moment or person in front of you), take a moment to survey your options and ask yourself, "Is there anything I can do differently to make this a more connected experience for myself?"

Sometimes the intervention you can apply is just inside your own mind, like taking a different mental approach, and other times it's actually changing your actions. You will be amazed at how intuitively you will be able to course correct and direct a disconnected moment into a more connected one.

We interviewed one research participant, "Linda," who told us that she noticed she had judgmental thoughts about her neighbors during her morning walk, which fueled her feelings of disconnection from her neighborhood and made her wish she could move. For the sake of experimentation, she agreed to the idea of stopping herself in her tracks and replacing the negative, disconnecting thoughts with completely opposite, loving thoughts.

Linda reported it felt contrived and awkward at first, but the trick did work. She felt warmer, more open, and connected to her neighbors and to herself. She also gained the self-awareness that those thoughts were just made-up stories that were mere habit and had nothing to do with reality, even though they had been causing her to feel painful disconnection for years.

In one of my own discoveries, I noticed that I often felt subtly disconnected while making dinner for my family. I approached it like a chore, never really tuning in to what I was cooking, and more or less tried to get through it as quickly as possible. When I asked myself how I could make this a more connected experience, the idea occurred to me that I could try to pick a recipe that was more exciting or one that maybe even drew the family into the equation.

My enthusiasm was immediately contagious in the household. We ended up making homemade pizza that night, and my boys got really involved with choosing their own toppings, rolling the dough, and watching it bake. This led to a Wednesday pizza night in our house, where my youngest is in charge of picking the menu, and we go shopping for groceries and cook together.

It was amazing to me how the simple act of noticing and arresting one small moment of disconnection within myself could lead to creating a much larger opportunity for deep connectedness throughout the entire family. Now dinnertime is something I look forward to with my family and a go-to way for us to reliably connect, when I remember to set the intention to do it.

You might notice that it requires more effort at first to enact your "intervention." Certainly, coming up with an exciting recipe and making a special trip to the store all required more energy than my usual short-shrift efforts. But that small investment of effort up front really paid off and ironically led to feeling a greater abundance of energy and time. I used to drag myself through the cooking process, feeling like it was always a drain on my time and energy to plan, grocery shop, cook, and clean up. But bringing mindful awareness and the intention to be more connected to the process has turned this chore into a labor of love.

My good friend and mentor, Philip McKernan, is fond of saying that it's really never about time and never about money. And I do think that's true.

When we are deeply connected to what we are doing, abundance is ours: the time, energy, motivation, money, and the *how* all show up. Joy, fulfillment, and tranquility are the welcome by-products of doing what brings us meaning.

Time Chunking

The second technique for reclaiming your time is called *chunking*: setting aside larger blocks of time for a single activity and protecting them from intrusion by other activities, like meetings or appointments.

For example, I started corralling all of my in-person appointments to Thursday (mornings, ideally) instead of scattering them throughout my week, which required tons of driving time and broke up my days. Everything from meeting with my accountant, web designer, writing partner, office manager, hairstylist, doctor, school teachers, and the kids' dentist got rescheduled to Thursday. It took some discipline since I would usually have to settle for an appointment further out in the future in order to get it on my desired day, but I was pleasantly surprised to discover that almost everything in life can be scheduled on a Thursday. This alone cut my low-priority driving time by over 50 percent.

But I also needed to find a way to purge from my schedule the countless weekly trips to the grocery store. Getting more organized about what I needed on a regular basis helped me realize I could chunk this too and get supplies twice a week—and have them delivered by the grocery store at regularly scheduled times (*outside* my chunked time for work, family, and self-care). Now I rarely have to head to the store in person, and when my kids come home from school, I can truly be with them because everything else is done.

Ritualize the Tough Stuff

Mustering up willpower is tough. Performing rituals, on the other hand, requires almost no willpower—once they're ingrained as a habit. David Rock, the brain performance specialist, suggests using the power of routine to conserve mental energy and overcome your biggest stumbling blocks. Because routines are stored, recognized, and executed by the basal ganglia part of our brains, rather than our energy-hungry prefrontal cortex, they require far less energy to remember or to do. They can operate in the background without needing conscious input from you.[5] I decided to use this wisdom to ritualize the things on my priority list that were hardest to motivate myself to do.

In the spirit of first things first, I created a new morning ritual for myself that enshrines certain priorities as inviolate: as soon as I wake up, I meditate for a few minutes, drink a huge glass of water, take my supplements, make a healthy breakfast for me and the family, and either walk the kids to school or hop on the treadmill. All of this happens before it's time for me to punch the clock and start writing at 9:00 a.m.

This routine has replaced our usual haphazard mornings, and each day I'm nourished by the feeling of starting out on the right foot. I also learned through this process that mornings are my most productive time for writing, so I committed to four hours of writing each morning—with email and phone turned off. My friends and family now know this is my routine and don't even try to get hold of me during my writing hours. Committing to this kind of ritual has led to an explosion in my productivity. My constant battle with procrastination is gone, and I am immediately productive the minute I sit down.

Paired Activities

The third strategy I like to use to reduce spending time in meaningless ways is pairing: combining complementary activities that are less meaningful to maximize their value, or matching a chore with a fun activity to make the time enjoyable as well as productive.

Although I told myself it was a priority in life, exercise almost never happened because I always ran out of time. But then I decided to pair exercising with emailing—two things I don't love but that, when done together, make the experience more meaningful. I "built" a makeshift desk on my treadmill by putting a piece of wood over the handrails, and my new rule is that if I'm at home, I'm only allowed to check email if I'm walking on the treadmill, even if it's at a snail's pace.

As someone who has successfully undermined and defeated every exercise initiative that's come down the pike, I'm amazed to say, three years in, that this strategy has actually worked. I now walk every day—sometimes a lot, sometimes a little—and occasionally I even turn it into a run. The point is, I found a way to ritualize it into my everyday experience by pairing it with another activity.

Looking at other pair-able activities, I started taking Uber for longer drives so that I could bring my laptop, be hands-free, and get through my phone calls and emails simultaneously. For a small cost, my time in the car is now incredibly productive. I also schedule my calls for when I will be on the road, so that the calls are less intrusive to the day. Podcasts or audiobooks are also great partners for otherwise boring or unpleasant activities, since they are hands-free and offer countless options to engage and absorb us.

Think about the activities in *your* day that feel meaningless, and see if there is a way to make them more palatable through pairing, either with something more fun or with another chore that makes the time spent doing it more productive. With a bit of creativity, this technique can help you make major strides toward living in alignment with your values.

SIMPLIFY TO CONNECT

It's incredible how complex our lives have become in this modern age, in ways we often don't even notice. Yet so many of our greatest thinkers—people like Confucius, Einstein, Henry David Thoreau, and Benjamin Franklin—have praised the importance, virtue, and joy of simplicity. This advice is truer now than ever before.

With the advance of technology, the internet, and cell phones, our lives are moving at a breakneck pace. We juggle, we multitask, we work long hours and spend increasing time commuting, forever bowing to the demands on our attention. In 1960, Americans spent about 7.4 hours a day taking in information. In 2008, we spent 11.8 hours each day and processed 33 gigabytes of information in our nonworking time alone.[6] By 2012, we were averaging 13.6 hours and 63 gigabytes of media consumption every day.[7] And yet the brain's processing speed maxes out at a lowly 120 bits (not bytes) per second. That's barely enough to understand two people talking to us at once.[8]

We complicate our lives at our own expense. We can no longer hear ourselves think. We lose touch with our true wants and needs. We lack clarity.

Complexity is having too many things in our lives. Specifically, it's about having too many thoughts, considerations, responsibilities, tasks, things, possessions, properties, to-dos, choices, and so forth. Numerous studies have confirmed the huge psychological costs to complexity.[9] We so often think that accumulating more and more things (e.g., vacations, experiences, houses) and taking on optional tasks in life, such as volunteering for the school auction or agreeing to help organize the next partner outing at work, is what helps us live a bigger and broader life. What we don't realize is that dividing our attention in too many directions, across too many areas, actually blocks connection. It prevents us from truly living and being able to savor the things that we care about the most.

Consider the totality of your life with brutal honesty. How complicated does your life feel to you?

I once participated in a group where we were asked to draw all of the important areas of our lives and responsibilities on a big poster board along with things that consume our time and attention. I was shocked to see how crowded and chaotic our poster boards looked. Person after person got up to share what they had drawn on their posters, and many welled up with tears as they looked at the portraits of their hugely complex lives. A picture is definitely worth a thousand words when analyzing complexity.

Letting Go of the Scarcity Myth

Ultimately, simplicity is about letting go. Clinging and hanging on are habits born of fear and what's called the *scarcity mentality*—the belief that there is not enough money, time, stuff, friends, love, and so on in the world to meet everyone's needs and that we therefore need to stockpile everything we can to ensure our own needs will be met.

Lynne Twist, author of *The Soul of Money*, theorizes that we often strive to get more than we need because we fear there is not enough. Once we let go of that scarcity outlook, we discover the abundance of sufficiency: "a knowing that there is enough, and that we are enough."[10]

"When you let go of trying to get more of what you don't really need, which is what we're all trying to get more of," says Twist, "it frees up immense energy to make a difference with what you have. When you make a difference with what you have, it expands."[11] The freeing up of this energy is what allows us to gain perspective, often enabling spontaneous connection to occur. When we reduce the sheer volume of things we are required to consider, we are better able to savor and cherish the true abundance that already exists—and take another step closer to authentic connection to our lives.

In his book *The Logic of Sufficiency*, Dr. Thomas Princen makes the case that contenting ourselves with enough when more is possible is both intuitive, rational, and ethical. Sufficiency isn't about denial, sacrifice, or doing without; rather, it's based on the simple truth that goods are only good for us up to a point. He notes that before nineteenth-century industrialists standardized working times, people intuitively knew this and lived their lives according to their natural rhythms. Workers would show up at a factory gate when they felt like working. They'd work until they had earned what they needed, and then they'd leave and do whatever else they wanted to do—fishing, playing with their children, going to town.

In this natural state, says Princen, "The owners could pay the workers more and, yes, they might work more . . . [b]ut at some point, no matter how high the wage, workers would offer *less* work; the supply curve bends backward."[12] Yet the modern business world assumes that more wages will inspire more work, more work will cause more productivity, and more productivity will cause more profits, without any natural breaking point. This infinite expansion theory ignores the fact that we live in a finite world, with finite natural resources, and finite human capabilities. There are many compelling logical, ethical, and ecological reasons why more is not always better. As one of my favorite all-time truisms goes, "The enemy of good is better."

The law of diminishing returns applies when we seek, acquire, collect, pay attention to, and hold onto more than is necessary. In the extreme, it can be wasteful, gluttonous, and burdensome. But even at more moderate levels, having more than we need in any category overcomplicates our lives and interferes with how we connect to our true priorities.

Excess in any capacity of our lives requires more bandwidth and more attention management, and it often translates to a subtle unease and chronic sense of inadequacy because of the myriad of things we are forgetting about, unable to attend to, or ignoring. It's one thing to learn the art of "good enough" and making peace with things that remain undone, but I'm talking about tossing out entire categories of things from your life. That's truly simplifying. Ask yourself: What types of things am I doing that I really *don't* need to be doing to feel that I'm living according to my personal values? Which activities are valuable to you personally, and which are just taking up space in your calendar?

Joshua Becker's book, *The More of Less*, defines minimalism as "the intentional promotion of the things we most value and the removal of anything that distracts us from them."[13] He argues that "de-owning" and decluttering help clarify our purpose and values and unburden our lives of the things that prevent us from living our values.[14] Becker's gorgeous website, becomingminimalist.com, will inspire and empower you to reorient the way you look at the patterns of behavior in your life.

My family and I moved to Bali for a year as a way to escape the rut of our daily living and to share a totally different life experience. It was nothing short of transformative. But the most positive aspect, by far, was the way it forced us to live a radically simplified life. Each of us brought just one large suitcase, with the clothes and belongings we'd deemed absolutely necessary. We were all so afraid of not having enough "stuff" for the year ahead, but after just a few weeks, every one of us felt that we had brought too much. Island life was about rising and going to sleep with the sun, seeing friends every day, living in your bathing suit, and reading lots of books. We were in an environment where things like makeup, hair products, and personal maintenance were pointless, and the type of clothing we wore was irrelevant. Bali life was about owning only what you needed and used. Nothing more.

The unburdening that came from this simplified lifestyle is difficult to put into words. I felt the happiest I'd ever felt in my life. It was amazing to watch my kids stop asking to buy things, stop caring about gifts during holidays and birthdays, and essentially shed their compulsions to be little consumers. They discovered they were actually more content when they had less stuff, and it was wonderful to witness. My kids also experienced the real me, the most relaxed and fun-loving mother they'd ever known—available for lengthy tuck-in conversations, marathon board games, or a dip in the ocean—because I wasn't consumed by endless to-dos relating to managing our stuff and our home. Living only with what we truly needed made connection of all kinds easy and inevitable.

Trusting that we are enough and that we have enough inspires us to let go more easily, freeing up the space to connect with what we truly need, want, and cherish.

Common Culprits for Needless Complexity

In my group workshops, simplicity is one of the first areas we focus on. I've noticed over time that complication tends to flourish in the same or similar areas for most people. These top ten areas, in no particular order, are:

1. *Real estate.* Do you have too much of it? More properties equal more hassle and degrees of complexity in your head, regardless of how you rationalize it.

2. *Multiple ventures.* Simultaneously pursuing multiple professional "ventures" and streams of income, versus doing one thing that you love and can devote all of your time and attention to, can stunt your ability to connect and grow in important ways.

3. *Overscheduling.* So many of us overcommit ourselves and our kids due to FOMO (fear of missing out).

4. *Yes.* It's common to say yes out of obligation or guilt when we should be saying no.

5. *Unrealistic expectations.* We need to get real about what is reasonable to take on or accomplish in a day, a month, and a year.

6. *Relationships.* Often we find ourselves spending an enormous amount of time and energy in relationships that no longer serve us.

7. *Too much stuff.* Here I'm referring to hoarding and collecting things that aren't beloved hobbies and that require time and energy and actual physical space (old clothes that don't fit, books you don't look at, art, wine, or automobiles, etc.).

8. *Ego.* Your ego may push you to accumulate, achieve, and acquire more and more. But in the chase for fool's gold, you may sacrifice the real gold in your life.

9. *Screen time.* An undisciplined relationship with technology allows our devices to fill up every spare nook and cranny of our lives. We are thoughtlessly carried away, surfing the web and engaging with social media, wasting our mental power (and time) on things that don't ultimately matter.

10. *General clutter.* There are likely things that occupy space in your home but that you no longer look at or consciously enjoy. Newspapers, magazines, or decorative things can quickly become clutter.

A life complicated by excess is a life not lived to its full potential. Attention, energy, time, and money that could be spent pursuing your most valued hopes and dreams are instead wasted on minutiae that—when we're honest with ourselves—don't contribute meaningfully to our lives or the legacy we most want to leave.

Once you are attuned to the dangers of a complicated life, you will start to spot needless complexity everywhere in your environment. Even seemingly innocent activities like a family vacation will be up for scrutiny. You will find yourself asking questions like, How do I imagine I will feel before, during, and after this vacation? Will it add ease to my life, or will it be a huge ordeal, disruption, needless expense, and require a big recovery after the fact? It's enormously empowering, and deeply connecting, to bring healthy skepticism to each potentially complex aspect of your life.

As I became more aware of the complexities in my own life, I launched a radical simplification experiment. I had already minimized things in my schedule that felt meaningless to me and used time chunking to make myself more efficient, but I began scouring my calendar more rigorously—challenging myself about what still might be an unnecessary drain on my time. Suddenly, it became clear to me that entire categories of time-sucking activities (such as managing home maintenance, participating in certain clubs and organizations) could be completely delegated, or deleted entirely, so that I could spend my time on activities that promoted connection to myself and my loved ones.

I began to make even larger decisions to delete and de-own aspects of my life that were taking a toll, such as asking my kids to play only two sports a year instead of three, selling my car, selling our family vacation property, and letting go of all the to-dos related to them all. Talk about an empowering exercise! It's amazing to look at your calendar through the lens of protecting your time and sanity. You'll find new ways of creating space, giving yourself adequate transition time, and ensuring you don't have too many movements in a day or too many things on your plate.

In the end, I was able to clear a massive amount from my calendar, but more importantly, I learned to be more discerning about which activities were important and life-enhancing and which ones would be life-draining. It also showed me how to be *much* more realistic in terms of what I could accomplish in one day for myself and for my family. I learned to put a value on myself and my sanity, which was a new, more self-connected way of thinking.

The greatest opportunity to simplify our lives is actually at the macro level. As I questioned and evaluated everything in my life in terms of complexity, I came to understand that large commitments like my home, automobiles, volunteering at school, certain friends, and, ultimately, even my work, were no longer serving me. A thousand little activities across these areas added up to a heavy burden of complications and complexity.

It's tempting to believe that a bigger house will make us happier, but having finally gotten a bigger house with room to spread out, I realized that it was creating huge burdens on me to clean it, to keep up with the maintenance, and to fill it with stuff. I also had the psychological burden that comes along with having all of that stuff—the responsibility for keeping it clean, safe, in working order, tidily put away, and worthwhile. Justifying its presence and expense complicated my life immensely. It soon became clear that, for me, living in a much smaller space would decrease my mental load and daily burden. So I moved to a place with one-third the square footage and felt an immediate wave of relief at the amount of stuff I had gotten rid of. Downsizing inspired me to get rid of my car and shifted us into being a one-vehicle family. I haven't looked back.

There is great beauty in living our lives more simply. When we cut out the nonessentials, the people and things that remain in our lives are those we truly care about and cherish—no more and no less. It's the old quality-over-quantity concept. Quality—and the deeper connection that simplicity enables—wins every time.

ELECTRONICS AND TECHNOLOGY

Simplicity, sadly, is often easier said than done in the modern world of smartphones, smart homes, and nonstop information sharing. Whether it's the twenty-four-hour news headlines, continual Facebook updates from friends and strangers, gaming, or the never-ending stream of tantalizing emails pouring into our inbox, technology is captivating to our brains. The release of dopamine when we get "likes" or search results or advance to the next level of a game is part of the reward system of the brain. The vastness of the internet and the options for electronic games—many specifically designed to be addictive in this way—make the feel-good hits easily available and essentially limitless, keeping us coming back for more and more and more.

Much has been written about internet and gaming addiction, and there is even a new dubious mental disorder called "internet addiction disorder" that's being diagnosed by some practitioners (though this "disorder" does not appear in the current *DSM-5*). While the validity and reliability of many diagnostic labels (including some in the *DSM-5*) are suspect, the fact that this issue has risen to such attention shows that there is a growing problem out there. For some people, this addiction feels very real, even life destroying. The sooner you acknowledge that technology can be, and often is, specifically designed to be addictive, the better you are able to guard against giving yourself over to that medium when it's incongruent with your values and your true wishes.

One of the great ironies of modern technology is that we are often the most disconnected from ourselves, our true priorities, and our environment when we are digitally "connected." Doctors Shoba Sreenivasan and Linda E. Weinberger put it beautifully: "While the digital age imbues our life with instantaneous and wide-ranging connectivity, it also creates pseudoconnectivity, where 'friends' may number in the 'thousands'; yet, there may not be a single living, breathing person with whom there is a true emotional connection."[15] In fact, almost 25 percent of Americans said that they didn't have a single person to discuss important matters with; compare this to 1985, when that number was just 10 percent.[16] Our relationship to electronics and screens has become one of the biggest, if not *the* biggest, relationship most people have in their lives.

In one of Connection Lab's research studies, we interviewed individuals who were considered highly self-connected by others and asked what their behaviors looked like when they felt connected, versus disconnected, from themselves. The vast majority of participants noted that when they were connected, they were disengaged from their addictions and spent time on higher, more purposeful pursuits. For some people, that meant healthy habits like avoiding drinking or smoking, but for others it meant having a more disciplined relationship with their devices—disconnecting from technology as much as possible and choosing to spend more time in nature instead. As one participant put it, "To be connected to ourselves we have to make the effort to separate ourselves from all the distractions."[17]

Digital communication seduces us to disconnect from ourselves, our present moment, and the people around us more completely than anything else. Nielsen Corporation reported that in 2020, adult Americans spent on average almost twelve and a half hours each day engaging with media through televisions, smartphones, tablets, gaming systems, radio, and the internet.[18] That's more time than most people spend on any other single activity, including work, interacting with others, or even sleep. It's a staggering amount of time.

If you're like most people, you couldn't say exactly how much time you spend interacting with your electronics. Likely, it's much more than you think. In one of my workshops, participants calculate hour by hour how they spend their time in a given week. The two areas they always drastically underestimate are (1) time in the car and (2) time engaging with technology.

We tend to think that time spent texting or responding to emails doesn't really count as a day's activity or is much faster than it really is. We tell ourselves, *I'll just quickly respond to a few emails, and it will only take a second . . . .* Forty-five minutes later, we wonder where the time has gone.

The truth is, most of us are not in the driver's seat when it comes to our relationship with technology. Media report an uptick in screen addiction and the deleterious side effects of too much technology, but no one is telling us how to cultivate a healthy relationship with technology. Technology is here to stay, and barring some kind of apocalyptic destruction of the world, it's going to be a permanent part of our lives. So, we've got to figure out how to live with it without losing ourselves.

The Big Picture

Start by accurately calculating how much time you spend on screens each day. You can't properly evaluate the situation without accurate data—as the saying goes, garbage in, garbage out. You need to log your screen time throughout the day.

While it may feel tedious to jot down every time you watch TV, open your laptop, or unlock your phone, the information you will have after just a day or two of tracking is well worth it. Once you've calculated the total number of daily screen hours, step back and ask yourself:

- Am I okay with this?
- Is this consistent with my priorities?
- Is this how I truly want to live my life?

If you are okay with the amount of time—and the proportion of your life that this represents—that's great. Many jobs these days require employees to interact constantly on their computer screens or smartphones, and there is no right or wrong about that. But the real problem occurs when people pile on more screen time during their evenings and weekends, without it ever really feeling like a conscious choice. This is how we disconnect from ourselves—when our choices stop being conscious.

There has also been a slow migration of many previously non-tech-dependent professions toward computer dependency. A photographer friend lamented that he chose a life of photography in order to be engaged with the real world, only to discover that the vast majority of his time is now spent in front of a computer, editing and organizing digital photos. This is true for doctors, marine biologists, artists, designers, architects, and many others who chose their careers ten, twenty, or thirty years ago, never knowing how much time they would eventually spend staring at the computer.

Take a step back and ask yourself whether this is the life you imagined for yourself. Is it one you're truly content to continue living?

My photographer friend answered no and decided to step away from digital photography. He went back to using real black-and-white film in order to spend his days in the dark room, working with his hands, which he loves. Are there options for you to reduce your screen time at work? If you're unhappy with the way your work has evolved, spend some time thinking about alternatives that tap into what you loved about your career in the first place.

High-Quality and Low-Quality Interaction

Even if you're not up for a total overhaul, there is a lot you can do to improve your relationship with technology. First, and most important, become more intentional and aware of it. Learn to tell the difference between high-quality digital interactions and low-quality ones. We do this by cultivating mindful awareness of the quality of our mood and physical state while we're engaging with our devices. Bring a curious attention and do a body scan to help identify the subtle feeling states that accompany different types of screen engagement. You'll quickly start to recognize the distinction.

I have discovered that when I am writing, I feel extremely connected to myself and my technology usage. I'm focused, feel on-task and often exhilarated, and I am able to be simultaneously aware of myself, my needs, and my surroundings. Even though I lose time significantly as I get into flow states, when I "come to," I am refreshed and fulfilled by the encounter. By contrast, I've noticed that unintentional (or too much) time spent on social media or aimlessly surfing the web easily pulls me into a disconnected state where I am no longer aware of my needs (such as noticing how tired or hungry I am). I feel slightly anxious or in an unpleasant mood, almost as though I am under a hypnotic spell. I regret the time spent in this way as soon as I awaken from the trance and realize I've lost an hour or more that could have been spent with family, a good book, or something else more aligned with my priorities.

Low-quality technological interactions can rob us of some of the most precious aspects of life. The slippery slope of social media feeds, YouTube videos, and overflowing inboxes can add up to a staggering amount of time spent mindlessly on devices instead of on our true priorities. These interactions deprive us of natural daydreaming and time to check in with ourselves. We tend to reach for a device the moment we hit a sliver of downtime. This is how we slip away from our true selves: we fill every spare second looking at our phones instead of looking inside—or outside, at the real world around us.

A 2014 study found that spending time on Facebook, the world's most popular online social network, negatively impacted mood.[19] The more time was spent on it, the worse the impact—apparently because the users felt that they had just spent all that time on something that wasn't meaningful.

Even just a small amount of self-observation makes it easy to see the price you pay for low-quality screen engagement. A mother in one of my parenting groups observed that although she was patting herself on the back for making it home in time from work to be with her children after school each day, she was actually frittering away that time by constantly checking her devices or responding to emails—which made her just as unavailable and disconnected from her kids as if she were still physically at work. Her solution was to start taking public transportation to and from her job, so she could honor both her need to blast through emails at the beginning and end of day and her need to put her devices away from 5:00 to 8:00 p.m. so she could be more present and available for human connection. This strategy worked well for her, and she discovered she rarely felt like she was missing any important electronic communication during the 5:00 to 8:00 p.m. window of true human connection.

Low-quality interactions with technology are, sadly, a given and part of our daily lives. While it would be great to transform all of our interactions into high-quality versions, that isn't realistic given the mundane realities of modern life. The best we can do is learn to harness these interactions and bring an intentionality to them—controlling when they happen, rather than having them happen haphazardly all day long.

I had become a slave to responding to emails at all times throughout the day, from the moment I woke up until right before falling asleep—sometimes even waking up with my phone still in the bed. I joked that my business card should say "email responder" rather than "writer." For me, responding to emails feels like low-quality time and not how I wanted to be spending my days. It was also no surprise that, during this phase, I had difficulties with procrastination and feeling chronically unsettled about the progress of my writing. I finally realized I was letting other people's email and text requests rule my day, causing me to continually defer and postpone my own priorities. So I developed several strategies to get out from under the constant barrage of emails while still keeping up with my work.

First, I decided that checking emails the moment I opened my eyes was not the ideal way to start the day and instead adopted a morning meditation practice to ensure I was able to get centered and feel a sense of connection to myself before my mind was off to the races in email land. Next, I decided I only wanted to spend around two hours a day on emails and that scheduling that time would be the most effective approach. I permitted myself one hour to respond to emails in the morning and one in the afternoon, and I stuck to the schedule. Knowing I only had an hour inspired me to work fast, work smart, and delegate wherever possible. In between email hours, I used simple tools, like the "do not disturb" feature on my laptop, to avoid seeing incoming calls, emails, or texts until I was ready to respond to them.

I also told my friends and colleagues that I would be writing from 9:00 a.m. to 1:00 p.m. each day and not to contact me during that time—which made a big difference. I requested that certain people, like my research partners, speak with me in person or over the phone instead of sending lengthy emails, and I made a conscious effort to reduce the number of emails I would receive on a given day—unsubscribing from old mailing lists, solicitations, and anything else that didn't feel relevant.

My research partners and I also agreed to stop maniacally checking our smartphones before and after a meeting or even during a bathroom break as we were in the habit of doing. Instead, we would take a moment to breathe, reflect on all that had just happened, look outside the window to take in the view, or make eye contact with and smile at others in our coworking space. We found that we were much more refreshed with this practice, no less productive, and never missed anything urgent. Rather, we felt more connected to ourselves for reclaiming that time instead of automatically sacrificing it to our devices.

Take stock of which technological interactions in your life are truly high quality and which are just wasting time you'd rather be spending on your priorities. Technology and electronics can be enormous forces for good, but also tremendously powerful forces for disconnection. Be aware of how they're impacting you and make the changes necessary for the life you want to lead.

Numbing vs. Active Engagement

We all, at times, use technology to zone out, decompress, or avoid our feelings. Zoning out and decompressing are reasonable by-products of screen time if you are intentional about it and if that is truly the desired outcome. Numbing can be problematic though.

When we are engaged in numbing behaviors, we are disconnected from ourselves emotionally, unaware and unable to feel our real feelings, and unable to see how our actions may be out of alignment with our deepest needs. Screens of some form are the numbing weapon of choice these days for most people. You might be mindlessly watching TV you don't really care about, surfing the web, or losing hours to social media. If you are using screens to avoid dealing with something, chances are you are numbing. Note the quality of attention and awareness you are bringing to the activity to determine whether it's a numbing strategy.

Mindlessly binge-watching Netflix can leave you feeling hungover, but a consciously savored and intentionally enjoyed show might leave you feeling connected and fulfilled by the encounter. The difference is the intention and awareness you bring to the encounter.

Scarcity and Fear Push Us Toward Our Devices

The constant contact that technology allows us to have with each other creates a false sense of urgency around even the most mundane communications. It also breeds a sense of fear and scarcity: fear that we are not responding fast enough, making someone wait too long, missing something important, fear of missing out, fear of looking like we have nothing to do, fear of being alone or bored, fear that there is not enough time to get it all done, or fear that we must constantly bat away emails, lest we drown in them.

When you are able to step away from technology, you can reclaim your power of personal choice. Reassure yourself that there is plenty of time for the things that truly matter, that both things and people can wait, and that things will get done. In short, return to a mindset of abundance and faith. I laugh now, noticing that the more I stay away from email, particularly group email chains, the more things seem to get resolved nicely without ever requiring my involvement.

Setting Healthy Boundaries

One of the most effective ways to deal with the fear of unplugging for longer periods is to manage people's expectations. I admire and respect people who let me know that they return calls at the end of the day, for example. If you let others know when you are usually plugged in or how long it usually takes you to reply, it can reduce the feeling that you are at everyone's beck and call—and ensure that the other person knows you are on top of things.

Many of us feel compelled to constantly check our phones because we're afraid we'll get in trouble if we miss responding immediately. It's a real challenge to let go of that and believe that you're not going to suffer professionally. While it's true that being immediately responsive is an important part of the job and nonnegotiable for some professions, I find that most people exaggerate this perceived obligation and its repercussions. While I like immediate responses from others just as much as the next person, I find I actually respect and admire people *more* who have the strength of character to set boundaries, be realistic, and let me know that it may take them some time to respond. That kind of statement suggests healthy self-worth, integrity, good judgment, and discernment. It also suggests an even higher quality of work when a busy professional refuses to entertain interruptions during her deep work on a project.

If you are willing to adjust for the technological communication styles and habits of others, you should expect others to be flexible for you. It often comes down to the question of who is training whom. Are you training others around how and when you will be plugged in, or are they training you?

Ask yourself also whether your tendency to respond to everything immediately might be fueled by a compulsive relationship with your technology, rather than an actual urgency. Setting boundaries with yourself to restrain compulsive email checking, email surfing, text responding, or channel switching on the TV is equally important. Compulsive behaviors are born from anxiety and breed even more of it. They feed on themselves and grow stronger over time. When you're operating from that place, notice how you are slightly on edge, how you feel tightly wound, and how your breathing is shallow. Next time you feel that powerful urge to check and reply, take a deep breath instead, and ask yourself: Is this really what I want to devote my attention to right now, or am I better served by sticking with my current train of thought? Resisting the urge in this way helps build mental muscle and helps you realize what a powerful force that "urge" really is.

Our complicated relationship to technology represents one of the largest areas of opportunity for most people to reconnect with their intentions and reclaim a domain that so often causes them to disconnect. Having a positive connection with technology is simply being clear about your why, how, and when of engagement and catching yourself when you get off track. For the average person in modern society, technology is a steadily rising tide that can flood the environment at any moment, without mindful awareness and intentional use. The addictive quality of technology requires us to frequently check in, reappraise, and course correct where needed to tame the beast and use technology for its intended purpose: bettering life, not owning it.

SLOWING DOWN TO CONNECT

Some of the greatest lessons in life are paradoxical in nature. Authentic connection as it relates to the notion of time is certainly one of them. We are compelled to believe that the more we do, the faster we run, or the more balls we juggle simultaneously, the more we accomplish, the more we achieve, and the more we really *live*. It's as if we are trying to get the most out of this life and then some; as if, by running as fast as we can, we might stuff the equivalent of 1.5 or 2 lives' worth into one. This is our desperate attempt to defeat mortality and stave off the looming fear that we are wasting this precious life.

One of our research participants described his own experience in this regard:

> When I'm disconnected . . . I feel way more confused . . . and my response to that confusion is to speed up. . . . Like for me, it's that I'm not connected to my wisdom, I feel really confused about what I should do, my perseveration goes up, my thoughts quicken, and I want to go faster and do more. And what I find is that it's usually the opposite that helps me back into connection with myself.[20]

What's interesting is that the more we slow down and learn to choose more wisely how we spend our time—picking meaningful experiences over meaningless ones, learning to be here now and savor what is right in front of us—the more time seems to be available.

Being busy, rushed, and stressed are diametrically opposed to being connected. When we are stressed, we are usually also impatient and making it all about us—and these emotions are connection killers.

Research shows that when we are rushing to get somewhere, even if we're on our way to talk about our priorities, we tend to forget about those priorities in the way we handle ourselves. One of our favorite psychology experiments on this tendency is nicknamed the Good Samaritan study.[21] The subjects were seminary students who were asked to prepare a short talk about either seminary jobs or the Good Samaritan parable in the Bible and then walk a short distance to the location where they would give their talk. Along the walking path, researchers planted a man slumped over on the ground, groaning in apparent pain. Before taking this walk past the "injured" confederate, some of the students were told that they were late and should hurry. Another group was told everything was ready and they should head right over, and the third group was told they had time to spare but should head over anyway.

You'd think that seminary students, of all people, would stop to offer help to a stranger in need, especially if they were on their way to give a talk about the Good Samaritan. But only 10 percent of the "late" seminarians stopped to offer help. One participant even stepped over the slumped body in his haste!

This experiment demonstrates how easily situational pressures can trump personal values in guiding our behaviors. Rushing to get somewhere on time, we forget who we are and what really matters to us. We no longer see our priorities or other people's needs—all that we see and prioritize is our rushing. In our state of tunnel vision, 90 percent of us do not live according to our values. We break the rules we want to live by and hurt the people we want to cherish. We have got to slow down.

When we take the time we need to connect to our present and our values, we feel unrushed, unhurried, unconcerned about how we spend our time—as if we have all the time in the world. When you feel more intrinsically satisfied with your choices about how you are spending your time, that satisfaction makes it less necessary to search constantly for fulfillment . . . because you already have it.

CONNECTION IS A PRACTICE

The beauty of intending to become more connected to your life and true self is that it doesn't matter where you begin the journey. Simply deciding that you crave more of this kind of clarity of purpose is enough to reset your compass and priorities in a new direction. This helps much of the process to unfold naturally from there.

It's important to put some targeted efforts forth in specific, particular areas to get the ball rolling (such as self-care or clarifying priorities). This book has taken you on a tour of the various areas of your life where you might examine your connection to yourself at the granular level and begin to make some of those targeted efforts. In reality, the unfolding of your own deeper connection with yourself will be more organic. As you discover which areas need reconnecting in your life, you will decide which need more concerted efforts and which need just simple awareness and curiosity.

What I love about this work is that progress can happen so quickly—you can see and feel results within a single day. Being in touch with our deepest truths and needs is a natural state of being for us and something that we gravitate toward. Shedding old, disconnecting habits is thus an inherently rewarding, self-perpetuating process. Connection spreads widely and easily across our lives. Once you open the door to an area that was previously blocked, you will likely notice how the urge to be awake and connected in other areas of your life rushes forth to carry you forward.

As you start down this path, consider what the right point of entry might be for you. Perhaps it is to take the slow, organic process described above, where you generally set your intention to become more aware and connected and allow opportunities to unfold in front of you. If you are like me and prefer a more structured approach to change, consider identifying one area of your life that's most in need of deeper connection. The thrill of conquest and positive transformation in this area will lead you to want to pursue other areas of deeper connection in your life with gusto.

Part of slowing down is also accepting that Rome wasn't built in a day. Building a life rich with connection takes time, practice, and persistence. If you are the type who likes to take on big change all at once, be aware that it may not be humanly possible to adopt all of the connecting practices described in this book simultaneously and sustain them right off the bat. A better approach for the ambitious sort is to start out with a few practices—maybe three or four—that span different areas of your life and that speak to you.

For example, maybe for the first month, focus on hydrating, clarifying your values, and being more mindful about your use of technology. Including at least one "easy" practice as part of your first batch gives you the opportunity for immediate success, which will encourage you to continue. After a month or so, you will hopefully have incorporated the first few practices as part of your routine and will find yourself with more energy to make additional changes—exploring sensory awareness, cultivating more meaning in your daily activities, and improving sleep hygiene, for example.

It's important to remember that connection takes practice. Changing habits and ingrained mindsets is difficult for nearly everyone. When you find yourself falling off the connection wagon, don't beat yourself up. Just regroup, and begin again.

Like meditation, connection actually offers tremendous value even when you "fail" at it—learning to redirect your attention and consciously reconnect after a lapse is helpful in and of itself for building up the "muscle" you need to get through the day. So don't bemoan your failures—celebrate them as learning opportunities. You are gaining a better understanding of yourself and giving your reconnection muscles another set of reps.

The good news is that once you have trained your attention and awareness to be on the lookout for opportunities for deeper connection or signs of disconnection, it becomes nearly effortless to sustain. It's worth repeating that mindful attention and intention doesn't cost us any additional time or effort. It's a gentle internal guidance system operating in the background that helps you pause to consider your options and make better, more aligned decisions moment by moment.

Connection is a lifelong practice, and it will be easier to achieve at some times than at others. But the peace and satisfaction it will bring to your life will be well worth the effort.

Conclusion

While the positive psychology movement has given us a myriad of gifts—including many of the forgiveness, mindfulness, and self-discovery practices mentioned in this book—these efforts didn't create a holistic framework to guide us to a life well lived. People hoping for a more satisfying, optimal existence are adrift in a sea of good intentions and advice, with no cohesive plan for applying that knowledge and creating a life that is satisfying to the core.

What connection theory offers is a guiding light to show you the way out of the dark woods. The intention it inspires, the attention it directs, and the simple question it invites together point the way to a life of profound and enduring well-being. *Am I feeling connected right now?* That one simple question helped me, and I believe it will help others find a path out of the darkness and into the radiance of the present moment, where authentic connection can take root.

When we shift our focus to connecting (with ourselves, others, our work, and the world we live in), we are empowered to access a level of contentment that's far richer, more rewarding, and lasting than mere happiness. Our lives fill with meaning and purpose. We experience the type of sustained wellness that only comes from living in alignment with our deepest wants and needs. Authentic connection helps us jump straight to what matters, teaches us to love our lives and each other, and allows us to make the most of our time on this earth. No life-threatening diagnosis is required.

It all starts with self-connection: developing an unbreakable, loving bond with our true selves. When we know who we are, what we stand for, and what makes our hearts soar, we claim the power to create a life filled with meaning, purpose, and meaningful connection with others as well as the world around us.

With connection theory, all you need to guide you in your journey is this: **Intention + Attention + One Simple Question.**

Set the *intention* to be more connected to yourself and your life.

Give it your *attention*, checking in with yourself throughout the day.

And just keep asking that *one simple question*: Am I feeling connected right now?

It does take time. It does take patience. It also takes practice and a willingness to make tough decisions and changes in furtherance of your priorities. But as you strengthen your awareness of connection and bring your life into alignment with your truths, thrumming with sensory awareness and vibrant energy, you will discover a joy, satisfaction, and freedom like no other.

Acknowledgments

I have many people to thank for helping me bring this book to life. But I must begin with my two boys, who are my inspiration and my ultimate "why." Watching their youthful exuberance, innocence, and easy connection in life so often helped show me *how* to connect in ways beyond what my research or textbooks could ever reveal. It also motivated me to create a guidebook for them, to help distill and share with them the best of what I've learned about true contentment—and, should they ever lose their way, help them reconnect with their hearts.

I also must thank my clinical training program, not just for their top-notch training but for simultaneously instilling in me a deep reverence for combining science with real-world clinical work, and for their continued contact and encouragement to this day. I appreciate Bram Fridhandler and my colleagues at California Pacific Medical Center for believing in the positive impact of health psychology programs and, of course, my many medical patients there who guided me just as much as I guided them. I'm deeply grateful to my postdoctoral fellows for their commitment and enthusiasm, in particular to Jeremy Bornstein for continuing that work and growing the program beyond my wildest dreams.

Massive thanks go to my research partners at the Connection Lab, who share my passion for understanding the causes and conditions of authentic connection and a meaningful life. I've enjoyed every aspect of our journey at the Lab, from publishing, presenting, and theorizing to taking turns watering the plants in the office. You are some of the smartest, most talented people I have ever worked with.

Like many things in life, we don't imagine we can do something until we see it done. My fellow psychologist, Rick Hanson, showed me the way—sharing so much of himself and his own book-writing journey with me over the years. Rick, your belief in me made me believe more in myself, and *you* are the reason I imagined that I could share my voice with the world. Your constant mentoring and caring presence have changed my life for the better, and I will never be able to thank you enough for that.

To the dear friends in Bali who became my family when my boys and I took a year abroad: You all were the greatest cheerleaders a girl could ever ask for. Your endless interest in the book topic and writing process kept me fueled and unwavering in my commitment. Our walks on the beach and swims in the ocean at the end of the day were also amazing incentives to get the job done. I love and miss you all dearly.

Through the hundreds (probably thousands, actually) of rounds of revisions, citations, and true grit moments, the one person I could always count on to do the heavy lifting with me was my supremely talented writing partner, Deirdre Bourdet. Deirdre, your combination of constant cheerfulness, willingness to dive in at a moment's notice, humor at all times, tough love, unconditional commitment, and friendship through many phases and stages of life over a ten-year period has meant more than words can express. I literally could not have written this book without you and wouldn't have wanted to. Your belief in the importance and message of this book kept me going and made this often solitary process a lovingly shared one. I bow deeply in gratitude to you for that, and for too many other things to even mention here.

One of the most pleasant surprises about the publishing industry was meeting so many new, talented, and wonderful people. Caroline Pincus, you were my first terrifying phone call into the big world of traditional publishing. Unlike the many people who filled my ears with negative predictions about a first-time author getting an agent—let alone a publisher—you took the time to give it to me straight, you read my work, and you shared all the inside scoop you had. Thank you for helping me craft a sixty-page book proposal, challenging me to make it sing, and ultimately finding my agent, Steve Harris. I couldn't have asked for a better literary agent. Steve, your guidance, advice, and strategy has been spot-on from the first moment. You made a potentially stressful process a complete joy and landed me with my dream publisher.

While I already felt lucky to work with Sounds True publishing, whose authors, content, and contribution to the world I've admired for years, I really hit the jackpot working with Diana Ventimiglia. Diana, your exuberance for bringing this kind of message to the world is infectious. Thank you for being such an astute advisor and bright beam of light throughout the whole process . . . all while recovering from broken bones during COVID-19 quarantine. I've loved working with you from the second we first spoke and have so appreciated the joy you bring to all interactions. Thank you for making this part so much fun.

Enormous thanks also go to Kendall Hinote, my proofreader, PR guru, TEDx coach, and now close friend for life. I am honored by how important you felt this message was to get out to the world and how deeply you mined with me to make sure we never strayed from the core truth. Thank you for the many thoughtful (and sometimes maddening) discussions of intonation and nuance, and for helping me through the times when I'd lost what I was trying to say. Our long, deep conversations are all in a treasure box for me and will always make me smile. You brought a depth and quality to this book that is profound, and your friendship across the distance is simply priceless. I'm so glad I met you, Kendall. You are a dear and special person in my life.

Finally, I'd like to thank my family, friends, and loved ones closer to home for the love and encouragement that sustained me through this long, winding book-writing process. Your patient willingness to test out novel connection-promoting activities, participate in pilot research studies, share your thoughts on drafts, drag me away from my laptop for a change of scenery, and share your love in countless other ways large and small was—and is—astounding in its generosity and grace. Thank you to everyone who shared their talent, time, and enthusiasm on this journey. I am exceedingly grateful to you.

Appendix

WORKSHEETS FOR CONNECTION

Understanding Your Values
and Priorities Worksheet

Set aside an hour to jot down some of the values that matter most to you in each category of your life. (Sample categories are provided below; feel free to rename or recategorize as needed to describe your life.)

Then, list your top priorities in each category and try to rank the top three. Ask yourself the tough questions in order to better figure out which priorities win out over others. If you had to choose between two, which would you pick? If money and other obstructive practicalities were no object, what would really mean the most to you?

Periodically, check in on your lists and ask yourself whether they are still a true reflection of what matters to you most or whether your feelings have changed. If you're not sure about a priority's position on the list, put a question mark next to it to remind yourself that this area needs further observation. This will become a living, breathing record that you populate and update over time.

Health

VALUES   PRIORITIES

Well-Being/Self-Care

VALUES   PRIORITIES

Work

VALUES   PRIORITIES

Finance

VALUES   PRIORITIES

Romantic Partnership

VALUES   PRIORITIES

Friendships

VALUES   PRIORITIES

Parenting

VALUES   PRIORITIES

Community Involvement/Service

VALUES   PRIORITIES

Learning/Personal Growth

VALUES   PRIORITIES

Play/Creativity

VALUES   PRIORITIES

Assessing Meaning Worksheet

When assessing meaning, it is helpful to use a ten-point scale, where one is utterly meaningless and ten is one of the most meaningful things you've ever experienced. Consider each of the major areas of your life separately, rather than trying to do a global assessment. The list of primary areas might vary from person to person but most commonly includes romantic partnership, family, work, social, and spiritual.

Level of Meaning (1 is lowest, 10 is highest)

Family

| 1 | 2 | 3 | 4 | 5 | 6 | 7 | 8 | 9 | 10 |

Work

| 1 | 2 | 3 | 4 | 5 | 6 | 7 | 8 | 9 | 10 |

Social

| 1 | 2 | 3 | 4 | 5 | 6 | 7 | 8 | 9 | 10 |

Spiritual

| 1 | 2 | 3 | 4 | 5 | 6 | 7 | 8 | 9 | 10 |

Romantic Partnership

| 1 | 2 | 3 | 4 | 5 | 6 | 7 | 8 | 9 | 10 |

Physical Self-Care Worksheet

*Why Do **You** Care about Your Physical Self-Care?*

Tapping into your "why" reveals the intrinsic motivations to tend to your body—the ones that are aligned with your deepest values. Powerful whys generally sound something like "to have some quality alone time with myself" or "in order for me to get out of my head and into my humanity" or "to celebrate my innate masculinity/femininity" or "to honor myself and my body with proper care" or "to forge physical connection to my body each day."

What's your why?
WRITE IT HERE:

_____

_____

_____

_____

_____

_____

_____

_____

_____

_____

_____

_____

Your Nonnegotiable Self-Care Fundamentals

Decide what your minimum daily requirements are to feel you're caring for your physical self in ways that matter to your "why." These fundamental touchpoints will become your self-care nonnegotiables.

How do you decide what your core areas of self-care are? Five common contributors are sensory awareness, nutrition, movement, sleep, and hydration. Take a few minutes to consider and journal about which activities in these realms, when done regularly, make you feel more whole, grounded, and cared for. (For example: eight hours of sleep each night, a large glass of water in the morning and before dinner, and ten minutes of aerobic activity each day.)

What are your nonnegotiables?

WRITE THEM HERE:

Emotional Self-Care Worksheet

Untangling Thoughts, Emotions, and Truths

Completing this template often helps to unpack and better understand emotionally charged beliefs.

Upsetting thought/belief #1:

_____

_____

How it makes me feel:

_____

_____

_____

_____

Evidence that thought/belief #1 is true:	Evidence it is false:
_____	_____
_____	_____
_____	_____
_____	_____

Revised, more reasonable belief:

_____

_____

_____

Upsetting thought/belief #2:

....

....

How it makes me feel:

....

....

....

Evidence that thought/belief #2 is true:	Evidence it is false:
....	....
....	....
....	....
....	....

Revised, more reasonable belief:

....

....

....

Upsetting thought/belief #3:

_____

_____

How it makes me feel:

_____

_____

_____

_____

Evidence that thought/belief #3 is true:	Evidence it is false:

Revised, more reasonable belief:

_____

_____

_____

Notes

Introduction

1. Allen Frances, *Saving Normal: An Insider's Revolt Against Out-of-Control Psychiatric Diagnosis, DSM-5, Big Pharma, and the Medicalization of Ordinary Life* (New York: William Morrow and Company, 2013).

2. "Authentic," Merriam-Webster Online Dictionary, merriam-webster .com/dictionary/authentic.

3. The term *hedonic treadmill* was coined by Brickman and Campbell in their 1971 article "Hedonic Relativism and Planning the Good Society," in *Adaptation-Level Theory*, ed. M. H. Appley (New York: Academic Press, 1971), 287–302. For more on the theory of hedonic adaptation, see S. Frederick and G. Loewenstein, "Hedonic Adaptation," in *Well-Being: The Foundations of Hedonic Psychology*, ed. D. Kahneman et al. (New York: Russell Sage, 1999), 302–329.

4. Baumeister et al., "Some Key Differences Between a Happy Life and a Meaningful Life," *Journal of Positive Psychology* 8, no. 6 (2013): 505–516, gsb.stanford.edu/faculty-research/publications/some-key-differences -between-happy-life-meaningful-life.

Chapter 1: Begin with Self-Connection

1. Vernon Howard, *The Power of Your Supermind* (New York: Prentice Hall, 1975), 160.

2. K. Klussman et al., "What's Stopping Us from Connecting with Ourselves? A Qualitative Examination of Barriers to Self-Connection," *International Journal of Applied Positive Psychology* (2020), doi.org/10.1007/s41042-020-00031-x.

3. Connection Lab Research, Summer 2017, Interview 007.

4. K. Klussman et al., "Examining the Effect of Mindfulness on Well-Being: Self-Connection as a Mediator," *Journal of Pacific Rim Psychology* 14, no. E5 (2020), doi.org/10.1017/prp.2019.29.

5. K. Klussman et al., "Fostering Stress Resilience among Business Students: The Role of Stress Mindset and Self-Connection," *Psychological Reports* (July 2020), doi:10.1177/0033294120937440.

6. Connection Lab Research, Summer 2017, Interview 005.

7. Connection Lab Journal Study, JR_023, Entry no. 1.

8. Klussman et al., "What's Stopping Us from Connecting with Ourselves?" In general, the barriers participants reported reflected both internal factors— feeling lost, negative self-judgment, a lack of motivation, avoidance, and prioritizing others, etc.—and external factors such as time, work, ability to meet basic needs, and powerlessness.

9. Supertramp, "The Logical Song," by Richard Davies and Roger Hodgson, Universal Music Publishing Group, available on YouTube at youtube.com /watch?v=low6Coqrw9Y.

10. Brené Brown, *Daring Greatly: How the Courage to be Vulnerable Transforms the Way We Live, Love, Parent, and Lead* (New York: Gotham Books, 2012), 136–137.

11. Rick Hanson, "Notice You're Alright Right Now," in *Just One Thing* newsletter, rickhanson.net/notice-youre-alright-right-now/.

12. Rick Hanson, *Hardwiring Happiness: The New Brain Science of Contentment, Calm, and Confidence* (New York: Harmony Books, 2013), 2, Kindle.

13. Klussman et al., "Examining the Effect of Mindfulness on Well-Being." Mindfulness predicted self-connection and well-being in both studies; self-connection also predicted well-being and partially mediated the relationship between mindfulness and well-being. K. Klussman, A. L. Nichols, and J. Langer, "The Role of Self-Connection in the Relationship Between Mindfulness and Meaning: A Longitudinal Examination," *Applied Psychology: Health and Well-Being* (2020), doi.org/10.1111/aphw.12200. Mindfulness predicts the presence of meaning, and those low in self-connection are more likely to benefit from mindfulness as a means to boosting meaning.

14. Jon Kabat-Zinn, *Mindfulness for Beginners: Reclaiming the Present Moment and Your Life* (Boulder, CO: Sounds True, 2016).

15. Kabat-Zinn, *Mindfulness for Beginners.*

16. Rainer Maria Rilke, *Letters to a Young Poet*, trans. M. D. Herter Norton (New York: W. W. Norton, 1993), Letter no. 4, 27.

Chapter 2: Connecting with Your True Self

1. Lissa Rankin, "Stop Should-ing Yourself," The Chopra Center, chopra.com /article/stop-should-ing-yourself#sm.001p5dz8p11ywemnzh41p4xkzl2ud.

2. Connection Lab Journal Study, JR_048, Entry no. 1.

3. Andre Agassi, *Open* (New York: Knopf Doubleday Publishing Group, 2009), 3.

4. Jiddu Krishnamurti, *Life Ahead: On Learning and the Search for Meaning* (Novato, CA: New World Library, 2014), 133.

Chapter 3: Connecting with Meaning

1. Emily Esfahani Smith, "There's More to Life than Being Happy," *The Atlantic*, January 9, 2013, theatlantic.com/health/archive/2013/01/theres -more-to-life-than-being-happy/266805/.

2. N. Krause, "Longitudinal Study of Social Support and Meaning in Life," *Psychology and Aging* 22 (2007): 456–469; M. F. Steger et al., "The Meaning in Life Questionnaire: Assessing the Presence of and Search for Meaning in Life," *Journal of Counseling Psychology* 53, no. 1 (2006): 80.

3. Irvin D. Yalom, *Existential Psychology* (Ann Arbor: University of Michigan, 1980).

4. Samantha Heintzelman and Laura King, "Life Is Pretty Meaningful," *American Psychologist* 69 (2014), doi.org/10.1037/a0035049.

5. K. Klussman et al., "Does Positive Affect Lead to Perceptions of Meaning in Life? The Moderating Role of Self-Connection," *European Journal of Applied Positive Psychology* 4, no. 7 (2020). Self-connection, and not positive affect, is reliably related to increased meaning in life.

6. K. Klussman, A. L. Nichols, and J. Langer, "Finding Meaning in Our Everyday Moments: Testing a Novel Intervention to Increase Job and Life Satisfaction" (unpublished manuscript). Our results suggested that listing daily activities and rating the meaningfulness of each hour was most beneficial. Compared to only listing daily activities, this

group experienced greater increases in job- and life-satisfaction. In K. Klussman et al., "The Effect of Daily Affect on Health: The Moderating Effect of Meaning Salience" (unpublished manuscript), participants either listed their daily activities or listed them and assigned meaning to each hour of their days. Results suggested that the intervention directly increased mental and physical health and moderated the effects of positive and negative affect in the desired direction.

7. Tim K. Blake, "Journaling: An Active Learning Technique," *International Journal of Nursing Education Scholarship* 2, no. 1 (April 15, 2005), doi.org/10.2202/1548-923X.1116.

8. Kelli A. Keough and Hazel Rose Markus, "On Being Well: The Role of the Self in Building the Bridge from Philosophy to Biology," *Psychological Inquiry* 9, no. 1 (1998): 49–53.

9. Geoffrey L. Cohen and David K. Sherman, "The Psychology of Change: Self-Affirmation and Social Psychological Intervention," *Annual Review of Psychology* 65 (2014): 333–371.

10. J. Cacioppo et al., "Social Isolation," *Annals of the New York Academy of Sciences* 1231 (2011): 17–22. For a fascinating exploration of the many ways human contact can positively impact our health and well-being, read Susan Pinker, *The Village Effect: How Face-to-Face Contact Can Make Us Healthier and Happier* (New York: Penguin Random House, 2014).

11. Connection Lab Journal Study, JR_54, Entry no. 3.

Chapter 4: Connecting with Your Life Purpose(s)

1. Brené Brown, "Appendix to *Daring Greatly*," brenebrown.com/the-research/.

2. L. S. George and C. L. Park, "Meaning in Life as Comprehension, Purpose, and Mattering: Toward Integration and New Research Questions," *Review of General Psychology* 20, no. 3 (2016): 205–220, doi.org/10.1037/gpr0000077.

3. Connection Lab Research, Summer 2017, Interview 001.

4. William Damon, *The Path to Purpose: Helping Our Children Find Their Calling in Life* (New York: Free Press, 2008), chapter 3.

5. Joseph Campbell, *The Hero with a Thousand Faces*, 3rd edition (Novato, CA: New World Library, 2008), 49.

6. Jiddu Krishnamurti, *Life Ahead: On Learning and the Search for Meaning* (Novato, CA: New World Library, 2014), 136.

7. Amy Wrzesniewski, Paul Rozin, and Gwen Bennett, "Working, Playing, and Eating: Making the Most of Most Moments," in *Flourishing: Positive Psychology and the Life Well-Lived*, ed. C. L. M. Keyes and J. Haidt (Washington, DC: American Psychological Association, 2003): 189, doi.org/10.1037/10594-008.

8. Richard Leider, "Author Q&A," richardleider.com/author-qa.

9. Ken Page, "How Our Insecurities Can Reveal Our Deepest Gifts," *Psychology Today*, psychologytoday.com/blog/finding-love/201109/how-our -insecurities-can-reveal-our-deepest-gifts.

10. Bronnie Ware, "Regrets of the Dying," bronnieware.com/blog/regrets-of -the-dying/.

11. A. H. Maslow, "A Theory of Human Motivation," *Psychological Review* 50 (1943): 370–396, psychclassics.yorku.ca/Maslow/motivation.htm.

12. David Brooks, *The Road to Character* (New York: Random House, 2016), 21.

13. "Episode 129," *The James Altucher Show*, mixcloud.com /thejamesaltuchershow/ep-129-dr-wayne-dyer-namaste/.

14. William Damon, *Noble Purpose: The Joy of Living a Meaningful Live* (West Conshohocken, PA: Templeton Foundation Press, 2003), 7.

15. Michael Bernard Beckwith, *The Answer Is You* (Culver City, CA: Agape Media International, 2009), 6.

16. Our team first found this exercise on the blog of Steve Pavlina, "How to Discover Your Life Purpose in About 20 Minutes," January 16, 2005, stevepavlina.com/blog/2005/01/how-to-discover-your-life-purpose-in -about-20-minutes/.

17. Pavlina, "How to Discover Your Life Purpose in About 20 Minutes."

18. Pavlina, "How to Discover Your Life Purpose in About 20 Minutes."

Chapter 5: Connecting with Your Physical Self

1. Buddha's first sermon, as quoted in B. R. Ambedkar, *The Buddha and His Dhamma: A Critical Edition* (Oxford: Oxford University Press, 2011).

2. John J. Ratey and Richard Manning, *Go Wild: Eat Fat, Run Free, Be Social, and Follow Evolution's Other Rules for Total Health and Well-Being* (New York: Little, Brown and Company, 2014), 26.

3. Russell T. Hurlburt, "Sensory Awareness: Why People (Including Scientists) Are Blind to It," *Psychology Today*, October 31, 2011, psychologytoday.com /blog/pristine-inner-experience/201110/sensory-awareness-why-people -including-scientists-are-blind-it. See also R. T. Hurlburt, C. L. Heavey, and A. Bensaheb, "Sensory Awareness," in *Investigating Pristine Inner Experience: Moments of Truth*, ed. R. T. Hurlburt (New York: Cambridge University Press, 2011), 309–324.

4. For an excellent summary of the benefits of cold shock and cryotherapy, with links to the underlying scientific studies, see Rhonda P. Patrick's 2015 paper "Cold Shocking the Body: Exploring Cryotherapy, Cold-Water Immersion, and Cold Stress," foundmyfitness.com/reports/cold-stress.pdf.

5. Brian Wansink and Jeffrey Sobal, "Hidden Persuaders and 200 Daily Decisions," *Environment and Behavior* 39, no. 1 (2007): 106–123.

6. For a cinematic overview of the economics and politics of Big Food, I recommend the documentary *Food, Inc.* Respected researcher Marion Nestle also offers meticulously detailed accounts of the food industry's political activity in her books, most notably *Food Politics: How the Food Industry Influences Nutrition and Health* (Berkeley: University of California Press, 2013).

7. Michael Pollan, *In Defense of Food: An Eater's Manifesto* (New York: Penguin, 2008), 10–11, 97–100.

8. Pollan, *In Defense of Food*, 89–90.

9. "The Brain-Gut Connection," Johns Hopkins School of Medicine, hopkinsmedicine.org/health/healthy_aging/healthy_body/the-brain-gut -connection.

10. Pollan, *In Defense of Food*, 1, 146.

11. Mark Hyman, "Fat: What I Got Wrong, What I Got Right," drhyman
.com/blog/2016/03/30/fat-what-i-got-wrong-what-i-got-right/.

12. The Connection Lab's research findings suggest that not all forms of
exercise may be equally beneficial to physical and mental well-being,
however. See K. Klussman, J. Langer, and A. L. Nichols, "The Tenuous
Relationship Between Physical Activity, Health, and Well-Being:
Examining the Type of Exercise and Self-Connection as Moderators"
(unpublished manuscript). We plan to further investigate whether exercise
forms that emphasize connection may, in fact, be the ones that make the
biggest positive impact.

13. Centers for Disease Control and Prevention, "Summary Health Statistics
for US Adults: National Health Interview Survey, 2009" (December 2010):
11, cdc.gov/nchs/data/series/sr_10/sr10_249.pdf.

14. Centers for Disease Control and Prevention, "Summary Health Statistics
for US Adults: National Health Interview Survey, 2017," table A-14a, 1,
cdc.gov/pub/Health_Statistics/NCHS/NHIS/SHS/2017_SHS
_Table_A-14.pdf.

15. K. Sheldon and T. Kasser, "Goals, Congruence, and Positive Well-Being:
New Empirical Support for Humanistic Theories," *Journal of Humanistic
Psychology* 41 (2001): 30–50.

16. For a good review of the research findings, see chapter 10 of David B. Agus,
The End of Illness (New York: The Free Press, 2012); and J. Eric Ahlskog et
al., "Physical Exercise as a Preventive or Disease-Modifying Treatment of
Dementia and Brain Aging," *Mayo Clinic Proceedings* 86, no. 9 (September
2011): 876–884.

17. K. Mandsager et al., "Association of Cardiorespiratory Fitness with Long-
Term Mortality among Adults Undergoing Exercise Treadmill Testing,"
JAMA Network Open 1, no. 6 (2018): e183605, doi.org/10.1001
/jamanetworkopen.2018.3605.

18. Michelle L. Segar, Jacquelynne S. Eccles, and Caroline R. Richardson,
"Rebranding Exercise: Closing the Gap Between Values and Behavior,"
International Journal of Behavioral Nutrition and Physical Activity 8, no.
94 (2011): 1–4.

19. See, for example, N. Zaer Ghodsi, M. R. Zolfaghari, and A. Fattah, "The Impact of High-Intensity Interval Training on Lipid Profile, Inflammatory Markers and Anthropometric Parameters in Inactive Women," *Medical Laboratory Journal* 10, no. 1 (2016): 56–60. See also J. B. Gillen et al., "Twelve Weeks of Sprint Interval Training Improves Indices of Cardiometabolic Health Similar to Traditional Endurance Training Despite a Five-Fold Lower Exercise Volume and Time Commitment," *PLoS ONE* 11, no. 4 (2106): e0154075, doi.org/10.1371/journal.pone.0154075.

20. Katy Bowman, *Don't Just Sit There* (Carlsborg, WA: Propriometrics Press, 2015), 4.

21. For more on this issue, consult R. M. A. Al-Dirini, M. O. Reed, and D. Thewlis, "Deformation of the Gluteal Soft Tissues During Sitting," *Clinical Biomechanics*, May 22, 2015, clinbiomech.com/article /S02680033(15)00144-8/abstract; N. Shoham et al., "Adipocyte Stiffness Increases with Accumulation of Lipid Droplets," *Biophysical Journal* 106, no. 6 (March 18, 2014): 1421–1431, doi.org/10.1016 /j.bpj.2014.01.045; N. Shoham et al., "Static Mechanical Stretching Accelerates Lipid Production in 3T3-L1 Adipocytes by Activating the MEK Signaling Pathway," *American Journal of Physiology—Cell Physiology* (October 2011).

22. Joan Vernikos, *Sitting Kills, Moving Heals: How Everyday Movement Will Prevent Pain, Illness, and Early Death—and Exercise Alone Won't* (Fresno, CA: Quill Driver Books, 2011), 248, Kindle.

23. Ellen J. Langer, *Counterclockwise: Mindful Health and the Power of Possibility* (New York: Ballantine Books, 2009).

24. Vernikos, *Sitting Kills, Moving Heals*, chapter 4.

25. Joseph Mercola, "The Gokhale Method: An Interview with Esther Gokhale," August 25, 2013, mercola.fileburst.com/PDF/ExpertInterviewTranscripts /GokhaleTranscript.pdf.

26. Agus, *The End of Illness*, chapter 11.

27. Michael Breus, "Alcohol Likely to Keep You Awake, Not Help You Sleep, When Drinking Before Bedtime," February 4, 2013, thesleepdoctor .com/2013/02/04/alcohol-likely-to-keep-you-awake-not-help-you-sleep -when-drinking-before-bedtime/.

28. Harvard Medical School, "The Importance of Staying Hydrated," *Harvard Health Letter*, June 2015, health.harvard.edu/staying-healthy/the -importance-of-staying-hydrated.

29. Tony Robbins is a prolific author, inspirational speaker, and world-famous performance coach who has worked with people like Bill Clinton, Oprah, and Nelson Mandela.

30. R. An and J. McCaffery, "Plain Water Consumption in Relation to Energy Intake and Diet Quality Among US Adults, 2005–2012," *Journal of Human Nutrition and Dietetics* 29 (2016): 624–632, doi.org/10.1111/jhn.12368.

31. Julia Abigail Fletcher Carney, "Little Things," in *Famous Poems from Bygone Days*, ed. Martin Gardner (New York: Dover Publications, 1995), 36.

32. Philip McKernan, "Meet Philip McKernan," philipmckernan.com/believe/.

Chapter 6: Connecting with Your Emotional Self

1. Joseph Fort Newton as quoted in Chaim Stern's *Day by Day: Reflections on the Themes of the Torah from Literature, Philosophy, and Religious Thought* (New York: Beacon Press, 1998), 202.

2. Kristin Neff, *Self-Compassion: The Proven Power of Being Kind to Yourself* (New York: William Morrow and Company, 2011), 6, Kindle.

3. Neff, *Self-Compassion*, 3–4.

4. Neff, *Self-Compassion*, 6.

5. Neff, *Self-Compassion*, 119.

6. John D. Mayer and Glenn Geher, "Emotional Intelligence and the Identification of Emotion," *Intelligence* 22, no. 2 (March–April 1996): 89–113, doi.org/10.1016/S0160-2896(96)90011-2.

7. Dr. Thomas Moore's quote is cited in Katrina Kenison, "Why You Must Have Time Alone," *Oprah.com*, oprah.com/spirit/why-you-must-have -solitude-and-time-for-yourself.

8. A conversation between Susan Cain and journalist Gareth Cook appears in "The Power of Introverts: A Manifesto for Quiet Brilliance," *Scientific American*, January 24, 2012, scientificamerican.com/article/the-power-of -introverts/.

9. Kenison, "Why You Must Have Time Alone."

10. M. Goyal et al., "Meditation Programs for Psychological Stress and Well-Being: A Systematic Review and Meta-Analysis," *JAMA Internal Medicine* 174, no. 3 (2014): 357–368, jamanetwork.com/journals /jamainternalmedicine/fullarticle/1809754.

11. M. Speca et al., "A Randomized, Wait-List Controlled Clinical Trial: The Effect of a Mindfulness Meditation-Based Stress Reduction Program on Mood and Symptoms of Stress in Cancer Outpatients," *Psychosomatic Medicine* 62 (2000): 613–622. This randomized controlled study demonstrated a clear association between mediation and a reduction in stress. See also S. Horowitz, "Health Benefits of Meditation: What the Newest Research Shows," *Alternative and Complementary Therapies* 16, no. 4 (2010): 223–228. This review of the literature reports research supporting a wide variety of benefits of meditation, including cardiovascular health, treatment of cancer, chronic pain disorders, menopausal symptoms, HIV/ AIDS, substance abuse, memory loss, and issues of youth populations, incarcerated populations, and psychological trauma.

12. L. Chu, "The Benefits of Meditation vis-à-vis Emotional Intelligence, Perceived Stress, and Negative Mental Health," *Stress and Health* 26 (2009): 169–180. See also H. S. Hodgins and K. C. Adair, "Attentional Processes and Meditation," *Consciousness and Cognition* 19 (2010): 872–878. This study found that meditation is associated with the development of superior attention skills ("more accurate, efficient, and flexible visual attentional processing across diverse tasks . . ."). See also F. Zeidan et al., "Mindfulness Meditation Improves Cognition: Evidence of Brief Mental Training," *Consciousness and Cognition* 19, no. 2 (2010): 597–605. This study finds connections between meditation and several outcome variables, including visual-spatial processing, working memory, executive functioning, and attention. See also A. Baltzell et al., "Qualitative Study of MMTS: Coaches' Experience," *Journal of Multidisciplinary Research* 7, no. 3 (Fall 2015): 5–20, jmrpublication.org /portals/jmr/Issues/JMR7-3.pdf. This qualitative/narrative study finds that participating in the Mindfulness Meditation Training for Sport (MMTS) program is associated with less emotional reactivity to negative thoughts and emotions while coaching and positive changes among players who are recovering emotionally from mistakes on the field.

13. Deepak Chopra, "Find Your True Self Through Meditation," chopracentermeditation.com/article/5-find_your_true_self_through _meditation.

14. Esther Hicks and Jerry Hicks, *Ask and It Is Given: Learning to Manifest Your Desires* (Carlsbad, CA: Hay House, 2009), 133.

15. Robert A. Emmons and Michael E. McCullough, *The Psychology of Gratitude* (New York: Oxford University Press, 2004), 158–159.

16. Brother David Steindl-Rast, *Gratefulness, The Heart of Prayer: An Approach to Life in Fullness* (New York: Paulist Press, 1984), 207.

17. See Sonja Lyubomirsky, *The How of Happiness: A New Approach to Getting the Life You Want* (New York: Penguin Press, 2007), 96–97.

18. George E. Vaillant, *Spiritual Evolution: A Scientific Defense of Faith* (New York: Broadway Books, 2008), 66.

19. William Damon and Anne Colby, *The Power of Ideals: The Real Power of Moral Choice* (Oxford: Oxford University Press, 2015), 148.

20. Thich Nhat Hanh, "What We Fund," Thich Nhat Hanh Foundation, thichnhathanhfoundation.org/what-we-fund.

21. Glenn Albrecht, "Eutierria," February 20, 2018, glennaalbrecht.com/2018 /02/20/eutierria/.

22. Author's private papers.

23. Julia Cameron, *The Artist's Way: A Spiritual Path to Higher Creativity* (New York: Penguin, 2016), 205.

24. K. G. Lambert, "Rising Rates of Depression in Today's Society: Consideration of the Roles of Effort-Based Rewards and Enhanced Resilience in Day-to-Day Functioning," *Neuroscience & Biobehavioral Reviews* 30, no. 4 (2006): 497–510, doi.org/10.1016/j.neubiorev.2005.09.002. See also Kelly Lambert, "Depressingly Easy," *Scientific American Mind* 19, no. 4 (August 2008): 30–37, doi.org/10.1038/scientificamericanmind0808-30.

25. Kelly Lambert, *Lifting Depression: A Neuroscientist's Hands-On Approach to Activating Your Brain's Healing Power* (New York: Basic Books, 2008), 33.

26. J. A. Egeland and A. M Hostetter, "Amish Study, I: Affective Disorders among the Amish, 1976–1980," *American Journal of Psychiatry* 140, no. 1 (January 1983): 56–61.

27. See, for example, Lambert, *Lifting Depression*; Carrie Barron and Alton Barron, *The Creativity Cure: How to Build Happiness with Your Own Two Hands* (New York: Scribner, 2012), 140–142.

28. See Carmine Iannaccone, "History, Humanity and Handwork," *Renewal, A Journal for Waldorf Education* 10, no. 2 (Fall 2011), waldorflibrary.org /articles/764-history-humanity-and-handwork; Eugene Schwartz, "Discover Waldorf Education: Knitting and Intellectual Development, the Role of Handwork in the Waldorf Curriculum," March 6, 2009, desertmarigold .org/curriculum/specialty-classes/handwork/.

29. National Public Radio, Forum, "Alonzo King's New Ballet Takes Its Soundtrack from the Animal Kingdom," April 3, 2015, 49:19.46, kqed .org/forum/201504031000/alonzo-kings-new-ballet-takes-its-soundtrack -from-the-animal-kingdom.

30. Brené Brown, *The Gifts of Imperfection: Let Go of Who You're Supposed to Be and Embrace Who You Are* (Center City, MN: Hazelden Publishing, 2010), 96.

31. Marian C. Diamond, "Successful Aging of the Healthy Brain," originally presented at the Conference of the American Society on Aging and the National Council on the Aging, March 10, 2001, New Orleans, LA, First Joint Conference, silverinnings.in/wp-content/uploads/2016/10/Successful -Aging-of-the-Healthy-Brain.pdf.

32. For a historical investigation of the origins of this adage, visit quoteinvestigator.com/2013/08/09/scare/.

33. "Enthusiasm," Online Etymology Dictionary, etymonline.com/word/enthusiasm.

34. K. Anders Ericsson and Robert Pool, *Peak: Secrets from the New Science of Expertise* (New York: Houghton Mifflin Harcourt Publishing, 2016), 258.

35. Mihaly Csikszentmihalyi, "Flow, the Secret to Happiness," TED talk, February 2004, ted.com/talks/mihaly_csikszentmihalyi_on_flow.

36. Mark Manson, "7 Strange Questions That Help You Find Your Life Purpose," September 18, 2014, markmanson.net/life-purpose.

37. Mihaly Csikszentmihalyi, "Finding Flow," *Psychology Today*, July 1, 1997, psychologytoday.com/articles/199707/finding-flow.

Chapter 7: Creating Time and Space to Connect

1. Stephen R. Covey, *The 7 Habits of Highly Effective People: Powerful Lessons in Personal Change* (New York: Simon and Schuster, 2004), 298.

2. David Rock, *Your Brain at Work: Strategies for Overcoming Distraction, Regaining Focus, and Working Smarter All Day Long* (New York: Harper Collins, 2009), 11.

3. Rock, *Your Brain at Work*, 11.

4. William Wan, "How Deadlines Thwart Our Ability to Do Important Work (and What We Can Do about It)," *Washington Post*, May 24, 2018, washingtonpost.com/news/speaking-of-science/wp/2018/05/24 /how-deadlines-thwart-our-ability-to-do-important-work-and-what-we-can -do-about-it.

5. Rock, *Your Brain at Work*, 40.

6. R. E. Bohn and J. E. Short, "How Much Information? 2009 Report on American Consumers," Global Information Industry Center Report (2010): 12, researchgate.net/publication/242562463_How_Much_Information _2009_Report_on_American_Consumers.

7. J. Smart, "How Much Media? 2013 Report on American Consumers," October 2013, business.tivo.com/content/dam/tivo/resources/tivo-HMM -Consumer-Report-2013_Release.pdf.

8. See Daniel J. Levitin, *The Organized Mind: Thinking Straight in the Age of Information Overload* (New York: Dutton, 2014), 6–7; M. Csikszentmihalyi and J. Nakamura, "Effortless Attention in Everyday Life: A Systematic Phenomenology," in *Effortless Attention: A New Perspective in the Cognitive Science of Attention and Action*, ed. B. Bruya (Cambridge, MA: MIT Press, 2010), 179–189.

9. See, for example, Galen V. Bodenhausen and Meryl Lichtenstein, "Social Stereotypes and Information-Processing Strategies: The Impact of Task Complexity," *Journal of Personality and Social Psychology* 52, no. 5 (May 1987): 871–880, which discusses how we often turn to stereotypes to

process complex decisions; Alexandre N. Tucha et al., "Visual Complexity of Websites: Effects on Users' Experience, Physiology, Performance, and Memory," *International Journal of Human-Computer Studies* 67, no. 9 (September 2009): 703–715, which shows that complex website design slows user reaction time and recognition and causes tension in facial musculature.

10. Lynne Twist, *The Soul of Money* (New York: W. W. Norton, 2003), 74.

11. Lynne Twist, "Sufficiency Is Not Abundance," February 1, 2016, awakin .org/read/view.php?tid=2097.

12. Thomas Princen, *The Logic of Sufficiency* (Cambridge, MA: MIT Press, 2005), chapter 5.

13. Joshua Becker, *The More of Less: Finding the Life You Want Under Everything You Own* (Colorado Springs: WaterBrook Press, 2016), 17.

14. Becker, *The More of Less*, 39, 83–85.

15. Shoba Sreenivasan and Linda E. Weinberger, "The Digital Psychological Disconnect: How Has This Impacted Face-to-Face Interpersonal Interactions?" *Psychology Today*, July 10, 2016, psychologytoday.com/us /blog/emotional-nourishment/201607/the-digital-psychological-disconnect.

16. M. McPherson, L. Smith-Lovin, and M. E. Brashears, "Social Isolation in America: Changes in Core Discussion Networks Over Two Decades," *American Sociological Review* 71, no. 3 (2006). The 25 percent figure was derived from a 2004 update to a previous 1985 survey.

17. Connection Lab Research, Summer 2017, Interview 002.

18. "The Nielsen Total Audience Report: April 2020," April 20, 2020, nielsen.com /us/en/insights/report/2020/the-nielsen-total-audience-report-april-2020/.

19. C. Sagioglou and T. Greitemeyer, "Facebook's Emotional Consequences: Why Facebook Causes a Decrease in Mood and Why People Still Use It," *Computers in Human Behavior* 35 (June 2014): 359–363, doi.org/10.1016/j .chb.2014.03.003.

20. Connection Lab Research, Summer 2017, Interview 017.

21. John M. Darley and Daniel C. Batson, "From Jerusalem to Jericho: A Study of Situational and Dispositional Variables in Helping Behavior," *Journal of Personality and Social Psychology* 27, no. 1 (July 1973): 100–108.

About the Author

K ristine Klussman, PhD, is a positive health psychology researcher, clinician, writer, and community organizer dedicated to helping others live more productive, authentic lives of meaning and purpose. She founded and leads Purpose Project, a nonprofit think tank committed to the scientific research, exploration, education, and practice of authentic connection. As director of its research arm, Connection Lab, Klussman explores the causes and conditions of authentic connection and what it means to live a meaningful life. She and her research team publish their findings in peer-reviewed academic journals and present at scientific conferences around the world.

Interest in her work has made Klussman a sought-after keynote, TEDx, and conference speaker on issues of connection, and she often presents at workshops and conferences for professional groups as well as the general public. Building on decades of experience as a clinician, she also offers coaching for individuals and groups around authentic connection to self, others, and work as the path to greater peace, purpose, and well-being. Her love of learning and experience as a teacher— as a former fellow and lecturer at Harvard's Cambridge Hospital, as director of postdoctoral teaching and training at the California Pacific Medical Center, and as the leader of community workshops—animate her engaging writing and fuel the wide-ranging initiatives of her Purpose Project.

Klussman earned graduate degrees and postgraduate training in clinical psychology from Palo Alto University, Medical College of Virginia, and Harvard Medical School. She returned to her native Bay Area to found and direct California Pacific Medical Center's Health Psychology Program, providing free behavioral and motivational counseling to seriously ill patients and their families. This experience, and observations of her private practice clients, prompted her interest in developing a new connection-based theory of well-being, which ultimately inspired the Purpose Project and Connection Lab, as well as this book.

Klussman lives with her family and tribe of rescue animals in the San Francisco Bay Area.

For more information, visit kristineklussman.com.

About Sounds True

Sounds True is a multimedia publisher whose mission is to inspire and support personal transformation and spiritual awakening. Founded in 1985 and located in Boulder, Colorado, we work with many of the leading spiritual teachers, thinkers, healers, and visionary artists of our time. We strive with every title to preserve the essential "living wisdom" of the author or artist. It is our goal to create products that not only provide information to a reader or listener but also embody the quality of a wisdom transmission.

For those seeking genuine transformation, Sounds True is your trusted partner. At SoundsTrue.com you will find a wealth of free resources to support your journey, including exclusive weekly audio interviews, free downloads, interactive learning tools, and other special savings on all our titles.

To learn more, please visit SoundsTrue.com/freegifts or call us toll-free at 800.333.9185.